Mexican food should be cheap

FICTION

Warning: this topic can really fire me up. Why is it okay to pay $40 for a plate of handmade pasta but not tacos? The basic ingredients are similar. People should pay a fair price for food that has been lovingly prepared with quality ingredients, tremendous skill and lots of passion. Traditional Mexican food takes time to prepare and cook. A proper tortilla, for example, will take a couple of days to make once you've converted the grains of maize into masa and then a tortilla. It's time Mexican food's cheap reputation gets thrown in the bin.

Chilli con carne is Tex-Mex

FACT

Chilli con carne isn't a Mexican dish but a Tex-Mex classic. There are many delicious Tex-Mex dishes out there, but my main gripe is that a lot of people outside of Mexico think Tex-Mex is Mexican when it is instead its own cuisine. Chilli con carne probably originated in San Antonio, Texas, and is the official dish of the Lone Star state. Although there is some debate around the origins of chilli con carne, I think we can let Texas have this one.

Fajitas are Mexican

FICTION

This might shock some of you, but fajitas are not Mexican. Tacos de alambre de res (page 118) is the closest dish to fajitas.

Mexican cuisine uses a lot of chillies

FACT

Yes, traditional Mexican cuisine features a lot of chillies, but this doesn't mean it's all spicy. Many chillies are used to add or enhance flavours without the heat. But for those who enjoy a kick, varieties such as the arbol chilli definitely deliver.

Margarita is Mexico's favourite cocktail

FICTION

We prefer a glass of Cuba libre campechana (page 213) or a Paloma (page 212) over a cheeky Marg (page 219).

Mexican food is homogenous

FICTION

Mexico has 31 states, and each state has its cuisine. Unfortunately this is not reflected in restaurants outside of Mexico. In 2010, Mexican cuisine was inscribed by UNESCO on their Representative List of the Intangible Cultural Heritage of Humanity, where it was described as an elaborate and symbol-laden cuisine.

We acknowledge the Traditional Owners of the lands on which this book was written and made: the Kaurna people of the Adelaide Plains, the Wurundjeri and Bunurong people of the Kulin nation, and the Gadigal and Cammeraygal people of the Eora Nation. We pay our respects to all Aboriginal and Torres Strait Islander Elders, past and present.

¡PROVECHO!

REAL MEXICAN FOOD at HOME

DANIELLA GUEVARA MUÑOZ
with David Knight

Photography by Simon Bajada

murdoch books
Sydney | London

¡Buenos días! 6
Utensilios de cocina mexicana / **Mexican cookware** 14
Alacena mexicana / **Mexican pantry** 18

1
Desayunos
Breakfast
27

2
Sopas y caldos
Soups + broths
47

3
Antojitos, garnachas y entradas
Snacks + starters
67

4
Tacos, tortas y tostadas
Tacos, loaded rolls + tostadas
109
Tacos 112
Tortas / Loaded rolls 122
Tostadas 128

5
Platos fuertes
Mains
137
Guisados / Stews 158
Enchiladas 170

6
Dulce
Sweet
177
Paletas / Ice blocks 194

7
Bebidas
Drinks
199

8
Lo básico
Essentials
215
Salsas 236
Maíz y masa / Corn and dough 248

Los menús 260
Some useful words 262
Stockists 263
Acknowledgements 264
Index 266

¡Buenos días!

I'm Daniella Guevara Muñoz, but everyone calls me Dani. I spent the first half of my life in the lively Iztapalapa borough of Mexico City (where my parents still live). I now enjoy a quieter life in Port Adelaide, South Australia, where I run a small eatery called La Popular Taqueria with my husband, Kor.

Clockwise from left: Mum, Dad and me in Michoacán, 1980; In my last year of primary school; Me at three years old with my sister, Maru, having something to eat at our house.

In Iztapalapa, I was surrounded by carts and stalls slinging tacos, gorditas, tamales, pozole, fresh seafood and so much more. To grow up immersed in one of the world's great street-food cities means I'll always feel connected to my roots, no matter where I am. Cooking and sharing the food I grew up with takes me back to the street carts, restaurants and family gatherings of home. The happiest moments of my childhood were connected to cooking. Food brought our family and friends together to share dishes, talk endlessly and laugh lots.

On a typical day, we would enjoy huevos rancheros, tamales or gorditas for breakfast. My mother would cook delicious chicken flautas or pork and zucchini (courgette) stew – my favourite! – for lunch, and we would head out for tacos at night. To this day, my dad buys huaraches or carnitas from the same neighbourhood street carts that my family has frequented for the past 40 years.

On weekends, we would go to the Portales market and have pancita (tripe soup) for breakfast, which is an important meal in Mexico. On a typical afternoon, we would gather at my aunty's house and order tacos or pozole from local eateries like Tapsa, or tortas from Tort-As.

Despite our eating out a lot, my mother was, and still is, a great cook. I would return from school to watch her in the kitchen (we liked to eat!) as she prepared family favourites or experimented with new recipes found in the cookbooks and magazines she would collect.

Growing up in Mexico City was the best food education that money can't buy. The city is huge and very cosmopolitan. The heartbeat of the city is its taquerías, food vendors, markets and taco carts, where people from all walks of life come together.

Perhaps the most important food lesson you learn in Mexico is that street food isn't fast food. People labour for hours over marinating, cooking and basting the meats for taco fillings. Many hours are spent stuffing corn husks with masa and fillings,

From left: Through the window of a home in Yucatán; Me as the director of the Arrecife de Puerto Morelos National Park, doing an interview for local television.

then folding them to make tamales. These are then steamed in a massive pot that is brought to the street corner to sell. This involves passion, knowledge and skill. It is the very opposite of junk food. It might not always be healthy, but every dish has a depth of flavour resulting from knowledge passed down through the generations and countless hours spent preparing the perfect bite to enjoy on the street.

Mexican food is zesty and fun to eat and, as you will gather from the pages of this book, a lot of fun to prepare. It is perfect to enjoy at a taquería with friends over a few drinks, or with your extended family at large gatherings. It can also be as easy or as difficult as you want it to be, depending on your skill set and what you choose to make.

The cuisine is also rich, diverse and historic. There are influences from all over the world: from the Middle East to France and from the ancient Mexican and Central American empires to, of course, Spain.

Before the Spanish arrived, corn was the main staple in Mexico, and its growing cycle would influence religious rituals, astronomy and even the timing of wars. Corn was domesticated more than 6000 years ago and became the most important ingredient of the ancient civilisations' diets in Mexico. Other important crops were beans, squash, fruits and herbs, grown in permaculture plots called milpas, which are still in use today.

Mexican cuisine changed radically after the Spanish arrived. They brought spices and produce from Europe, Asia and the Middle East, and Mexican food started to evolve into what we know today.

Mexico has had a complex history, and every change has left its mark on its gastronomy. This is still happening today. For example, the famous tacos al pastor is the result of Lebanese migration in the early 20th century, as is alambre de res.

Although I've been obsessed with food since I was little, it wasn't until I was half a world away from my hometown, living the dream as a marine biologist on the Great Barrier Reef in Australia, that the idea first hit me: should I give all this up to open a restaurant?

I was not a trained chef. I had never even set foot in a commercial kitchen! I just wanted to show people real Mexican food, as I believe Mexican food is one of the most misunderstood cuisines in the world. What passed for Mexican cuisine in Australia was not the food I grew up with. On a good day, let's just say it was more on the Tex-Mex side of things.

For me, 40 and living on the other side of the world, it was a huge decision to change careers and start again. However, something in me needed to do it. I wanted to connect with my past, my family, and share the food of my home with the world.

To get my hands dirty (not literally) and get experience – any experience – I worked as a dishie in Adelaide. Then came Mi Mero Mole, the underground dinners Kor and I curated before we opened our restaurant, La Popular Taqueria, in Port Adelaide in 2017. My journey from marine biologist to chef brings us to the cookbook you now hold in your hands.

Provecho is for everyone who loves Mexican food but finds it hard to source authentic (and delicious) recipes to cook and enjoy at home; it's for every food lover who has wasted countless hours searching for real Mexican recipes online (a task that can be especially difficult if English is your first language, as most Mexican recipes in English are a hybrid of Western cuisines with Mexican flavours, rather than true Mexican); it's for anyone who wants to learn about a rich and ancient food culture and, most importantly, have fun while doing it.

You will find all the recipes in this book in Mexico's taquerías, street carts and homes; there is no Tex-Mex or Oz-Mex here. These are some of the essential Mexican dishes I cook at home, for friends at parties and for guests of our little restaurant. Some of the ingredients here might be slightly different due to geographic constraints, but I've tried to make every recipe as close to authentic as I possibly can.

Of course, this is by no means the definitive Mexican cookbook – that would take many volumes and decades to write – and Mexicans will squabble over certain recipes because their grandmothers would have done it differently, but these debates are healthy, as food should elicit passion!

When I cook food from another culture, I always worry that I'm not doing it right. I feel the gaze of people across the country as they shake their heads and mouth, 'No, that's wrong'. But I keep going. I keep cooking, hoping that it will taste like the real thing. You may feel the same when it comes to cooking Mexican food, but this is my way of introducing you to authentic dishes that you can replicate easily at home, no matter where you live.

Looking back, I think my destiny was to eventually call Australia home, and living here has made me realise how unique and special my childhood was.

My upbringing seems even more profound when we go back to Mexico. On our last trip, we visited a tiny family-run restaurant (or fonda) in Zacatlán de las Manzanas Puebla, where I was reminded of the custom of saying 'provecho' to your fellow diners, even if they're complete strangers.

'Provecho' roughly translates to 'enjoy your meal'. It's a beautiful tradition I miss when I'm in Australia, as all diners utter this customary salutation to each other when they walk into or leave eateries in Mexico.

Below: My tiny kitchen at La Popular Taqueria.
Opposite: Me chatting with some of our regulars at La Popular Taqueria.

This is why we've called the book *Provecho*. The word encapsulates everything that's special about Mexican hospitality.

Thank you for picking up this book and trusting me to guide you through some of the essentials of Mexican food. It's an absolute privilege that I get to share these recipes from my loved ones and my restaurant with you.

Enjoy, and remember to say 'provecho' to friends and family before you devour the recipes from this book or when you visit a taquería or Mexican restaurant. It's one simple word, but it makes your meal so much more meaningful.

Daniella

Mexico: a culinary timeline

21000 BCE
Humans arrive in Central America

10000–7000 BCE
Corn is cultivated

3500 BCE
Indigenous Mexicans and Central Americans begin cultivating chillies

1500 BCE
First Mesoamerican civilisation

1200 BCE
Mesoamericans begin eating tortillas

1200–400 BCE
The Olmecs drink chocolate

250 CE
Mayan civilisation dominates

1400 CE
Aztecs dominate central Mexico

1519
The Spanish arrive

1521
The Spanish defeat the Aztecs

1795
Tequila is first produced commercially

1810–21
War of Independence

1824
Mexico becomes a federal republic

1846
Mexican–American war begins

1861
The French invade Mexico

1910
Zapata leads the Mexican Revolution

2017
La Popular Taqueria opens

•PORTAR ARMAS.

Utensilios de cocina mexicana

—

Mexican cookware

Want to make handmade tortillas and up your salsa game but don't know where to start? You've come to the right place. Don't worry, you don't have to buy a professional kitchen's worth of appliances; you'll find you have some of the necessary tools in your cabinets and drawers already. For tools that aren't found in typical Western kitchens, you might need to work your credit card just a little to order online or head to your trusty Latin American or Asian supermarket.

The great thing about Mexican cooking is that you can usually find something in your kitchen that can act as a substitute, and it won't make much difference.

One of the reasons I wanted to write this book was to show that Mexican cooking isn't daunting. It's super approachable once you have the right tools and tricks. With just a few essentials, you're all set to conquer most of the classics.

All the tools mentioned here are used for recipes in this book, but this is just a sample of common utensils used in Mexican cooking. Handmade clay pots, for example, are found in most Mexican kitchens. They can be big, up to 1 metre (40 inches) wide and 50 cm (20 inches) deep, depending what you are going to use them for. I wish I had more of them in Australia. They are decorative and great to cook with, but I have not had much luck travelling with them on the long-haul flight from Mexico to Australia; they are extremely fragile, so a few of my favourites haven't completed the journey. Because of this I haven't included clay pots, or other large common cooking tools, such as a metate (a millstone for grinding corn, chillies or cacao).

Some of these tools, such as the comal, are pre-Hispanic, while others, such as the tortilla press, are more recent inventions.

Remember, while it's handy to have these in your kitchen, there are always substitutes; you just need to know what they are and how to use them. Here I have included all this information.

Blender

A Mexican kitchen without a blender (or la licuadora) is like Simon without Garfunkel; it works but it's just not the same. The classic Oster brand blender with a plastic or (luxury) glass jar is the convenient, modern substitute for the metate (see page 14) or molcajete (pictured opposite). You don't need anything fancy, just something functional. In our house we have two jar blenders, one for sweet and one for savoury. Bullet blenders are also great, especially if you want to make a quick salsa. Just a note on bullet blenders: their power can affect your control over the blend. If you like a chunkier salsa, use a different blender or do it by hand.

Chiquihuite

This little woven basket is a godsend for tortilla lovers. A chiquihuite is a small-to-medium basket made from straw, pine needles or palm leaves. It is used to keep tortillas warm and complete the cooking process, while allowing the tortillas to 'breathe' so they don't become soggy. Just place a large cotton napkin or small tea (dish) towel in the basket before adding the tortillas. You can find chiquihuites online or in specialty shops, and they are fairly cheap. If you don't have a chiquihuite, use a small basket with a clean tea towel – make sure it is fabric softener–free (when you wash it) so you don't ruin the taste and aroma of your tortillas.

Citrus press

You don't need a fancy citrus press to do the job. But what a job! Lime juice is vital for salsas, marinades, drinks and desserts, and adds vibrancy and complexity to Mexican cooking. If you don't have a citrus press, you'll be scraping a lot of seeds out of your food processor. When squeezing, place the fruit cut-side down, towards the holes, then press. You can get a citrus press at most supermarkets for less than $10.

Comal

A comal is a flat pan/griddle that is usually round and shallow or has no edge. It can be made of cast-iron, (heavy) clay or carbon steel. We use it to cook tortillas, sopes, quesadillas and other masa products. It is also used to char veggies and roast spices and chillies. So, kinda important, no? Comal comes from the Nahuatl word comalli and is of pre-Hispanic origin. Traditionally, a clay comal sits over three stones on a woodfire, and the surface of the comal is cured with a slaked lime slurry. It is considered one of the most important tools of Mexican cuisine. My dream kitchen is a cocina de humo (smoke kitchen) with a clay comal heated by a wood fire as the centrepiece. Every household in Mexico has a comal. The best one for home cooking is 25–28 cm (10–11¼ inches) in diameter. If you don't have one, use a large non-stick frying pan with no oil.

Fine-mesh strainer

El colador, although simple and present in most kitchens around the world, plays a significant role in Mexican cuisine, which really relies on the good ol' strainer. The blender is often used for making sauces or juicing, and removing those fibrous bits afterwards is an important step.

Molcajete

A molcajete (pictured opposite) is Mexico's pre-Hispanic version of a mortar and pestle. Most are made out of rough, porous volcanic stone or basalt, and are chiselled by hand. A classic molcajete is a heavy bowl standing on three legs, sometimes in the shape of a pig, with a large stone pestle known as a tejolote. Molcajetes are primarily used to make salsas and grind spices. The texture of a salsa made in a molcajete is different from a blended one, as the seeds are not cut to pieces and the texture is chunkier. Molcajete salsas always seem to taste better, too – like most things made by hand.

Tortilla press

If you're serious about making tortillas, I recommend getting one of these. A tortilla press – prensa tortilladora – is just a simple cast-iron or aluminium press with a lever to apply pressure. A word of advice: when pressing your corn tortillas, you will need two small plastic sheets to stop the dough sticking to the press (see page 253). Without them, making tortillas is impossible. This is because masa (corn dough) is super soft and doesn't hold like other flour doughs. The sheets allow you to transfer tortillas from the press to the palm of your hand. If you don't have a press, you can use a hardcover book or a thick chopping board on a flat surface, but you still need to use plastic sheets. I make mine out of sandwich bags, as they are just the right thickness.

Alacena mexicana

—

Mexican pantry

If you want to cook authentic Mexican food at home, here is a list of pantry non-negotiables. Some, such as avocados and limes, are easy to get, while others require some travelling beyond your local supermarket. When I arrived in Australia in 2009, it was difficult to find basic ingredients. Fortunately, online Mexican specialty shops (see page 263) have made this much easier and, with a bit of planning, you can make almost any dish. Fresh produce is still the hardest to get, so I grow some myself, including epazote and tomatillos. Online seed shops are where you'll find the more exotic species and varieties. Many Mexican ingredients are also used in Asian cuisines but might have a different name (jícamas are called yam beans, for example), so it's always good to pay regular visits to Asian supermarkets. I have given substitutes for some of the harder-to-find ingredients.

Achiote paste

Achiote is a paste made of annatto, small waxy seeds that come out of a spiny pod from the small *Bixa orellana* tree. Annatto is used as a spice and colourant. The Zo'e tribe from the Amazon rainforests of north Brazil, for example, paint their bodies with it. If you can't find the paste, look for annatto in Asian supermarkets. Achiote paste is common in the Mayan cuisine around the Yucatán Peninsula, and is sold in small packets. The paste contains not only annatto seeds but spices such as oregano, cumin and allspice, as well as vinegar. Achiote has a very earthy flavour. It is principally used to marinate meats such as Cochinita pibil (page 146), pollo adobado (see page 119), Pescado tikin xik (page 154) and pork for pastor tacos.

Allspice

Known in Mexico as pimienta gorda, or fat peppercorns, allspice is a fragrant and slightly sweet spice that is used in Mexican and other international cuisines. Due to its flavour profile (reminiscent of cinnamon, nutmeg and clove), I once thought it originated from Asia but, no, it is a tree (*Pimenta dioica*) native to southern Mexico, Guatemala and the Caribbean islands. Allspice is an important ingredient in Mayan cuisine around the Yucatán Peninsula and is one of the distinctive ingredients of achiote paste (see left).

Avocado

Like most delicious things in the fruit and vegetable world, avocados hail from Mexico (well, Mesoamerica to be precise). To say Mexicans love avocados is an understatement. They are as vital to our cooking as corn or tomatoes. From tacos to salsas and salads to desserts, avocados are one of the wonders of the food world, especially in the hands of a Mexican cook! You can do so much more with your humble hass or shepard besides guacamole or smashed avo! In Mexico you find many types of avocados, including the curiously delicious aguacatillo, a tiny fruit you can eat with the skin on.

Beans

For Mexicans, beans (frijoles) are an essential part of life; so much so that they are responsible for more than one-third of the population's protein intake! Breakfast, lunch, dinner, snacks, starters and mains, you name it, beans will be part of it. There are many types of beans in Mexico, and there are also local varieties, but black (turtle), bayo and pinto are the most common and easiest to find on Australian grocers' shelves. The earliest evidence of beans in Mexico dates back some 8000 years ago. They are an essential crop in the permaculture plots, called milpas, as they have nitrogen-fixing bacteria (rhizobia) in their roots, which return essential nutrients into the soil that are taken up by other crops. Enough biology for now; the main reason they are in this book is because they are delicious! If you don't have time to cook your own, buy quality tinned Mexican beans. Avoid beans that have been prepared with cumin.

Chamoy

Chamoy, mmm Chamoy. This goopy sauce is so Mexican in its flavour profile – sour, sweet, salty and spicy – though it finds its origin in China as a fruit snack. It is made with fruit, chillies, sugar and the vinegary brine that comes from the process of making saladitos, a salty, sweet and sour dried fruit snack generally made with apricots or plums. Chamoy is used to spice things up, including fruit, potato chips (crisps) and the delicious chamoyadas, which is a fruit sorbet made with Chamoy. You could also rim your glass with it and make a Michelada (page 208). Just the thought of Chamoy makes my mouth water.

Cheese

Queso is the Spanish word for cheese. Mexico has around 40 varieties of cheese, the majority being fresh or young cheeses. Most of these are hard to find outside of Mexican borders. The most famous cheese is probably queso oaxaca, also known as quesillo or queso de hebra. The following cheeses have all been mentioned in recipes in this book, where they are generally used as a garnish or a filling. I have suggested substitutes if they are hard to find.

AÑEJO

This is basically an aged queso fresco (see below). It's a touch dry but packs a punch and crumbles easily. It's hard to find outside of Mexico, so I like to use grated ricotta salata as a substitute, as it has that same salty umami deliciousness you want.

COTIJA

This is quite a salty fresh cheese and is often used to add some punch to a dish. It is made from cow's milk and gets its name from the village Cotija de la Paz in Michoacán. I like to use ricotta salata or Cyprus haloumi as a replacement.

FRESCO

Queso fresco is one of the most popular cheeses in Mexico. Fresco means fresh, so it's a very young cheese. It has a neutral, milky flavour and is like queso panela (see below): a bit rubbery in mouthfeel. Need to replace it? Substitute La Casa del Formaggio brand's Homestyle Fresh Cheese (if in Australia), or use Indian paneer cheese.

OAXACA

This cheese, as the name suggests, is originally from Oaxaca but is ubiquitous throughout Mexico. It's also known as quesillo and queso de hebra. There are various theories about its origin, but the one I like most is that a 14-year-old girl, Leobarda Castellanos Garcia, made a mistake and invented this stringy young cheese that melts rather nicely, hence its use in quesadillas. If you can't get a hold of it, replace it with mozzarella, which is similarly boiled and stretched but not as funky.

PANELA

Panela is a young basket cheese made of pasteurised cow's milk. It has a chewy, rubbery mouthfeel and is light in flavour. As with queso fresco, substitute with La Casa del Formaggio brand's Homestyle Fresh Cheese (if in Australia), or use Indian paneer cheese. Queso panela is more about texture than flavour.

Chicharrón

I've included chicharrón (pork skin crackling; pictured above) here as it's quite tricky to make yourself. (However, I have included a meaty recipe in the book – see Chicharrón en salsa verde on page 160.) You can also source crackling in Asian supermarkets if you can't find a Mexican version. It's best to try out the different crackling available in Asian supermarkets, but avoid types with additional flavours like soy. A good chicharrón should be dry, not fatty, and have a good crunch.

Chillies

Chillies play a hugely important role in Mexican cuisine. The word chile derives from the Nahuatl word chīlli, while the Spanish call it pimentón, as it had a spiciness similar to pepper. Chillies belong to the genus *Capsicum* and are part of the nightshade family like many other domesticated species, such as tomatoes and potatoes. Five *Capsicum* species have been domesticated and most Mexican chillies derive from *Capsicum annuum*. All chilli species are native to Mesoamerica and have only been used in other cultures for approximately 500 years. Imagine what South-East Asian cuisine would taste like without them! One of the earliest discoveries of domesticated chillies dates back to about 6900 BCE, where they were found in Coxcatlán, Puebla.

I don't know the exact number of chilli varieties in Mexico, but my guess is close to 60. Many chillies are only known locally and used for just a few dishes. I, for example, just discovered simojovel chilli thanks to my cousins from Chiapas, who brought it with them last time I was in Mexico. The types of chillies increase when you account for the form they are in. For example, jalapeños are called jalapeños when fresh but become morita (if red) or chipotle (if green) when dried in a wood oven.

Sourcing the right chillies can be challenging. I have found that buying dried chillies is not so hard if you look online, so some planning might be needed. The dried chillies I always have in my pantry are guajillo, pasilla, morita and ancho. A tin of chipotle will be hiding somewhere, too. Another important detail is that your dried chillies need to be freshly dried. A good dried chilli is leathery and should not crack when pressure is put on it. Fresh chillies are more challenging, so I like to grow them at home, as the seeds are easy to find online.

Below are descriptions of the chillies I use in this book. I list the names for both fresh and dried.

ÁRBOL (FRESH) / ÁRBOL SECO (DRIED)

This is a hot red chilli. I never bother getting chile de árbol. I just use bird's eye or dried red chillies from the Asian supermarket, fresh or dried. See the photograph opposite – árbol seco is the small, red, thin chilli at the top.

CHILACA (FRESH) / PASILLA (DRIED)

Generally used dry, chilaca is a fruity chilli that adds a depth of flavour to salsas and moles, as it is quite mild. If you can't find pasilla, you can replace it with ancho, which is milder and a little sweeter. See the photograph opposite – pasilla is the large, black chilli in the centre.

GÜERO (FRESH) / CHILHUACLE (DRIED)

It's called banana chilli here in Australia and is a mild chilli that I generally use fresh for stuffing – see Chile güero relleno de picadillo (page 142).

HABANERO (FRESH) / HABANERO SECO (DRIED)
This chilli is the hottest of them all. Habanero is best known for its use in Mayan cuisine, around the Yucatán Peninsula. It's extremely hot, but it's not just about the heat – it carries a lot of flavour and is very fragrant. It's mainly served as a side and eaten raw, and it's great to make salsa with. If you can't find it fresh, use bottled habanero salsa. Similar varieties are Hainan yellow lantern chilli and Carolina reaper.

JALAPEÑO (FRESH) / MORITA (RED, DRIED) / CHIPOTLE (GREEN, DRIED)
This is probably the easiest chilli to find fresh outside Mexico. It's a great all-rounder, but it's best to try before you buy, as it can either be extremely hot or have little to no bite at all. The morita chilli (also known as chipotle morita) is a small, dried red jalapeño that has been slowly smoked. It has a mild, fruity flavour and is not very hot. The chipotle most people are familiar with is chipotle meco, made from green or ripening jalapeños. These are smoked for a longer period for a more intense flavour. Chipotle meco is not easy to find dried and is typically sold tinned, rehydrated with cane sugar, and labelled as chipotle chilli in adobo. You can substitute one dried chipotle meco for every two moritas. See the photograph on the right – morita is the black chilli at the bottom.

MIRASOL (FRESH) / GUAJILLO (DRIED)
This chilli is generally used dry. You will find it in the base of soups or moles, and it is a great addition to salsas. It has a bit of heat but not too much. If you don't have guajillo, you could use ancho. See the photograph on the right – guajillo is the red chilli at centre left.

POBLANO (FRESH) / ANCHO (DRIED)
I use ancho chillies a lot. Sometimes I'm lucky and can score fresh poblanos at my local grocery store, but they're not that common here in Australia. There's no real replacement, but it's easy to find online. Use tinned poblano chillies if you can't get them fresh; they're not the same, but they're still good. See page 231 to learn how to roast and peel the chilli before use.

SERRANO (FRESH)
A popular green chilli known for its freshness. I like it for fresh salsas. If you can't get it, use jalapeño.

Chocolate

The Aztecs called chocolate (pictured above) the 'food of the gods' and, according to legend, a cacao tree was given to them by the god Quetzalcōātl. Chocolate comes from the Nahuatl word xocolatl, and the fermented seeds have been used by both Mayans and Aztecs for more than 2500 years.

Traditionally, cacao is processed into unrefined chocolate, which is very different from chocolate in countries other than Mexico. You find 'molinos' around the central plazas of every town in Oaxaca, where they grind fermented beans with sugar, and sometimes cinnamon, to make chocolate. You can find chocolate tablets at Mexican supermarkets; they are primarily used as a spice, for Oaxacan mole, for example. There are many drinks made with cacao and chocolate. I use it in my Chocolate caliente mexicano (page 206) and champurrado (see page 184), and it is also used in tejate, tascalate and pozol.

Chorizo

To my great regret, I have never been able to find Mexican chorizo in Australia. I even had to make it myself, but it is a lot of work. Spanish chorizo is the easiest to find and is a good substitute, but it's not the same. (Spanish chorizo is a cured meat, while Mexican chorizo is raw.) If looking for Spanish chorizo, pick a brand or a butcher that makes the softest/freshest sausage. Chorizo is generally removed from its casing and fried until crisp. What I do is fry Spanish chorizo in little chunks and, once it is half-fried, mince (grind) it in a food processor to get a minced meat–like consistency, and then fry it further.

Coriander

Coriander (cilantro) is a herb that polarises, and if you're one of the 10 per cent who thinks coriander takes like soap, I'm sorry. Truly sorry. But if you're one of the 90 per cent who loves it, count your lucky stars, as it's frequently used in Mexican cuisine, adding that fresh bite to salsas and tacos. Originally a herb from the Mediterranean, it was brought to Mexico by the Spanish in the 16th century and is now one of the essential flavours of Mexican cooking.

Cream

When you think of cream and Mexican food, your mind might immediately go to sour cream, or crema agria. Truth is, we only use that type of cream for a handful of dishes. Thickened (heavy) cream and cooking cream are more appropriate to use in traditional dishes. At the market in Mexico, you find cremerías where they specialise in creams and cheeses. Cream is mostly used as a topping or a garnish to enrich the flavour and mouthfeel of dishes, such as sopes, flautas, tostadas, mole and enchiladas.

Epazote

Don't let the English names for epazote fool you. It might be known as goosefoot, skunk weed, wormseed and Mexican tea, but it's not that kind of herb. Instead it's a fresh herb used to add a strong flavour and aroma to cooked beans, mushrooms and quesadillas. There isn't a substitute, so just omit it from recipes if you can't source it. You can buy seeds online, so you might like to try growing your own, which is what I do.

Jamaica flowers

Not actually flowers, Jamaica flowers are the calyx or fleshy base of *Hibiscus sabdariffa*, also known as rosella or hibiscus rosella. The calyxes are dried and used to make infusions, and they have a tangy/tart taste. In Mexico, they are mainly used for Agua de jamaica (page 202). You can find it in the vegetable section of the supermarket. The left-over/spent flowers (after making agua de jamaica) are a great meat substitute for vegetarians and vegans, and can be used as a taco filling.

Lard

Lard, or manteca, just makes food taste better. Luckily, you can generally find lard in the supermarket but, if you can't, you can always make it yourself. Head to your local Asian supermarket, where you can get pork fat for a few dollars. Get 2 or 3 kilograms (4 or 6 pounds), cut it into small pieces, then simmer over a low heat or in a slow-cooker for a couple of hours. Ladle off the fat and strain through muslin (cheesecloth). You can keep lard at room temperature for 6 months.

Limes

If you don't have a few limes kicking around your kitchen, then you're in a bit of trouble when it comes to Mexican cooking. They are essential. They add a citrus kick as a condiment for tacos and soups, while also being the principal ingredient for ceviches and aguachiles.

Masa harina

Masa harina, or nixtamalised corn flour, is a special flour used to make tortillas (and any other masa derivative). It is a must-have for your pantry. I almost forgot to include it here, as it is second nature for Mexicans living overseas to have it in their kitchens (in Mexico, they will simply buy the tortillas freshly made!). Do not confuse masa harina with P.A.N. white/yellow corn flour – they are not the same. I will explain a bit more about masa and tortilla-making in the Essentials chapter (see Maíz y masa, page 248).

Mexican oregano

It looks like oregano, it smells like oregano, but Mexican oregano ain't oregano. It belongs to a whole different plant family, and its flavour and aroma are way more intense and complex. If you can't find Mexican oregano, you can substitute it with its Mediterranean namesake, but you'll need to add more than the recipe lists and be aware it will taste slightly different.

Mole

One of Mexico's gifts to the world. Mole, from the Nahuatl word mōlli, translates to 'sauce' and is made with chillies, herbs, seeds and tomatoes. It was made by pre-Hispanic cultures in Mexico and would be offered to the gods in thanks for their help. When the Spanish arrived, different spices were added to the sauce, including anise seeds, cinnamon, cloves and ginger, to mention a few, plus Mexican chocolate. This changed the game.

In Mexico, if you're getting married or celebrating a birthday, you need to have mole on the menu; we had it at our wedding. Unlike salsa, which also translates to 'sauce', moles are a dish on their own, not just used as an accompaniment. There are many types of mole. Poblano is the most famous, but there is also oaxaqueño, almendrado (almond), verde (green), rojo (red) and amarillo (yellow). Making mole is complicated and involves hours of charring, grinding and cooking. Therefore most people don't make their own; they go to the market and buy the mole base and finish the sauce at home.

Nopal

Nopal are tender cactus pads from the *Opuntia ficus-indica* cactus, also known as prickly pear. The young pads are soft and tender, but the spines need to be removed before you use them. (You will always find someone despining pads in the greens section of Mexican supermarkets and markets.) They are similar in flavour to green beans or asparagus, but what makes them different from other greens is that they can be a bit slimy – not unpleasantly, though. According to archaeological finds, nopal was domesticated approximately 9000 years ago, together with maize, beans and agave. When the Spanish arrived at Tenochtitlan (now Mexico City), it was translated to nopal from the Nahuatl word nohpalli.

It is such an iconic plant in Mexico that even the national coat of arms has an *Opuntia* cactus on it. I can't find any fresh nopal here in Adelaide, so I use tinned. However, if using tinned, make sure you give it a good rinse with water before using. I am growing a prickly pear in the garden now, so hopefully one day I will have some fresh nopal!

Pepita

Meaning 'little pit' in Spanish, pepitas are the husked seeds of pumpkins, also known as pumpkin seeds. They are very popular in Mexico and commonly eaten as a snack – they are the earliest known snack in Mexico, in fact – or used in sweets. As a main, they are found as an ingredient in mole verde (or pipian, see Pozole verde on page 56). Pumpkins or squash were one of the first domesticated plants in Mexico and have been on the menus of pre-Hispanic cultures for more than 10,000 years.

Tajín

If you've never tasted Tajín, run to the shop now and get yourself a bottle. And then get another one. Tajín is a chilli powder made with árbol, guajillo and pasilla chillies mixed with citric acid and salt. It's spicy, tangy and salty all at once, Mexicans put it on everything, particularly fruit. Visit the market in Mexico, and the stalls will have peeled fruit with Tajín ready to go. Have you ever tried a jícama? In Asian supermarkets, you can find it as yam bean. Peel it, cut it in chunks, add lime juice and Tajín. So good. You can also use Tajín to rim cocktail glasses.

Tomatillos

Tomatillos (pictured opposite) look like tomatoes but are far less juicy and contain smaller seeds. They are closer to cape gooseberries than a roma (plum) or truss tommy. Part of the nightshade family, *Physalis ixocarpa* is sometimes called husk tomato, as the fruit is covered by a papery husk. In Mexico City, we call them tomates, and if you're after the red ones you'll need to ask for jitomates. The word tomate comes from Nahuatl again and means 'watery fruit': tomahuac, 'fruit' and atl, 'water'. Jitomate comes from xictomatl, and xi means 'belly button' or 'navel', so 'watery fruit with a navel'. One big mistake I have seen here in Adelaide, and probably one of the reasons you can't find it here, is that people use tomatillo in salads. It is very sour and unpleasant to eat raw. It is really meant for saucing, either raw (see Salsa verde cruda on page 242) or cooked (see Salsa verde cocida on page 245), and in Entomatado de res (page 167). If you can't find it fresh, get it in a tin – it's easy to find online.

Valentina sauce

Valentina is an everyday dry chilli and vinegar hot sauce that you find everywhere in Mexico – and I mean everywhere! Grab a box of popcorn at the movies and you will drizzle loads of Valentina sauce from the pump dispenser onto your buttery puffed corn goodness. It's always good to have a bottle of Valentina sauce in your cupboard. It's seemingly indestructible as well and never seems to go off. Buy a bag of sea salt potato chips (crisps), dip them into some Valentina and you're hooked for life.

Vanilla

Vanilla comes from an orchid, the flat-leaf *Vanilla planifolia* to be precise. You can find it naturally grown all the way from Mexico to the northern part of South America. It was cultivated by the Totonac people in the state of Veracruz. The Totonacs were conquered by the Aztecs, who then used vanilla to give flavour to xocolatl, a cacao-based drink. This drink was reserved for royalty. When Hernán Cortés arrived in Tenochtitlan, now Mexico City, in 1519, xocolatl was offered by Moctezuma Xocoyotzin to welcome him.

Worcestershire sauce

What's Worcestershire sauce doing in a Mexican cookbook? Surely it's as English as a Sunday lamb roast or village cricket! Interestingly, Worcestershire sauce is a popular condiment in Mexico that we call salsa inglesa, 'English sauce'. Worcestershire sauce is an example of how Mexican cooking evolves uniquely by incorporating influences from all over the world – for example, when ordering a pizza, you will get a handful of salsa inglesa sachets. It is also popular as a marinade ingredient for meats and drinks. I use salsa inglesa for my Michelada (page 208).

Desayunos

—

Breakfast

The one thing Mexicans love more than breakfast is eggs. Mexico is among the top five consumers of eggs in the world. We're talking 21 kg (46 lb) per year for every single Mexican! This is roughly 345 eggs per person, per year! That's a lot of eggs. So, of course, we enjoy plenty of eggs for breakfast; it's one of the reasons it's such an important meal in Mexico, one we go out for regularly. Many of the recipes in the Essentials chapter (page 215) form the basis of a great Mexican breakfast. If you're planning to cook a feast for dinner, make sure you have left-over salsas, beans or corn chips to cure the next morning's hangover with a delicious breakfast.

We generally have fruit, juice, coffee and sweet breads (don't worry, Mexican sweet bread is not the sweetbread you're thinking of!) before the main dish: eggs, with spicy sauces on top, and sometimes soups or stews.

Serves 4

Preparation time 20 minutes

Cooking time 30 minutes

Dietaries Gluten free, vegetarian

Difficulty Easy

Chilaquiles

—

Corn chips with salsa

It wasn't love at first sight for me and chilaquiles; I was more a huaraches or pancita girl. But when I started making chilaquiles in Australia, I realised just how incredible they are. I guess I love them because they remind me of home, as well as being super easy to make.

Chilaquiles is a popular breakfast dish in Mexico made with tortilla chips simmered in a flavourful sauce. The tortilla chips are usually topped with queso fresco, cream and other garnishes. The name comes from the Nahuatl words chil and aquilli, translating to 'submerged in chilli'. For this recipe, I use salsa tatemada, but you can go with salsa roja or salsa verde cocida, too.

I like my chilaquiles crispy, but lots of people in Mexico like them soggy. It's up to you. You can serve them with a dollop of Refried beans (page 220) on the side. Chilaquiles can easily be served for lunch or dinner, too. If you do, add something heartier like grilled steak or shredded chicken.

- 750 g (1 lb 10 oz) Salsa tatemada (page 241), Salsa roja (page 238) or Salsa verde cocida (page 245)
- 60 ml (¼ cup) vegetable oil, to fry the eggs (if using)
- 4 eggs (optional)
- 800 g (1 lb 12 oz) corn chips (shop-bought or see page 252 for homemade)
- 150 ml (5 fl oz) thickened (heavy) cream
- 100 g (3½ oz) queso fresco, crumbled (in Australia you can substitute La Casa del Formaggio brand's Homestyle Fresh Cheese, otherwise use Indian paneer cheese)
- 1 small white onion, thinly sliced
- ½ bunch roughly chopped coriander (cilantro)

Add the salsa tatemada, salsa roja or salsa verde cocida to a large frying pan over medium heat and bring to a simmer. If it's too thick, add water – you want it a little bit runny, but not too much. Keep it warm.

(If you would like to include eggs, make them now. Add the oil to a medium frying pan over medium heat. Once hot, add the eggs and fry them to your liking. I like mine runny, especially for this dish. Once ready, transfer the eggs to a warm plate and cover them with foil until you have the chilaquiles ready.)

Now it's time to put the corn chips in a salsa bath! Add the corn chips to the salsa and toss to coat.

Transfer to four deep (preheated) plates. Top the chilaquiles with cream, crumbled cheese, raw white onion and chopped coriander (and the egg, if using).

Serves 4

Preparation time 10 minutes

Cooking time 20 minutes

Dietaries Gluten free, vegetarian

Difficulty Easy

Huevos rancheros — Ranch-style eggs

There are a couple of reasons huevos rancheros is arguably the most famous Mexican breakfast of them all: it's easy to make and incredibly tasty. Huevos rancheros are basically fried eggs on a bed of lightly fried tortillas with warm salsa roja on top.

For this recipe, you will need to have made your salsa roja and some refried beans. It is also a great recipe for using left-over tortillas from the night before. Serve huevos rancheros with a glass of freshly squeezed orange juice and a cup of coffee. In Mexico, you often get a crusty roll with butter on the side to dip into the yolk.

500 g (1 lb 2 oz) smooth Salsa roja (page 238)
500 g (1 lb 2 oz) Refried beans (page 220)
60 ml (¼ cup) vegetable oil
8 corn tortillas, preferably stale (shop-bought or see page 253 for homemade)
8 eggs
salt, to taste

TO SERVE (OPTIONAL)
queso añejo or ricotta salata
corn chips (shop-bought or see page 252 for homemade)

Heat the salsa in a small saucepan over low heat until it comes to the boil. Set aside.

Reheat the refried beans in a small saucepan. Set aside.

Heat the vegetable oil in a large frying pan over medium heat. Fry the tortillas, one by one, for about 10 seconds on each side, using tongs to flip. They need to stay soft, not become crunchy. Place the tortillas on a warm plate.

In the same frying pan, fry the eggs in pairs to your liking, salting to taste. I prefer mine sunny-side up with runny yolks.

Place two cooked tortillas side by side on a warm plate, followed by the fried eggs on top. Pour a good scoop of salsa roja over the eggs and add a dollop of refried beans on the side. Grate some cheese over the beans and finish with a couple of corn chips, if desired.

Serves 4

Preparation time 10 minutes

Cooking time 20 minutes

Dietaries Gluten free, vegetarian

Difficulty Easy

Huaraches con huevos y salsa verde

—

Huarache with eggs and salsa verde

This is huarache in easy mode – it's just eggs and salsa on a huarache. Effortless, quick and delicious, the hallmark of a great breakfast! If you're hungry, you can add a fried minute (sizzle/cube) steak instead of the eggs. Pair with a cup of coffee and some fresh orange juice.

- 400 g (14 oz) Salsa verde cocida (page 245)
- 8 eggs
- salt, to taste
- lard or vegetable oil
- 4 Huaraches (page 259)
- ½ white onion, finely diced
- 150 g (5½ oz) queso añejo or ricotta salata (optional)
- 10 g (⅓ cup) coriander (cilantro), finely chopped

Heat the salsa verde in a small saucepan over low heat just until it comes to the boil. Remove from the heat and set aside.

In a separate frying pan, fry the eggs in pairs, sunny-side up, or to your liking. Salt to taste.

Heat the lard or oil in a large frying pan over medium heat until hot. Add one or two huaraches and fry them until they are hot, about a couple of minutes each.

Pour a scoop of salsa verde on a huarache while it's still in the frying pan. Transfer to a plate using a spatula, then top with two eggs, some white onion, cheese (if using) and a sprinkle of coriander.

Serve any left-over salsa verde in a bowl on the table, as you might want to add more. ¡Buen provecho!

GRAMOSA

YUCATÁN
YWZ-487-E

Serves 2

Preparation time 20 minutes

Cooking time 20 minutes

Dietaries Gluten free

Difficulty Easy

Huevos motuleños — Motul-style eggs

Huevos motuleños are crispy tortillas topped with refried beans, two fried eggs and salsa roja yucateca. You then garnish them with peas, ham and gouda, ans serve with a side of fried ripe plantains. They remind me of the Caribbean coast as they are originally from a very small town called Motul in Yucatán. It is common to see them on menus around the peninsula for weekend breakfast.

This dish brings me back to our wedding in Mexico and specifically my friend Kate. We booked a large house in Puerto Morelos that we shared with friends. When going out for breakfast, Kate would always order huevos motuleños. Afterwards, she would ask me to make them when we returned to the holiday home, which I happily obliged. Kor would go to the cornershop to fetch plantains and eggs. Even back in Adelaide, Kate often requests this breakfast!

While plantains look like bananas, you can't substitute them with bananas, as they are too sweet – the flavours are completely different. Just go without. Enjoy with a cup of coffee and fresh orange juice.

1 ripe plantain
150 ml (5 fl oz) vegetable oil
4 stale corn tortillas (shop-bought or see page 253 for homemade)
300 g (10½ oz) Salsa roja yucateca (page 240)
200 g (7 oz) Refried beans (page 220)
4 eggs
100 g (⅔ cup) frozen peas, thawed
100 g (3½ oz) cubed ham (ensure ham is gluten-free if necessary)
50 g (1¾ oz) gouda, grated
fresh habanero, to garnish (optional)

Start by peeling the ripe plantain and cutting it diagonally into 1 cm (½ inch) thick oval slices. Cook in a frying pan with 2 tablespoons of the oil until golden brown. Set aside.

Give the frying pan a wipe with paper towel. Heat the rest of the oil and fry the tortillas until crispy, then set aside.

Heat the salsa in a small saucepan over medium heat until it comes to the boil. Set aside.

Reheat the refried beans in a small frying pan over medium heat until they start bubbling.

Now it is time to fry the eggs. Do this in pairs in the same frying pan used for frying the tortillas. I like my eggs sunny-side up.

Serve the motuleños on preheated plates. To build, place two crispy tortillas on each plate, then spread 1–2 tablespoons of refried beans on each tortilla. Add two fried eggs on top, then add a generous scoop of the salsa. Top with the peas, ham and grated cheese.

Finish by placing the plantain slices on one side of the plate, then eat immediately. If you like, you can garnish with a fresh habanero.

Serves 4

Preparation time 20 minutes

Cooking time 10 minutes

Dietaries Vegetarian

Difficulty Easy

Molletes – Toasted bread roll with beans and cheese

Molletes are one of the easiest and cheapest dishes to make and, because of this, they are pretty much an essential food group for students all over Mexico. They are an open sandwich covered with refried beans and melted cheese, served with zesty pico de gallo. These are generally served for breakfast or lunch, but I can eat them any time of the day just like I did in my student years!

When I was a student, I used to go to different restaurants for breakfast with my girlfriends. One of the options was called the 'uni student breakfast' – that was literally the name. Going out for breakfast is a tradition in Mexico, and all the restaurants have combos that include fresh fruit or a glass of juice and an Americano (as many cups as you want). The combo you choose determines the price, and the cheapest breakfast was always molletes – the uni brekkie!

- 4 large crusty bread rolls (bolillos) – think Vietnamese bánh mì rolls
- 30 g (1 oz) butter, softened
- 500 g (1 lb 2 oz) Refried beans (page 220), warm or cold
- 400 g (14 oz) queso oaxaca or mozzarella, shredded
- Pico de gallo (page 246), to serve

Preheat the oven to 200°C (400°F).

Heat a large frying pan over medium heat. Slice the bread rolls in half lengthways. Spread the butter over the bread halves, then place them, cut-side down, in the pan and cook until they are lightly golden brown and crispy, 1–2 minutes.

Spread each side of the rolls with a layer of refried beans and add some cheese on top.

Arrange the molletes on a baking tray, then bake in the oven (or under the oven grill (broiler) until the cheese has melted and turned golden.

Place the molletes on a large plate, top with pico de gallo and serve.

Serves 4

Preparation time 10 minutes

Cooking time 10 minutes

Dietaries Vegetarian

Difficulty Easy

Huevos con mole

—

Mole eggs

This is the ultimate breakfast if you have left-over mole. Eggs and mole are a match made in heaven, with the yolk and rich chocolate flavours combining into a blend that is greater than the sum of its parts. A bread roll is essential to mop up the sauce. Eggs must be runny for this and for life in general – eating hard eggs is like enjoying a steak well done: not right. Serve with fresh orange juice and coffee.

600 g (1 lb 5 oz) prepared mole from the Mole con pollo recipe on page 165
60 ml (¼ cup) vegetable oil
8 stale corn tortillas (shop-bought or see page 253 for homemade)
8 eggs
salt, to taste
200 ml (7 fl oz) thickened (heavy) cream
½ white onion, thinly sliced
4 crusty white bread rolls

Heat up the mole in a small saucepan over low heat, stirring and adding water to thin it if necessary.

Heat the oil in a large frying pan over medium heat. One at a time, fry the tortillas for about 10 seconds on each side, using tongs to flip. They need to be soft, not crunchy. Keep the tortillas warm by stacking them on a preheated plate.

Fry the eggs in pairs to your liking in the same pan, salting to taste. I prefer mine sunny-side up with runny yolks.

Place two cooked tortillas side by side on a warm plate followed by two fried eggs on top. Pour a good scoop of mole over the eggs so they are fully covered. Add a dollop of cream over the mole and garnish with thinly sliced white onion – this is not optional; it really needs the raw onion.

Serve the eggs with a crusty white bread roll – don't eat the bread roll all at once, as you will need it to mop up what's on the plate.

Enjoy. Trust me, you will thank me for this recipe.

SA
Great

Serves 2

Preparation time 15 minutes

Cooking time 5 minutes

Dietaries n/a

Difficulty Medium

Machaca con huevo

—

Eggs with machaca

This is a typical northern Mexican dish (pictured on page 233). When doing research for this book, I asked a friend from Chihuahua: 'What would you traditionally have for breakfast?' 'Machaca con huevo' was the answer. It's painless to make if you have machaca (dried and salted beef meat pulled to shreds) on hand. There is a recipe to make your own machaca in the Essentials chapter (page 232), so you might need to do some prep before you start. If you're lucky, your local Mexican shop might stock machaca. I'm yet to find it in Australia, unfortunately.

- 1 tablespoon vegetable oil
- ½ white onion, finely diced
- 4 jalapeños, deseeded and finely diced
- 80 g (2¾ oz) Machaca (page 232)
- 160 g (5½ oz) roma (plum) tomatoes, finely diced
- 4 eggs, beaten
- 250 g (9 oz) Refried beans, made using pinto beans (page 220)
- 50 g (1¾ oz) ricotta salata, grated
- 6 wheat tortillas (shop-bought or see page 234 for homemade), warm
- 100 g (3½ oz) Salsa roja (page 238)

Heat the oil in a frying pan over medium heat. Fry the onion until translucent, then add the jalapeños. Saute the jalapeños for a minute before adding the machaca, then cook for a minute or two.

Add the tomato and give it a good stir. (I like to add the tomato at this stage as I don't want it to disintegrate – I want to still feel the texture.)

Immediately add the beaten egg, and mix it with the machaca mixture until the eggs are to your liking.

Heat the refried beans in a small saucepan over low heat.

Place the scrambled eggs on a serving plate, then place the refried beans next to the eggs. Sprinkle some grated cheese on the beans.

Serve the eggs with the warm wheat tortillas and salsa roja.

If you fill a tortilla with some refried beans, followed by the egg with machaca and some salsa, you'll have a burrito de machaca con huevo.

Makes / serves	**Preparation time**	**Cooking time**	**Dietaries** Can be vegetarian	**Difficulty** Easy
8 / 4	5 minutes	10 minutes		

Simple quesadillas

—

Quesadillas de harina

This is our default breakfast dish at home. Kor: 'What do you want for brekkie today? Me: 'A couple of quecas' – short for quesadillas. It's as easy to make as a grilled cheese sandwich and much, much tastier. The quesadillas used for this recipe are basically folded wheat tortillas with ham and cheese. However, quesadillas can be complex, as the way they are made and the ingredients used change from state to state in Mexico. Literally, quesadillas translate to 'cheesy tortillas', but the funny thing is that not all quesadillas have cheese. Then again, this is only true for Mexico City. It can get very confusing, even for Mexicans! Children love quesadillas, so they are a great addition to your Mexican dinner party if the kids are coming along. If you're vegetarian, replace the ham with slices of mushroom or Refried beans (page 220).

8 wheat tortillas (shop-bought or see page 234 for homemade)
300 g (10½ oz) grated mozzarella or other melting cheese
4 slices of ham (or sliced mushroom or Refried beans, page 220, for a vegetarian option)
slices of avocado
Chiles en escabeche (page 229) or Salsa macha (page 244)

Place a comal, hotplate or large non-stick frying pan over medium–low heat.

Fill one half of the cold tortillas with a handful of cheese and half a slice of ham, then fold. Place the would-be quesadilla in the pan – no butter, no oil, you just want dry heat – and cook it for a couple of minutes, then flip. Continue until the cheese has melted and the tortilla has a lightly charred surface. Depending on the size of your pan, you can cook two to four quesadillas at a time.

Cut the quesadillas in half, if you want, then place them on a plate with slices of avocado and chiles en escabeche or salsa macha.

Sopas y caldos

—

Soups + broths

Mexico isn't the first country people tend to name-drop when they talk about the world's great soup nations, but it should be right up there. Soup ranks number one in the list of underappreciated Mexican foods as, for some strange reason, it's not recognised outside of Mexico's borders. What gives?! I wish more people knew about our rich history and traditions when it comes to soup.

We slurp soups as full meals and enjoy them at all times of the day. There are breakfast soups, such as pancita (tripe soup), while we enjoy sopa de pasta (pasta soup) and chicken consommé at comida time (2–3 pm); cena (8–10 pm) is for pozole (hominy soup). The Aztecs and Mayans were big slurpers before the Spanish arrived, but Mexico's soups are now heavily influenced by other cuisines.

Soups in Mexico have huge regional diversity. On my last visit, I went to Maíz de Cacao, a restaurant that specialises in regional dishes of the Huasteca Veracruzana. They recommended we try the wedding soup, or albóndigas de boda de la Huasteca, a light meatball soup. It was a revelation. I'm working on a recipe at the moment, so fingers crossed it will be on our restaurant's menu soon or in a future book.

Soups like Pozole verde (page 56) and Mole de olla (page 61) find their origins in pre-Hispanic dishes, where the local produce from the milpas – traditional permaculture plots – and meats were boiled into a broth. The soups we find in Mexico today are the result of 500 years of trial and error.

Makes / serves 2 litres (8 cups) / 6

Preparation time 1 day

Cooking time 1½ hours

Dietaries n/a

Difficulty Medium

Sopa de migas
—
Mexican bread soup

Sopa de migas, which translates to Mexican bread soup, isn't the sexiest of soups. Besides not having a very appealing name, I must warn you, it doesn't look great. I know I'm not selling it but, believe me, this soup is the food version of 'you can't judge a book by its cover'. It's what David Chang would call 'ugly delicious'. We'd always have this at home when my mother made Tostadas de salpicón (page 131). For salpicón, you boil flank steak for 1½ hours and the resulting beef broth is then converted into sopa de migas with left-over stale bread rolls. There is no wastage here. The side products just become the base for the next dish. Unsexy. Unglamourous. But delicious.

3 stale white bread rolls
1 tablespoon vegetable oil
½ whole garlic bulb, halved horizontally
6 árbol chillies, whole
4 morita chillies, seeds and stems removed
1 Mexican or Spanish chorizo (about 160 g/5½ oz), cut into cubes
1 white onion, diced
2 litres (8 cups) beef stock (see Tostadas de salpicón on page 131 if you want to make your own)
1 teaspoon dried Mexican oregano
handful of epazote (optional)
2 eggs, lightly beaten
15 g (½ oz) salt, or to taste
3 limes, halved
dry chilli flakes or chilli powder, to serve

Start by placing the stale bread rolls in water to soak. My mum always told me it's best to do this the day before making the soup, but a couple of hours works, too (just don't tell my mum!).

Before you start making the soup, take the bread rolls out of the water, squeeze the water out of them and set aside.

Add the oil to a large stockpot over medium heat. Place the halved garlic bulb face-down in the oil and fry until golden brown. Add the chillies and chorizo and cook, stirring, until the chorizo is crispy. Don't let the chillies burn, as this will make the soup taste bitter.

Add the onion and fry until translucent, about 2 minutes. Add the bread and let it soak up some of the flavour.

Add the stock, oregano and epazote (if using). Once the broth comes to the boil, turn the heat down to a simmer and slowly pour the beaten egg in while gently stirring. You want the egg to form threads. Season with salt to taste. Remove the garlic and discard.

Serve the soup in individual bowls, with a bowl of limes and dry chilli flakes or chilli powder on the side. Squeeze the lime into your soup, top with the chilli and enjoy.

Makes / serves About 2.75 litres (11 cups) / 6

Preparation time 20 minutes

Cooking time 40 minutes

Dietaries Gluten free, can be vegetarian

Difficulty Easy

Crema de chile poblano

—

Poblano chilli soup

I used to make this soup at our underground dinner parties, Mi Mero Mole. I wanted people to experience the full flavour of poblano chillies. Because these chillies are hard to find fresh in Australia, and can be very expensive, I decided to serve them as a soup to not waste anything.

1 kg (2 lb 4 oz) charred poblano chillies (see page 231); if you can't get fresh, use tinned
90 g (3¼ oz) unsalted butter
1 large brown onion, diced
1 celery stalk, diced
1 carrot, diced
100 g (3½ oz) baby spinach leaves
10 g (¼ oz) flat-leaf parsley, chopped
1 litre (4 cups) chicken stock (see page 221 for homemade) or vegetable stock
500 ml (2 cups) full-cream (whole) milk
300 ml (10½ fl oz) cooking cream, plus extra to serve
3 teaspoons table salt

TO SERVE

splash of extra-virgin olive oil
strips of fried corn tortilla (see page 55)
roasted or charred corn kernels

Make sure the stems are removed from the chillies. If you don't want the chillies to be too spicy, take the veins and seeds out as well. Reserve one chilli for garnish (cut into strips), then chop the rest into chunks.

Heat the butter in a large stockpot over medium heat. Add the onion, celery and carrot and cook until the carrot is soft. Add the chillies, spinach and parsley and saute for 5 minutes.

Add the stock and milk, reduce the heat to medium–low and simmer for 15 minutes.

Turn the heat off, add the cooking cream and stir it through. Let the soup cool down a little before processing the soup in batches in a blender or food processor (or use a stick blender in the pot) until smooth and silky.

Before serving, return the soup to the same pot and reheat. Season with salt.

Serve the soup in bowls and garnish with the reserved poblano chilli strips and a dollop of extra cream on top. Add a splash of good olive oil, strips of fried tortilla and roasted or charred corn kernels.

Makes / serves 2 litres (8 cups) / 6

Preparation time 30 minutes

Cooking time 30 minutes if you have the stock

Dietaries Gluten free, can be vegetarian

Difficulty Medium

Sopa de tortilla — Tortilla soup

Sopa de tortilla is also known as sopa azteca or Aztec soup. It is a simple but delicious soup and, as the name hints, is full of tortillas. This soup has been on La Popular's menu for years. Whenever we take it off, we get complaints. So it stays on. What makes this soup so delicious are the different textures – crispy tortilla strips, soft avocado, chewy cheese and a dollop of cream. The soup is made in two stages. First is the soup base (which you can pre-make and keep in the freezer) and the second is the assembly. This recipe is traditionally made with chicken stock, but if you are vegetarian you can use vegetable stock instead.

2 litres (8 cups) chicken stock (see page 221 for homemade) or vegetable stock

SOUP BASE

8 guajillo chillies, deseeded
2 garlic cloves
1½ brown onions, cut into chunks
700 g (1 lb 9 oz) ripe tomatoes
½ bunch coriander (cilantro), leaves picked
1 teaspoon dried Mexican oregano
1 teaspoon ground cumin
6 corn tortillas (shop-bought or see page 253 for homemade), cut into quarters
20 g (¾ oz) salt

TO GARNISH

1 guajillo chilli, to garnish
6 stale corn tortillas, (shop-bought or see page 253 for homemade), to garnish
200 ml (7 fl oz) vegetable oil
1 avocado
200 g (7 oz) cheese (queso panela if you can get it, but mozzarella works, too)
100 g (3½ oz) chicharrón or pork crackling (omit for vegetarian)
100 ml (3½ fl oz) thickened (heavy) cream

For the soup base, soak the guajillo chillies in boiling water until soft, about 5 minutes. Once soft, drain them and put them in a blender or food processor with the rest of the soup base ingredients. Blend on high until you have a soft paste – it shouldn't have any grittiness. Pass the base through a fine-mesh strainer.

For the soup, bring the stock to a slow boil in a stockpot, then add the soup base. Simmer until the soup thickens, about 30 minutes.

Meanwhile, prepare the garnishes. Using scissors, carefully cut the guajillo chilli into thin rings and cut the stale tortillas into 5 mm (¼ inch) wide strips.

Pour the vegetable oil into a small saucepan and heat to about 180°C (350°F). I use a thermometer to test the oil, but if a piece of bread dropped in the oil browns in about 15 seconds, the oil is at the correct temperature. Fry the chilli until crispy – don't let the chilli burn, this happens in about 5–10 seconds – then place on paper towel to drain.

In the same oil, fry the tortilla strips until crispy, about 3 minutes – these won't burn as easily. Place the strips on paper towel.

Halve the avocado, remove the seed and cut into slices.

Put all the garnishes in separate bowls on the table. Serve the soup in a large bowl. Each person can add whichever garnishes they want. I recommend: a handful of tortilla strips, cheese, avocado, chicharrón, a drizzle of cream, then the fried chilli. Keep adding more as you eat.

Makes / serves 3–4 litres (12–16 cups) / 8 | **Preparation time** 30 minutes | **Cooking time** 3 hours | **Dietaries** Gluten free | **Difficulty** Medium

Pozole verde – Green pork hominy soup

Just around the corner from my parents' place in Iztapalapa is a restaurant called Tapsa. It's nothing fancy for Mexico City, but it's our local for pozole, which we would enjoy there or take home, depending on the occasion. Pozole is enjoyed as an evening meal or made specifically for a celebration, and is a traditional dish from the state of Guerrero. You commonly eat it on Independence Day or during the Christmas holidays. Restaurants that specialise in pozole are called pozolerías.

Pozole finds its origin in the pre-Hispanic Aztec culture, where maize would be boiled to make a stew. Cacahuazintle is the maize used for pozole. It's a large-kernelled heirloom maize, which is nixtamalised (treated in an alkaline solution), then beheaded or descabezado (a process where the base of the corn kernel is removed for it to open or bloom when boiled).

There are many versions of pozole, including white and red soups. The pozole I present here, pozole verde, is not the simplest to make, but if you use the pork stock without the mole verde, you will have the basic pozole blanco or white pozole. The 'verde', or green, comes from the mole verde (a green vegetable and nut paste) that is added to the soup.

PORK STOCK

1 pork trotter, cut in half lengthways by your butcher
1 kg (2 lb 4 oz) pork bones
1 kg (2 lb 4 oz) pork shoulder, skin and fat removed, cut into 5 cm (2 inch) chunks
1 large brown onion, quartered
1 whole garlic bulb, halved horizontally
4 litres (16 cups) water
4 bay leaves
10 g (¼ oz) salt
800 g (1 lb 12 oz) tinned hominy

MOLE VERDE

150 g (1 cup) pepitas (pumpkin seeds)
300 g (10½ oz) tomatillos, fresh or tinned
50 g (1¾ oz) poblano chillies, fresh or tinned
80 g (2¾ oz) jalapeños
30 g (1 oz) radish leaves (use the leaves from the garnish radishes)
80 g (1⅔ cups) baby spinach leaves
½ teaspoon dried Mexican oregano
handful of epazote (optional)
2 teaspoons table salt
50 g (1¾ oz) lard
1 large brown onion, cut into chunks
2 garlic cloves

TO GARNISH

16 Tostadas (page 256)
½ iceberg lettuce, thinly sliced
8–12 radishes, sliced into thin rounds (use the leaves in the mole verde)
1 white onion, finely diced
2 avocados, halved and thickly sliced
4 limes, halved
100 g (3½ oz) pork crackling (optional)
chilli powder – piquín if possible
20 g (¾ oz) dried Mexican oregano

Place all the stock ingredients, except the hominy, in a large stockpot over high heat. Bring to the boil, then lower the heat and leave it on a rapid simmer for 2 hours. While the meat and bones are cooking, skim any scum that rises to the surface.

Remove all the bones and meats from the pot. Let the meats cool down a bit so you can shred them. If you like the fatty bits, leave a few; if not just shred the solid meat. Place the meat in a separate bowl and reserve. Strain all the stock and return it to the pot on a slow simmer.

While the stock is cooking, make the mole verde. Dry-roast the pepitas in a small frying pan over medium heat for 2–3 minutes. When nicely toasted, place the seeds in a blender with the tomatillos, both chillies, the radish leaves, spinach leaves, oregano,

epazote (if using) and salt, and process to a fine paste. Set aside.

In a medium frying pan, add the lard and fry the onion and garlic over medium heat until blackened – this will give more flavour to the lard.

Remove the onion and garlic from the pan, squeezing them as much as possible to keep most of the lard in the pan. Discard the onion and garlic.

Add the blended green paste to the lard and cook over medium heat for about 10 minutes until thoroughly cooked. Stir the frying paste constantly, as it will burn easily.

Transfer the paste to the stockpot. Once it boils, lower the heat to medium and add the shredded meat together with the hominy. Cook for 15 minutes more or until the maize blooms. The pozole is ready to serve.

Place the tostadas, lettuce, radish, onion, avocado, limes, pork crackling, chilli powder and oregano in bowls and plates on the table. Serve a large bowl of steaming hot pozole followed by the rest of the ingredients. The oregano is generally rubbed between the hands above the plate so it reduces in size. (If you see someone rubbing the oregano, you know they are from Mexico.) Mix and keep on adding until you are happy with the flavour. ¡Provecho!

Makes / serves
About 2.5 litres (10 cups) / 4

Preparation time
30 minutes, plus time to make the stock

Cooking time
2–3 hours

Dietaries
Gluten free

Difficulty Medium

Caldo de pollo estilo Yucatán — Yucatán-style chicken soup

This dish takes me back to when I first met my husband, Kor, at a marine research station in Puerto Morelos, Quintana Roo, in 1997. We had no car, just old bicycles. The only way we could get to the closest village, El Puerto, about 2–3 km (1–2 miles) away, was on our trusty bikes. The roads were horrible to ride on, but the scenery was beautiful. You'd never see cars, just endless mangroves and an abundance of animal life, including crocodiles, snakes, monkeys, migrating crabs and mozzies – lots of mozzies. It was always an adventure, and sweaty and humid. At around comida time – 2–3 pm – we would jump on our bikes and ride to El Puerto to eat a caldo de pollo at Antojitos Yucatecos El Tío, a tiny hole-in-the-wall with plastic tables and chairs near the old leaning Puerto Morelos Lighthouse, which nearly fell over in 1967 after a hurricane. Yes, we would eat soup on a hot and humid day after a bike ride! In Mexico, it doesn't matter if it's hot or not, it's always time for caldos or sopas.

This recipe is a whole meal. The soup is a hearty chicken broth with charred pollo adobado (see page 119), lettuce, diced avocado and a side of toasted (not fried) tostadas, served in a cheap plastic bowl. Serve with half a lime and some habanero hot sauce to add more heat to the heat. Just thinking about caldo de pollo estilo Yucatán makes me time travel to the Mexican Caribbean in the '90s. This is my spin on the soup, an ode to that time.

stock from a whole chicken about 2 litres/8 cups (see page 221 for recipe)
whole chicken from the stock (above)
50 g (1¾ oz) Recado rojo (page 223)
1 tablespoon vegetable oil

TO SERVE

12 oven-toasted Tostadas (page 256)
3 limes, halved
habanero hot sauce (shop-bought or see page 247 for homemade)
200 g (7 oz) White rice (page 224)
1 white onion, finely diced
½ iceberg lettuce, thinly sliced
½ bunch coriander (cilantro), chopped
2 avocados, halved and cut into cubes

Start by making the stock with a whole chicken. This will take a couple of hours, so do this early in the day, or the day before. When the chicken is cooked, remove the chicken breast and leg quarters and set them aside.

Use the recado rojo to cover the two cooked boneless, skinless chicken breasts and leg quarters.

Heat the oil in a frying pan over medium heat and fry the meat until nicely charred. Let the chicken cool, then shred it. Set aside in a bowl.

Once you are happy with the intensity and seasoning of your stock, pass it through a strainer set over a large bowl, then return the liquid to the empty pan over medium–low heat.

Get everything ready for serving. Place the tostadas, limes and habanero hot sauce on the table.

To each serving bowl, add a scoop of the white rice and a handful of the chicken, then fill the bowls with the boiling hot soup. Add some onion, lettuce and coriander. Finish by squeezing in some lime, adding some avocado cubes and a splash or two of habanero hot sauce – it needs to be spicy – then crumble a tostada in. Add more tostadas once you run out of these 'Mexican croutons'.

Makes / serves 2 litres (8 cups) / 4

Preparation time 30 minutes

Cooking time 2½ hours

Dietaries Gluten free

Difficulty Medium

Mole de olla — Pot mole soup

This dish has very little to do with the other moles, as it's not a sauce but a soup. Mole de olla was a comforting meal that my mother made often. My mum and sister would fight for the marrow as soon as the mole de olla hit the table. If one of them was lucky enough to find a bit that had not melted into the stock, they would immediately spread it on a tortilla, add some salt and make a taco. I wasn't a fan of the marrow back then, but now I love it.

It's believed that this dish, originally from the central parts of Mexico (Mexico City and surrounding states), finds its origin in the fusion of Spanish meat stews with produce from the milpas – the traditional agricultural system – such as corn, chillies and squash. The goal is for the meat to become fall-off-the-bone tender and full of flavour.

It's traditionally served with xoconostle, a fibrous cactus fruit or prickly pear, but I have not found anything similar to it in Australia as yet. There are lots of sayings in Mexico related to food; we have one that goes: A darle que es mole de olla. This means: 'Get on with it', 'Don't hesitate as there is some urgency', or 'Chop chop'! So, stop what you're doing and try this: ¡A darle que es mole de olla!

- 1.5 kg (3 lb 5 oz) osso buco, about 4 slices
- 1 brown onion, cut into large chunks
- 4 garlic cloves
- handful of epazote (optional)
- 15 g (½ oz) salt, plus extra if needed
- 2 all-purpose potatoes (I like brushed Dutch cream), peeled and cut into 3 cm (1¼ inch) chunks
- 1 choko (chayote), cut into 2 cm (¾ inch) chunks (if you can find it, otherwise omit)
- 1 corn cob, cut into 4 pieces
- 250 g (9 oz) zucchini (courgette), cut into 2 cm (¾ inch) chunks
- 100 g (3½ oz) green beans, halved
- 2 limes, halved
- 12 corn tortillas (shop-bought or see page 253 for homemade)

SOUP BASE

- 11 pasilla chillies, deseeded
- 3 garlic cloves
- 1 small brown onion
- 400 ml (14 fl oz) water

Add 2 litres (8 cups) of water to a stockpot and place it over high heat. Add the osso buco, onion, garlic, epazote (if using) and salt. Once boiling, turn the heat down and let the meat cook on a slow simmer for approximately 1½ hours, covered. Skim any foam that forms on top and discard it.

Meanwhile, prepare the soup base. Place all the ingredients in a medium saucepan over medium–low heat. Simmer for 20 minutes.

Drain the ingredients from the stockpot through a colander and into a bowl (reserve the liquid) and place the solids in a blender or food processor. Add 200 ml (7 fl oz) of the reserved liquid to the blender and keep the rest of the liquid for later. Blend until the base becomes smooth, and you don't see any bits and pieces. Set aside.

Remove the chunks of onion and the garlic cloves from the stockpot and discard. Add the blended soup base to the pot with the meat and stir. Keep cooking for 30 minutes. Once the meat is ready, it should fall apart easily. Check for salt and add more if needed. Add the potatoes, choko and corn and allow to boil for another 20 minutes.

Add the zucchini and green beans and cook for 10 more minutes. The soup should be ready to serve – check the salt and add extra if needed.

If the soup is very thick, add the remaining reserved liquid from the soup base. If you need more, add some water.

Serve the soup in large bowls and distribute the meat and vegetables among them. Place the lime halves in a bowl to serve on the side, and heat up a small basket of corn tortillas.

Squeeze the lime into the soup and eat the meat with the tortillas.

Makes / serves 750 ml (3 cups) / 10 shots

Preparation time 30 minutes

Cooking time 2 hours

Dietaries Gluten free

Difficulty Medium

Caldito de camarón – estilo cantina

—

Cantina-style prawn stock

High school changed my life. It's when I started travelling with friends and exploring Mexico City's cinemas, cultural events and music festivals. One of our favourite places to visit was the City Centre's cantinas. In these cantinas, also known as centros botaneros or salones familiares, the premise is simple: as long as you keep ordering beers or bottles of rum and coke, you'll be served snacks for free. For a group of students, this was heaven! This is where I tried caldito de camarón for the first time, served in a shot glass. It was a revelation! Caldito, which translates to 'little broth', needs to be super intense and full of umami and prawn (shrimp) flavour. Serve the soup in a tequila shot glass with a wedge of lime.

1 tablespoon vegetable oil
1 brown onion, chopped
½ carrot, finely diced
100 g (3½) small dried prawns (shrimp)
150 g (5½ oz) fresh school prawns (shrimp)
4 coriander (cilantro) shoots, finely chopped
500 ml (2 cups) very cold water
2 guajillo chillies
4 árbol chillies
1 garlic clove
salt, to taste
2 limes, quartered

Add the oil to a medium saucepan over medium heat. Add half the chopped onion and all the diced carrot, then cook for 10 minutes. Add the dried and fresh prawns and coriander, together with the very cold water, and cook for 30 minutes until everything is soft. You want to extract as much flavour as possible from the prawns.

Meanwhile, bring 500 ml (2 cups) of water to a slow boil in a small saucepan over medium heat. Add the chillies, the remaining onion and the garlic and cook for 10 minutes. Remove the saucepan from the heat and leave it to rest for 5 minutes. Drain and reserve the liquid. Put the cooked chillies, garlic and onion, along with 100 ml (3½ fl oz) of the reserved cooking liquid, in a blender and process until creamy. Pass through a fine-mesh strainer and set aside.

Once the prawn stock is ready, pass it through a colander lined with muslin (cheesecloth). Do this step in batches to collect as much of the stock as possible. Once the liquid has passed through, squeeze the muslin to ensure all the delicious juices come out – this is the intense flavour we are after. Discard all the solids and reserve the liquid.

Add the prawn stock to a medium saucepan over high heat. Add the chilli mixture, together with the salt, and cook until it starts boiling. Turn the heat down to low and cook for 25 more minutes. While cooking, taste the stock and add more salt if needed, but be careful not to add too much as the stock will intensify as it evaporates.

Once you're happy with the flavour, stop simmering and store until serving time. The flavours will get more intense if you keep it in the fridge overnight.

Heat up the stock, pour it into shot glasses and place a wedge of lime on top. Squeeze the lime juice into the broth and serve.

Makes / serves 1.5 litres (6 cups) / 4

Preparation time 30 minutes

Cooking time 30 minutes

Dietaries Gluten free, can be vegetarian

Difficulty Easy

Crema de frijol – Black bean soup

Crema de frijol is an easy soup to make, perfect for the cold, dark days of winter. It's also a great way to use left-over beans from the night before. I make mine with black beans, but you can use any type of bean. Throw in chochoyotes, little masa balls (corn dumplings), and let them cook in the soup for a few minutes to take this dish to another level.

1 tablespoon vegetable oil
50 g (1¾ oz) bacon, cut into cubes (optional, omit for vegetarian)
2 large tomatoes
½ white onion
1 garlic clove
500 g (1 lb 2 oz) cooked black beans (see page 218)
½ teaspoon dried Mexican oregano
½ teaspoon ground cumin
1½ teaspoons table salt, plus extra to taste
300 ml (10½ fl oz) full-cream (whole) milk
8 epazote leaves (optional)

CHOCHOYOTES

100 g (3½ oz) Masa (page 250)
½ teaspoon dried Mexican oregano

TO SERVE

100 g (3½ oz) queso panela or Italian fresh cheese, crumbled
100 ml (3½ fl oz) thickened (heavy) cream
olive oil for drizzling

Heat the oil in a medium frying pan over medium heat and cook the bacon (if using) until crispy. Transfer to a bowl and set aside.

In a large frying pan, char the tomatoes, onion and garlic until blackened – don't use any oil.

Working in batches, add the charred tomatoes, onion and garlic, beans, bacon, oregano, cumin and salt to a large blender or food processor and blend into a smooth sauce. Remove the centre cap of the blender lid and slowly pour the milk into the black bean cream as it processes. The end result should be frothy.

For the chochoyotes, mix the masa with the oregano and form the dough into 5–10 g (⅛–¼ oz) balls – approximately the size of grapes. Apply pressure with your finger to create an indentation in the centre of each ball.

Place a medium saucepan over medium–low heat and add the soup and the epazote (if using). Let the soup come to a gentle boil. Add the chochoyotes and keep stirring carefully, as you don't want to break up the little dough balls. Cook for 15 more minutes or until the chochoyotes are cooked. Season with salt to your liking.

Serve the soup in a large bowl, crumble some cheese over the top and add a dollop of cream. Drizzle with olive oil and serve.

Antojitos, garnachas y entradas

—

Snacks + starters

This chapter is like a produce market: it has a bit of everything. It's hard to pigeonhole some dishes in this book, or in Mexican cuisine in general, into a category like starters or mains. Some of these can be a snack – an antojito – but if you eat more, then it becomes a main.

Antojo means 'feeling peckish'. Antojitos is the diminutive – 'little snacks'. They are snacks eaten for the pleasure of eating them, not necessarily because you feel hungry. There is some debate about what a garnacha actually is. Garnachas are a special kind of antojito, derivatives of masa (corn dough) that have been fried – think flautas, sopes, empanadas and quesadillas. They are generally sold on street carts. Entradas is a more general term for starters, which you are more likely to find in a restaurant rather than at a street cart. Some of the recipes, such as guacamole and ceviche, are not a garnacha or an antojito.

Makes / serves
500 g (1 lb 2 oz) / 4

Preparation time
10 minutes

Cooking time
Nil

Dietaries Gluten free, vegan

Difficulty Easy

Guacamole

Do I even need to give this an introduction? Everyone knows guacamole, right? Ubiquitous and simple it might be, this is a party staple that many get wrong due to the endless recipes that are out there. The key to this dish lies in its simplicity. The hero of guacamole is the avocado, of course, so choose carefully. I like to use hass avocados, as they are creamy. I've used shepard avocados in the horror months when hass avocados are out of season, but the flavour and texture are just not the same. Lots of people don't realise that guacamole is a mole, or sauce – a sauce of avocados. The Aztec word mōlli means 'sauce' in Nahuatl, and ahuacatl means 'avocado'. (Fun fact: ahuacatl is also a Nahuatl word for 'testicle'.)

2 medium-ripe avocados, halved
salt, to taste
pinch of freshly ground black pepper
juice of 1 lime
¼ white onion, diced
½ bunch coriander (cilantro), finely chopped
1 tomato, cut into small dice
corn chips (shop-bought or see page 252 for homemade), to serve

Place the avocado flesh in a bowl and mash a little using a fork – I like this guacamole a bit chunky.

Add the salt, pepper and lime juice – at this point, I like it well seasoned. Add the rest of the ingredients and mix well.

This guacamole recipe is meant to be served with corn chips as a starter or a snack. You could use it on tacos, but Guacamole estilo mercado (page 72) is more suitable for that.

It's best to eat the guacamole immediately. Don't keep it overnight as the flavours degrade quickly, and if you've ever seen an overnight guacamole the morning after, you know what I mean.

Left to right: Guacamole estilo mercado (page 72), Guacamole (opposite)

Makes / serves 400 g (14 oz) / 4 | **Preparation time** 10 minutes | **Cooking time** Nil | **Dietaries** Gluten free, vegan | **Difficulty** Easy

Guacamole estilo mercado

—

Market-style guacamole

When you go to the markets in Mexico, you will see big molcajetes (mortars and pestles) full of guacamole without tomatoes. I guess it's easier for the avocado not to turn – that's my theory anyway. This recipe is similar to the guacamole on page 70, but here the tomatoes make way for chillies. Guacamole estilo mercado (pictured on page 71) is generally finer than an everyday guacamole, as it is ground in a molcajete.

¼ white onion, diced
¼ bunch coriander (cilantro), finely chopped
2 jalapeños or serrano chillies
juice of 1 lime
salt, to taste
2 medium-ripe avocados, halved, then chopped
corn chips (shop-bought or see page 252 for homemade), to serve (optional)

Add the onion, coriander, chillies, lime juice and salt to a mortar and mash with a pestle until you have a paste.

Add the avocado, a little at a time, to the mortar and mash it through the mix, continuing until you again have a paste.

You can serve this guacamole with corn chips, but I prefer it as a topping for tacos.

Makes 500 g (1 lb 2 oz) **Preparation time** 10 minutes **Cooking time** 1 hour 20 minutes **Dietaries** Gluten free, vegan **Difficulty** Easy

Cacahuates enchilados

—

Spicy peanuts

This recipe (pictured on page 63) comes with a warning; as a famous American snack slogan goes – once you pop, you can't stop. Simple, salty and smashable, this is perfect party food. Best of all, you can make cacahuates enchilados a few days in advance, as they will keep for a couple of weeks in a well-sealed container. But trust me, they won't last that long! Best enjoyed with a cold beer (or two).

20 g (¾ oz) fine salt
5 g (⅛ oz) citric acid powder
5 g (⅛ oz) chilli powder
500 g (1 lb 2 oz) raw peanuts
2 tablespoons peanut oil or vegetable oil

Preheat the oven to 160°C (325°F). Mix the salt and citric acid powder, then grind to a fine powder. I like to use my spice grinder for this, but you could use a mortar and pestle.

Place the mixture in a small bowl, then add the chilli powder. Mix well and set aside.

Arrange the peanuts on a large baking tray, so the nuts are not on top of each other. It is best to have a tray with four sides, as this will make tossing the hot nuts easier.

Place in the middle of the oven and bake for 30 minutes, then toss. Place back in the oven and toss every 10 minutes until the peanuts are roasted. This can take up to an hour, depending on the type, size and age of the peanuts.

Check the peanuts do not taste raw by biting into one. They won't be crunchy yet; this will happen as they cool down. When you're happy with the taste, place the nuts in a large bowl.

You need to do this next step when the peanuts are still hot, otherwise the coating won't stick. Add the oil – just enough for the peanuts to be coated but not drenched. Add the spicy mix and toss, then leave in the bowl to cool down.

Makes / serves	**Preparation time**	**Cooking time**	**Dietaries** n/a	**Difficulty** Easy
500 g (1 lb 2 oz) / 8	30 minutes	10 minutes		

Charales enchilados

—

Crispy whitebait with chilli

This is another easy-to-make snack that goes wonderfully with beer, and is great to kick off a dinner party. Generally whitebait is used, but small school prawns (shrimp) are also excellent. The idea is to fry these little fish until they become crispy – you don't need to worry about guts, heads or scales, as it all turns into crispy goodness! Make sure the whitebait comes sand-free, as a mouthful of sand makes for a deeply unpleasant eating experience. If you can't find whitebait, Asian supermarkets generally have packs of frozen school prawns – one 500 g (1 lb 2 oz) pack will make a bowlful.

500 g (1 lb 2 oz) frozen whitebait, or small school prawns (shrimp), thawed
1 litre (4 cups) vegetable oil
200 g (1⅓ cups) plain (all-purpose) flour
2 teaspoons table salt
2 teaspoons chilli powder
10 g (¼ oz) fine salt
2 limes, cut into wedges

Pat the thawed fish or prawns dry with paper towel. Set aside.

Heat the oil to 180°C (350°F) in a medium pan – I like to use an enamelled cast-iron pan, as the oil temperature is easier to control in a thick pan. I use a thermometer to test the oil temperature, but if a piece of bread dropped in the oil browns in 15 seconds, the oil is the correct temperature. You can also use a deep-fryer.

Place the flour in a bowl, add the table salt and mix to combine. Prepare a second large bowl by lining it with paper towel.

Grab a handful of fish and place them in the bowl with the flour mixture, tossing them so they are lightly dusted.

Take the fish out with a strainer spoon and place them in the hot oil. Cook for approximately 5 minutes. The cooking time will depend on the size of the fish. Test a fish every now and then to make sure they are cooked through and crunchy.

Place the fried fish in the second bowl with the paper towel, then repeat with the next batch. Transfer all the fried fish to a clean bowl and dust with chilli powder and fine salt. Mix well.

Serve warm with the lime wedges on the side. Squeeze the lime over the fried fish before eating. Accompany with a cold beer (essential).

Makes / serves	**Preparation time**	**Cooking time**	**Dietaries**	**Difficulty** Easy
1 kg (2 lb 4 oz) / 8	20 minutes	3½ hours	Gluten free, vegetarian	

Esquites

–

Corn in a cup

With its name derived from the Nahuatl word izquitl, meaning 'toasted corn', esquites (pictured on page 77) can be described as a deconstructed Elote callejero (page 76). Served in a cup, esquites evolved with the introduction of mayonnaise, cheese and lime into the street-food snack we know and love today. You find these at the same cart or stall where elotes are made. Esquites are made from corn kernels and are cooked with butter, onions, epazote and chillies. They are then served in a cup with lime, mayonnaise, chilli powder and cheese. As it is hard to find savoury corn in Australia, I use popping corn to make esquites. This will take a fair bit of boiling, but the result is very good – if you use a pressure cooker you will have a faster result. I like to add pickling lime – food-grade calcium hydroxide powder – to the mix, to break down the seed coat. If you don't have it, cook for a little longer.

500 g (1 lb 2 oz) popping corn
1 teaspoon pickling lime (food-grade calcium hydroxide; optional)
4 teaspoons table salt, plus extra to taste
3 árbol chillies
50 g (1¾ oz) unsalted butter
1 small white onion, finely chopped
handful of epazote leaves (optional)

GARNISH PER 150 G (5½ OZ) SERVE

200 g (7 oz) whole-egg mayonnaise
40 g (1½ oz) queso cotija or cyprus haloumi, grated
8 g (¼ oz) chilli powder
4 limes, halved

Add the corn, 2.5 litres (6 cups) of water, the pickling lime, salt and árbol chillies to a large pot over medium heat and bring to a slow boil. Cook for approximately 3 hours with the lid on. The cooking time might vary, depending on the age and hardness of the corn. Add extra water if necessary. Taste a kernel now and then to check if it is fully cooked. It needs to be soft but with a firm bite. If using a pressure cooker, add the same ingredients but cook for 30 minutes.

When the corn is ready, drain and set aside with the chillies.

In a medium pot over medium heat, add the butter and fry the onion until translucent. Add the cooked corn, chillies and the epazote (if using) and fry for 5 minutes. Add 1 litre (4 cups) of water, bring to the boil and cook for another 20 minutes. Taste and season with extra salt if needed.

Serve esquites hot in small cups. Traditionally, they are served in takeaway cups as a street snack. My serves are quite large – 150 g (5½ oz) – but you can make them smaller if you prefer.

To finish, add a dollop of whole-egg mayonnaise, then grated cheese and chilli powder. Squeeze the lime juice in and mix well. Enjoy!

Serves 4

Preparation time 5 minutes

Cooking time 20 minutes

Dietaries Gluten free, vegetarian

Difficulty Easy

Elote callejero

–

Grilled corn on the cob

Walk around any plaza or market in Mexico and you will find a corn stall or puesto de elotes. Elotes are fresh cobs of corn roasted on a little barbecue or boiled on a street cart – hence callejero, which means 'from the street'.

At high school, my friends and I would walk to the nearby Plaza Coyoacán just to have one of these – or Esquites (page 75) – while we loitered around or sat on a park bench to people-watch and gossip.

These aren't too dissimilar to the corn on the cob you'll find in other parts of the world, but Mexicans like to go a bit extra and bold with the flavours. We cover the cooked cob with mayonnaise and sprinkle it with crumbled cheese, chilli and lime. A messy but delicious business.

I don't know why, but the only fresh corn you find in Australia is sweet corn, while in Mexico this type of corn is not common. The flavour of Mexican fresh corn is more starchy and not so sweet; the kernels are also less juicy. If you can't find non-sweet corn or fresh maize, use sweet corn. Usually, the corn is boiled, and some places sell them charred, which I prefer for sweet corn.

4 corn cobs with husks on
4 wooden skewers (see Tip)
150 g (5½ oz) whole-egg mayonnaise
200 g (7 oz) grated queso cotija or ricotta salata
chilli powder, to sprinkle
2 limes, halved

Place the corn cobs on a hot barbecue and grill for 30 minutes, turning regularly. The husk will protect the corn from burning.

After 20 minutes, remove the burnt husks and fibres and char the cob until the kernels get some colour, about 10 more minutes.

Remove from the fire and stick the wooden skewers into the cobs. Cover the warm cobs with mayonnaise and sprinkle with cheese until fully covered. Sprinkle with chilli powder. Squeeze a little lime over the corn and enjoy.

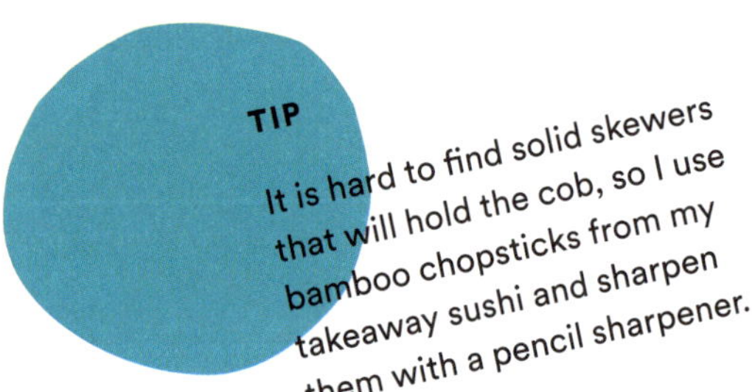

TIP

It is hard to find solid skewers that will hold the cob, so I use bamboo chopsticks from my takeaway sushi and sharpen them with a pencil sharpener.

Left to right: Elote callejero (opposite), Esquites (page 75)

Serves 4

Preparation time 5 minutes

Cooking time 20–30 minutes

Dietaries Gluten free, vegan

Difficulty Easy

Cebollitas cambray

—

Grilled spring onions

These are a must when you are hosting a carne asada (barbecue). A simple dish that you find in many taquerías, cebollitas cambray is really a side or a starter. The white bulb spring onions (scallions) are grilled on the barbecue until they are soft, then served with a wedge of lime. I find it very hard to source the right-sized spring onions here in Australia. Generally, they are spring onions without a bulb, and once I find them with a bulb they are too big! So I just use whatever is available.

8 bulb spring onions (scallions with bulbs) or regular spring onions (scallions)
vegetable oil
salt, to taste
1 lime

Cut off and remove the floppy green leaves from the spring onions, but keep the thicker stem and bulb. Also remove any roots. The onions with greens should be about 15 cm (6 inches) long.

Place the onions in a large bowl and drizzle with some oil and season with salt to taste.

Heat a barbecue, preferably coal, to high heat. Place the onions on the grill and cook for 20–30 minutes, turning frequently. The goal is to cook them all the way through so they become sweet. A few char marks are fine, but don't let them go black. Once cooked, keep them on the side until ready to serve.

Place the onions in a bowl and squeeze over the juice of the lime, adding more salt to taste. If the bulbs are very large, slice them lengthways.

It's best to eat these with Tacos de asada (page 114) at a barbecue with friends. You can place the onions with the meat in a tortilla or just eat them as is.

CLARA

Serves 1

Preparation time 20 minutes

Cooking time 10 minutes

Dietaries Gluten free, vegetarian

Difficulty Medium

Chicharrón de queso — Cheese crackling

This dish has the shortest list of ingredients – just cheddar. It is not the easiest dish to make, though – it took me a couple of tries to get it right. It's commonly served as a starter at a taquería with some salsa or pico de gallo. I made this a single-serve recipe, but you can easily make more if you need to. The goal is for a crispy cheese crust – it shouldn't be oily. Try some of your local cheeses to see which one works best. In Adelaide, I have found that sharp cheddar gives the best result. I suggest buying packaged cheese slices, which will be easier to cook because they are even in thickness.

4 slices of packed sliced sharp cheddar

TO SERVE (OPTIONAL)

Pico de gallo (page 246), Salsa tatemada (page 241) or Guacamole estilo mercado (page 72)

Heat a large non-stick frying pan over low heat. Arrange the four slices of cheese in the pan to form one large square. The edges of the slices need to touch but not overlap. Cook for about 5 minutes until the cheese starts to split (releasing oil). If there is an excess of oil, tip it out of the pan.

Turn up the heat to medium and keep cooking for about 5 minutes more until the cheese turns golden brown. With a thin spatula, try to get under the crust so you can flip it – it should not be melted cheese but a crispy crust approximately 1 mm ($\frac{1}{32}$ inch) thick and 20 cm (8 inches) in diameter. Flip the cheese crust and cook for a minute to make sure it is all crispy. Flip it back onto the other side.

With the spatula, take the cheese crust out of the pan and place on a chopping board. The next step should happen immediately (before the cheese becomes hard).

Take a round object – I use my narrow rolling pin – and roll the crust into a tube. Use an oven mitt or tea (dish) towel to do this, as the cheese is very hot.

Don't worry if you can't get the crust into a tube form – it took me a couple of goes. If you have a fail, simply break the cheese into shards and serve in a bowl instead.

You can make chicharrón de queso a couple of hours in advance; just let it cool down, then store in a sealed container.

Chicharrón de queso makes a great sharing dish, so cook a few, then serve on a nice plate. Serve with a bowl of pico de gallo, salsa tatemada or guacamole estilo mercado. Break into pieces and enjoy!

Makes 250 g (9 oz)

Preparation time 10 minutes

Cooking time 15 minutes

Dietaries Gluten free, vegan

Difficulty Easy

Sikil p'aak – Pepita dip

Sikil p'aak is a classic paste/dip from the Yucatán peninsula (to be more precise, Campeche). It comes from the Mayan words p 'aak, which means 'tomato', and sikil, which means 'pumpkin seed' – a toasted pumpkin seed dip with tomato, if you will. If you like hummus you'll be into sikil p'aak, although this is much spicier!

80 g (2¾ oz) pepitas (pumpkin seeds)
140 g (5 oz) very ripe tomatoes
¼ small red onion
1 small habanero
¼ bunch coriander (cilantro)
½ teaspoon table salt
corn chips (shop-bought or see page 252 for homemade), to serve (optional)

Start by toasting the pepitas in a dry frying pan over high heat for about 2 minutes. Keep tossing the pepitas, as they will burn easily. They are ready when fragrant and slightly charred. Transfer to a bowl and set aside. Reserve a few pepitas for decoration.

In the same pan (no oil), char the tomato, onion and habanero. The habanero and onion will be ready after 5–6 minutes, so remove them from the pan when they are ready. The tomatoes will take up to 10 minutes to char fully. Keep turning so they don't burn.

Add all the ingredients, except the reserved pepitas, to a bullet blender and blend until you have a smooth sauce. It is okay if it's a little gritty.

Place the sikil p'aak in a bowl and sprinkle with the remaining pepitas. You can serve the sikil p'aak with corn chips as a dip.

A DELICIOUS SIDE

I have also found other uses for the paste. The following is not a traditional recipe, but I created it for one of my Mi Mero Mole dinners and it is a delicious side to impress. Pan-fry some green beans with white onion. Next add a dollop of sikil p'aak to a nice plate, then add the fried beans. Garnish with wedges of peeled mandarin or orange and some toasted pepitas.

Serves 4

Preparation time 30 minutes

Cooking time 3 minutes

Dietaries Gluten free

Difficulty Medium

Aguachile

—

Prawns in chilli water

This is a perfect summer dish that is as refreshing as a dip in the Gulf of California on a hot day. It is a kind of ceviche, the difference being that it needs to be served immediately once you mix the prawns (shrimp) with the cucumber, lime and onion. It should also be very spicy. The prawns will be 'cooked' in the lime juice, but they still need to be rawish, so quality prawns are essential – never use frozen or pre-cooked prawns. Here in Adelaide, I like to use tiger prawns. Recently we created a miniature version – a sort of canapé – using fresh scallops, where we used the shell as a serving plate.

The name aguachile literally means 'chilli water'. This comes from the blitz of lime, cucumber, jalapeños and lime juice that becomes something similar to water (agua in Spanish). Serve with corn chips or tostadas and some tequila or mezcal.

800 g (1 lb 12 oz) large raw prawns (shrimp; 3 prawns per person)
1½ telegraph (long) cucumbers
250 ml (1 cup) freshly squeezed lime juice
½ white onion, for the marinade
¼ bunch coriander (cilantro)
1 jalapeño or 2 serrano chillies – or any other green chilli (but make sure they're hot)
1½ teaspoons table salt

TO SERVE

½ red onion, thinly sliced into half moons
2 tablespoons extra-virgin olive oil
200 g (7 oz) corn chips (shop-bought or see page 252 for homemade) or 4 Tostadas (page 256)

Peel and remove the veins from the prawns. Butterfly the prawns lengthways, cutting from the back to the belly but not all the way through. Set aside.

Cut one cucumber in half lengthways and slice both halves thinly (into 3 mm/⅛ inch thick half moons) for the garnish. Keep the slices in the shape of the cucumber.

Peel the remaining half with a potato peeler – a bit of skin is okay – then cut into rough chunks. Add the cucumber, lime juice, white onion, coriander, jalapeños and salt to a blender or food processor. Blend for 1 minute until liquified. Taste – it should blast with lime, spice and salt. If happy, place in a glass bowl.

Just before serving, place the prawns into the mix, toss them to cover with the aguachile sauce and leave them to 'cook' for 3 minutes.

Serve the prawns on a platter with all the sauce and place the slices of cucumber all around the platter. Finally, dress the plate with the thinly sliced red onion and a drizzle of olive oil. Serve the aguachile with corn chips or tostadas.

Makes / serves About 800 g (1 lb 12 oz) / 6

Preparation time 5 minutes

Cooking time 20 minutes

Dietaries Can be vegetarian

Difficulty Medium

Pasta seca enchipotlada

—

Chipotle dry pasta

This recipe will seem odd to someone who is not from Mexico. 'Dani, pasta's not Mexican!' I hear you say. But we take influences from all over the world and make it our own, and chipotle dry pasta is a great example of this. Made with tomatoes and chipotle, this is usually served as a starter, but you can enjoy it as a main, too. I also like to stuff poblano or ancho chillies with it, then cook them in the oven.

- 400 g (14 oz) ripe tomatoes, roughly chopped
- ⅓ brown onion
- 1 garlic clove
- 50 g (1¾ oz) tinned chipotle in adobo
- ¼ teaspoon dried Mexican oregano
- 30 ml (1 fl oz) vegetable oil
- 250 g (9 oz) short-cut angel hair pasta
- 350 ml (12 fl oz) chicken stock (see page 221 for homemade) or vegetable stock
- 1 teaspoon table salt
- 400 g (14 oz) Refried beans (page 220; (optional)
- 150 g (5½ oz) queso fresco (in Australia you can substitute La Casa del Formaggio brand's Homestyle Fresh Cheese, otherwise use Indian paneer cheese)

Place the tomato, onion, garlic, chipotle chilli (and juice) and oregano in a blender and process until liquefied.

Add the oil to a medium or large saucepan over medium heat. When the oil is hot, add the dry pasta! You have probably never cooked pasta this way, but trust me – fry the pasta.

Keep it moving until it is all toasty, about 5 minutes. It will change colour slightly to brown. Now, add the tomato mixture to the saucepan and coat all the pasta with the liquid, moving it with a spatula. Cook the pasta for 1 minute, then add the chicken stock and salt. Reduce the heat to medium–low and simmer for 6 minutes. The pasta is ready.

I like to serve the pasta over a bed of refried beans and crumble some cheese on top before serving.

La langosta está

Serves 4

Preparation time 20 minutes

Cooking time 20 minutes

Dietaries Gluten free, vegetarian

Difficulty Medium

Chile ancho relleno de queso de cabra

—

Stuffed ancho chilli with goat's cheese

Ancho chillies are the ripe, dried version of the poblano chilli, and are generally mild with a raisin-like taste. This dish bursts with flavour and is a guaranteed crowd-pleaser as a starter. You can prep the chillies a couple of hours in advance – just don't let them go dry.

- 100 g (3½ oz) piloncillo (raw cane sugar)
- 4 ancho chillies
- 120 g (4¼ oz) goat's cheese, aged not fresh
- 350 g (12 oz) Refried beans (page 220)
- handful of coriander (cilantro) leaves, to garnish

Break up the piloncillo into chunks and add it, together with 500 ml (2 cups) of water, to a small or medium saucepan over medium heat. Bring to a gentle boil and stir until the sugar dissolves.

Ancho chillies are dry and need to be rehydrated. We also need to clean them without damaging the chilli too much. So I dip the chillies in the hot sugary liquid for just a couple of seconds, until the skin softens.

Lay the chillies on a chopping board and slit them open along the side, lengthways, using a small paring knife. Dislodge the seeds near the stems and remove any veins. Leave the stems on.

Rinse the chillies under cold, running water to float the seeds out. Place all the clean chillies in the saucepan with the sugar water and let them simmer for 5 minutes. Remove carefully from the water with tongs, then transfer to a bowl. The chillies will now be rehydrated but also very fragile.

Preheat the oven to 160°C (325°F).

Cut the cheese into 30 g (1 oz) sticks – the same size as the rehydrated chillies. Insert a cheese stick into each chilli through the slit, then place the chillies on a small baking tray. Cover the tray with foil.

Heat up the chillies on the tray for 10 minutes. While the chillies are in the oven, reheat your refried beans in a small frying pan over low heat, stirring, for about 5 minutes. Add some water if necessary to loosen.

I like to serve the chillies individually on small, preheated plates. Add a scoop of refried beans to each plate and lay a chilli on top. Garnish with coriander leaves.

Makes / serves	Preparation time	Cooking time	Dietaries	Difficulty Easy
350 g (12 oz) / 8	10 minutes	20 minutes	Gluten free	

Gordita de chorizo con papa — Chorizo and potato gordita

Chorizo con papa (chorizo and potatoes), pictured on page 90, is a classic combination for a reason. I like to serve it with gorditas – as chorizo, potatoes and gorditas thrown together with salsa verde is a mouthful of heaven! I like to chop the potatoes into tiny cubes so you can fit them in the gorditas. Chorizo con papa can also be a filling for a taco or a sope and is a great addition to a taquiza (see Tip). They're so versatile and delicious that you'll want to serve them with pretty much anything! Mexican chorizo is a raw sausage, not cured, and can be crumbled, like minced (ground) meat, into a frying pan. You're unlikely to find this type of chorizo in Australia, but it doesn't matter too much as Spanish chorizo will work, too– just pick the softest you can find.

1 Mexican or Spanish chorizo, about 150 g (5½ oz), cut into 1 cm (½ inch) dice (ensure chorizo is gluten free if necessary)
1 tablespoon vegetable oil
300 g (10½ oz) baking potatoes, peeled and diced into 1 cm (½ inch) cubes
1 small white onion, finely diced
½ teaspoon table salt
8 Gorditas (page 258), warm
¼ iceberg lettuce, thinly sliced
150 g (5½ oz) Salsa roja (page 238), Salsa verde cruda (page 242) or Salsa verde cocida (page 245)
100 g (3½ oz) queso fresco, crumbled (in Australia you can substitute La Casa del Formaggio brand's Homestyle Fresh Cheese, otherwise use Indian paneer cheese)

Fry the chorizo in the oil in a frying pan over medium heat for about 5 minutes until half-cooked. Add the cubes to a food processor (not a blender) and chop until it's a minced (ground) meat consistency. Reserve the oil in the pan.

In the same frying pan, fry the diced potato for 5 minutes, then return the chorizo to the pan, along with the onion, and fry for another 10–15 minutes. Taste and add salt only if necessary, as sometimes chorizo can be really salty.

To the warm gordita pockets, add the chorizo con papa mixture, followed by thinly sliced lettuce, a tablespoon of salsa and some crumbled queso fresco. Keep a bowl of salsa nearby, as you might need more as you go!

A taquiza is a buffet-style dinner that is generally held on special occasions, such as birthdays and weddings. Guests can make their own tacos with a variety of tortillas, fillings, toppings and salsas. I usually include guisados (stews), a couple of starters and salsas and some grilled meat. Taquizas are a great way to throw Mexican parties at home. See page 260 for a suggested menu.

Left side of plate: Gorditas de chorizo con papa (page 89). Right side of plate: Gorditas de chorizo de hongos (opposite)

Makes / serves
450 g (1 lb) / 8

Preparation time
10 minutes

Cooking time
20 minutes

Dietaries Gluten free, vegetarian

Difficulty Easy

Gorditas de chorizo de hongos — Mushroom 'chorizo' gordita

This vegetarian chorizo is more than just a mere substitute for the meaty version. Of course it's not real chorizo, but the taste is so similar that it will even have carnivores asking for more. Because this goes so well in a gordita, it's in this section. However, feel free to add my mushroom chorizo to sopes or tacos, or stuff it in a quesadilla.

- 4 pasilla chillies, deseeded
- 2 guajillo chillies, deseeded
- 750 ml (3 cups) boiling water
- 4 garlic cloves
- ½ teaspoon dried Mexican oregano
- 3 peppercorns
- ¼ teaspoon cumin seeds
- 1 tablespoon white vinegar
- 2 teaspoons table salt
- 1 small white onion, finely diced
- 4 tablespoons vegetable oil
- 500 g (1 lb 2 oz) Swiss brown mushrooms, finely diced or chopped in a food processor
- 300 g (10½ oz) baking potatoes, peeled and cut into 1 cm (½ inch) cubes
- 8 Gorditas (page 258), warm
- ¼ iceberg lettuce, shredded
- 200 g (7 oz) Salsa roja (page 238), Salsa verde cruda (page 242) or Salsa verde cocida (page 245)
- 100 g (3½ oz) queso fresco, crumbled or cut into small cubes (in Australia you can substitute La Casa del Formaggio brand's Homestyle Fresh Cheese, otherwise use Indian paneer cheese)

Toast the pasilla chillies in a dry frying pan over medium heat for 30–45 seconds. Turn them regularly, as they burn easily. Set aside on a plate, then repeat the process with the guajillo chillies. Place all the chillies in a bowl, cover with the boiling water and let sit for 10 minutes.

Char the garlic in the same pan over the same heat for approximately 10 minutes. Drain the chillies and reserve ½ cup (125 ml) of the water.

Place the chillies, garlic, oregano, peppercorns, cumin, vinegar, salt and reserved soaking water in a food processor and blitz to a paste.

In a large frying pan over medium heat, fry the onion in 2 tablespoons of the oil until translucent, about 5 minutes, then add the mushrooms. Let the mix cook until all the liquids released have evaporated – this will take about 5 minutes.

Add the chilli paste and cook until the liquids have evaporated again, about 10 minutes more. It should now have a thick consistency. You can store this mix/paste in the fridge for at least a week.

In a separate large frying pan over medium heat, fry the potato in the remaining 2 tablespoons of oil until golden, about 10 minutes. Add the mushrooms and chilli paste, then mix and fry for another 5 minutes.

To serve, add some of the chorizo de hongos with potato to the warm gordita pockets, followed by the thinly sliced lettuce. Add a tablespoon of the salsa of your choice and some crumbled queso fresco. Keep a bowl of salsa nearby, as you might need more as you go!

Makes / serves 12 / 4–6

Preparation time About 1 day

Cooking time 10 minutes

Dietaries Gluten free, vegetarian

Difficulty Medium

Codzitos

—

Fried tortilla rolls with Yucatán-style tomato salsa

Also known as taquitos de nada or 'empty/nothing tacos', codzitos are perfect as a little snack before dinner. Hailing from the Yucatán Peninsula, they are deep-fried, rolled-up tortillas sprinkled with salsa and cheese with ... nothing inside. Koots means 'rolled up' in Mayan and ito is diminutive in Spanish, so codzito is a hybrid word meaning 'little rolled-up things'. You will need some sewing thread to keep the tortillas rolled up. It's best to dry the codzitos in the sun, so they don't open when fried. I recommend doing this a day in advance.

- 12 thin corn tortillas (shop-bought or see page 253 for homemade)
- 12 × 10–15 cm (4–6 inch) lengths of sewing thread
- 200 g (7 oz) Salsa roja yucateca (page 240)
- vegetable oil
- 150 g (5½ oz) queso sopero or haloumi, crumbled

The first step is to make the tortillas, or heat-up some shop-bought ones. Keep the warm tortillas in a tea (dish) towel while making the codzitos. Each tortilla needs to be rolled up tightly, then secured by winding some thread around it. Do this a day in advance, because we need to dry the tortillas – it's best to leave them in the sun for a couple of hours. Once the codzitos are dry, remove the thread. Set aside until ready to fry and serve.

Warm the salsa in a small saucepan over low heat.

Shallow-fry the codzitos (in about 1 cm/½ inch of oil) for approximately 5 minutes in a medium frying pan over medium heat, until golden brown and crunchy. Let them drain in a bowl lined with paper towel.

Place the codzitos on a long, oval serving plate and pour the warm salsa over them. Top with the crumbled cheese. Eat with your hands.

Makes / serves 12 / 6

Preparation time 30 minutes

Cooking time 20 minutes

Dietaries Gluten free

Difficulty Easy

Pescadillas – Acapulco fish fritters

Pescadillas are street food, which you often get on a plastic plate placed inside a plastic sandwich bag. (This way your food vendors don't need to wash the plate, but just slip the plate into a clean bag.) When enjoying these crisp tacos, make sure you have a slice of lime to add a refreshing tang, as well as a side of Valentina sauce for a kick of heat. This is a great dish for when you need to make use of left-over fish. You can prepare pescadillas a day or two in advance, then freeze and fry on the day, as they will keep if the fish mix is not too damp.

1 tablespoon vegetable oil, plus extra for frying
1 small brown onion, finely diced
1 garlic clove, minced
350 g (12 oz) tomatoes, diced
salt, to taste
freshly ground black pepper, to taste
350 g (12 oz) firm white fish fillets (you can use left-over cooked fish)
12 corn tortillas (shop-bought or see page 253 for homemade)
toothpicks
cabbage, thinly sliced
2 limes, cut into wedges
Valentina sauce

Heat the oil in a large frying pan over medium heat. Add the diced onion and cook until translucent, about 3 minutes. Add the minced garlic and cook for another minute.

Stir in the tomato and cook the sauce, stirring, for 5–10 minutes, allowing the flavours to combine. Season with salt and pepper.

Add the fish to the pan and keep cooking until the fish is well incorporated and flakes easily with a fork, about 5–10 minutes depending on the fish. Break up the fish – but not too much, as we want chunky bits of fish in the pescadillas.

Reduce the heat to low and cook for another 5 minutes or until the sauce reduces and there's no liquid left. Taste and check the seasoning.

Warm the tortillas in a dry frying pan over medium heat and place in a tea (dish) towel. Add a tablespoon of cooked fish to a tortilla, fold in half, then secure the sides with toothpicks. Repeat with the remaining tortillas and fish.

Add the oil for frying (about a 3 cm/1¼ inch depth) to a heavy-based pan over medium heat – I like to use an enamelled cast-iron pan, as the oil temperature is easier to control in a thick pan. Heat the oil to 180°C (350°F). I use a thermometer to test the oil, but if a piece of bread dropped in the oil browns in about 15 seconds, the oil is at the correct temperature.

Place the pescadillas into the oil and fry for 3–4 minutes – turning them to cook evenly on each side – or until golden brown and crispy.

Remove the pescadillas from the pan and place them on paper towels to drain any excess oil. Remove the toothpicks.

To eat, open the pescadillas, add some cabbage, squeeze over some lime juice and finally top with some Valentina sauce.

Makes / serves 8 / 4

Preparation time 30 minutes

Cooking time 40 minutes

Dietaries Gluten free, vegetarian

Difficulty Medium

Quesadillas fritas

—

Fried quesadillas

This is a typical garnacha, a deep-fried masa sold on the street. Quesadillas are usually cheesy tortillas, but not all quesadillas have cheese. The quesadillas in this recipe are made from raw masa and not tortillas, so they are uncooked when you make them. You can fill quesadillas with ingredients such as mushrooms, Picadillo (page 164), zucchini (courgette) flowers or Gorditas de chorizo de hongos (page 91). This recipe is for mushrooms and epazote, but feel free to replace with zucchini (courgette) flowers if in season.

1 tablespoon vegetable oil, plus extra for frying
½ brown onion, finely chopped
1 garlic clove
250 g (9 oz) button mushrooms, sliced
½ teaspoon table salt, plus extra to taste
pinch of freshly ground black pepper
500 g (1 lb 2 oz) Masa (page 250)
200 g (7 oz) queso oaxaca or mozzarella, pulled or grated
8 epazote leaves (optional)
¼ iceberg lettuce, thinly sliced
150 g (5½ oz) Salsa verde cruda (page 242), Salsa verde cocida (page 245) or Salsa roja (page 238)
100 ml (3½ fl oz) thickened (heavy) cream
150 g (5½ oz) queso fresco (in Australia you can substitute La Casa del Formaggio brand's Homestyle Fresh Cheese, otherwise use Indian paneer cheese)

For the filling, heat 1 tablespoon of oil in a medium frying pan over medium heat and fry the onion and garlic until translucent. Add the mushrooms, salt and pepper and fry until the mushrooms are soft, 5–10 minutes. Taste and season with more salt if necessary.

To make the quesadillas, take 60 g (2 oz) portions of the masa dough and form them into balls about the size of a golf ball.

Place a ball between two sheets of sandwich-bag plastic (about 20 cm/8 inches square) in a tortilla press. Press down firmly to flatten the dough into a circle about 15 cm (6 inches) in diameter and 3 mm (⅛ inch) thick. Rotate the flattened dough with the plastic sheets 180 degrees, then press again gently. Remove the top sheet of plastic.

Fill the middle of each dough disc with a scoop of cheese (about 20 g/¾ oz), some mushroom mix (about 20 g/¾ oz) and an epazote leaf (if using). I suggest you do a couple of trial runs to test the dough and your folding skills before you cook.

Now it's time to close the quesadillas using the bottom plastic sheet to help you. Fold the dough over, creating a half circle, making sure the edges meet perfectly. With the plastic sheet still in place, seal the quesadilla along the edge with your fingers. There should be no cavities in the quesadilla, or you will lose the cheese and the oil might spatter. The quesadilla is ready to fry.

Add oil (about a 3 cm/1¼ inch depth) to a heavy-based pan over medium heat – I like to use an enamelled cast-iron pan, as the oil temperature is easier to control in a thick pan. Heat the oil to 200°C (400°F). I use a thermometer to test the oil, but if a piece of bread dropped in the oil browns in about 10 seconds, the oil is at the correct temperature.

Remove the quesadilla from the plastic and fry in the hot oil on both sides until golden brown. This will take about 3 minutes – I like to splash the top side with hot oil while frying. Let the quesadillas drain on some paper towel.

Place the hot quesadillas on a plate and make an opening in the top with your fingers. Add lettuce, then salsa and cream, and finish with some crumbled cheese.

Makes / serves	Preparation time	Cooking time	Dietaries	Difficulty Medium
8 / 4	30 minutes	30 minutes	Gluten free	

Panuchos

When I lived in the Mexican Caribbean as a biology student, we were just 2 kilometres (just over a mile) away from the village of Puerto Morelos. Here, we enjoyed the traditional Yucatán/Mayan dish of panuchos and salbutes after a nice bike ride. These are thick tortillas (panuchos are stuffed with beans while salbutes are not), which are fried in lard, then topped with lettuce, adobo chicken (see page 119), pickled red onions and avocado. Add a drop of habanero hot sauce and I'm back in my Caribbean paradise. We would eat these as appetisers before tackling a Caldo de pollo (page 58) from El Tío, a small eatery in Puerto Morelos that we would frequent regularly.

1 boiled chicken breast (see page 222)
30 ml (1 fl oz) Recado rojo (page 223)
1 tablespoon vegetable oil, to fry the chicken
350 g (12 oz) Masa (page 250)
160 g (5½ oz) Refried beans (page 220)
3 tablespoons lard or vegetable oil

TOPPINGS

30 g (1 oz) thinly sliced white cabbage or iceberg lettuce
2 tomatoes, thinly sliced
100 g (3½ oz) Salsa roja yucateca (page 240)
80 g (2¾ oz) Cebolla curtida (page 228)
1 avocado, sliced
habanero hot sauce (shop-bought or see page 247 for homemade)

Cover the chicken breast with the recado rojo. Heat the 1 tablespoon of oil in a small frying pan over medium heat and fry the chicken until it has a nice caramelised coating, about 3 minutes per side. (You can also grill the marinated chicken on a barbecue.)

Let the chicken cool, then shred it and place in a bowl – it does not need to be hot when served; warm is fine.

To make the panuchos, roll portions of the masa (about 40 g/1½ oz) into balls.

Place a ball between two sheets of sandwich-bag plastic (about 20 cm/8 inches square) in a tortilla press. Press down firmly to flatten the dough into a circle about 10 cm (4 inches) in diameter and about 5 mm (¼ inch) thick. Rotate the flattened dough with the plastic sheets 180 degrees, then press again gently. Repeat with the remaining dough balls.

Cook the soon-to-be panuchos on a comal, hotplate or in a non-stick frying pan for 3–5 minutes on each side. Make sure they are cooked in the middle. Let them cool for a couple of minutes, but don't let them go cold.

Slice through the side about halfway through to make a pocket. Open the pocket and fill with refried beans. Set aside.

Prepare all the toppings and place them and the shredded chicken in separate bowls.

Once you are ready to serve, heat a medium frying pan over medium heat and add the lard or oil. Fry the panuchos until they are golden brown, about 2 minutes each side. When ready, the panuchos should still be soft but with a bit of crisp. Drain the panuchos on a plate lined with paper towel.

To serve, place the panuchos on a plate. On top of each, add a handful of cabbage or lettuce, some shredded chicken, a slice of tomato and some salsa roja yucateca. Finish with the slice of avocado and some cebolla curtida, and you're done.

Place all the panuchos on a serving plate and place a bowl of habanero hot sauce on the side. I suggest napkins, too, as it can get messy.

Makes / serves 16 / 4–8

Preparation time 30 minutes (1 day if making ahead)

Cooking time 40 minutes

Dietaries Gluten free, vegetarian

Difficulty Easy

Flautas de papa – Crispy potato tacos

Flautas simply mean flutes, and they are named for their shape. They are shallow-fried rolled tortillas with a filling – in this case potato mash. In some parts of Mexico, these would be called tacos dorados. Flautas can be served at lunch or dinner, but they are also used as a side with pozole and other dishes. They are easy to make but take a bit of time and planning. They are also a clever way to use your leftovers. Another very common flauta filling is cooked and shredded chicken or beef (if you're a carnivore by nature).

My mum always prepared the uncooked flautas a day in advance, so the flutes would hold their shape when shallow-frying.

3 mashing potatoes, peeled and cut into cubes
salt, to taste
16 corn tortillas about 15 cm (6 inches) in diameter (shop-bought or see page 253 for homemade)
500 ml (2 cups) vegetable oil
500 g (1 lb 2 oz) Salsa roja (page 238), Salsa verde cruda (page 242) or Salsa verde cocida (page 245)
150 ml (5 fl oz) thickened (heavy) cream
½ iceberg lettuce, thinly sliced
50 g (1¾ oz) ricotta salata, grated

Cook the potato in a saucepan of salted water over high heat until tender. Drain, making sure to save a few tablespoons of the cooking water. Mash the potato (adding some of the cooking water if the mash feels dry). Add more salt to taste, if necessary, then set aside.

Working in batches, heat the tortillas on a comal, hotplate or in a non-stick frying pan for a few seconds on each side, then place in a clean tea (dish) towel. This process will make the tortillas softer and easier to roll – if you roll cold tortillas they will split.

To make a flauta, take about 1½ tablespoons of the mashed potato filling and place in a tortilla, slightly off centre, but do not overfill. Roll the tortilla up very tightly. Repeat with the remaining tortillas and mash.

Place the flautas in an airtight container that is just big enough to hold all 16 flautas. Place them closely together so they don't unroll. You will have a better result if you make the flautas the day before, as they will hold their shape when frying.

Add the oil for frying (a depth of about 1–2 cm/½–¾ inch) to a medium heavy-based frying pan – the oil temperature is easier to control in a thick pan. Heat the oil to 180°C (350°F). I use a thermometer to test, but if a piece of bread dropped into the oil browns in 15 seconds, the oil is at the correct temperature.

Working in batches of four, fry the flautas until golden and crispy, about 3–5 minutes, using tongs to turn them over while frying. Place the flautas on a plate lined with paper towel to drain. You can keep the freshly fried flautas in a low oven, as they will stay crisp – just keep an eye on them, as they will dry out if you keep them in too long.

Place four crispy flautas on a plate, top with salsa, cream, lettuce and cheese. Repeat for the remaining flautas. Serve flautas as a starter or main. The easiest way to eat flautas is with your hands, although you'll want to use a spoon to scoop up all the goodness that will spill out when you eat them. It's always messy, so have napkins on hand.

Serves 4 | **Preparation time** 30 minutes | **Cooking time** 20 minutes | **Dietaries** Gluten free | **Difficulty** Medium

Ceviche de pescado con mango y aguacate

—

Fish ceviche with mango and avocado

This ceviche has the perfect balance of sweetness, creaminess and tanginess. It's delicious and super fresh (especially with some drops of habanero hot sauce). This dish always takes me back to cave diving near Akumal in the Yucatán Peninsula. A friend of ours would make this at home and bring it to the dive site. After the dive, we'd get stuck into the cold beers and this delicious fish ceviche with mango and avocado. Perfect for coastal summer entertaining.

300 g (10½ oz) sashimi-grade, firm white fish fillets (such as kingfish or snapper – or sea bass for the UK and US), cut into small 1 cm (½ inch) cubes
120 ml (4 fl oz) lime juice (from about 4–5 limes)
1 teaspoon table salt, plus extra to taste
1 small red onion, diced
1 bunch coriander (cilantro), chopped
200 g (7 oz) ripe but firm mango, peeled and diced
1½ hass avocados, diced
1 tablespoon olive oil
freshly ground black pepper, to taste

TO SERVE
corn chips (shop-bought or see page 252 for homemade) or Tostadas (page 256)
habanero hot sauce (shop-bought or see page 247 for homemade; optional)

In a glass or ceramic bowl, combine the fish with half the lime juice and 1 teaspoon of salt. Let the fish 'cook' for 15 minutes.

Strain the juices from the fish. Add the onion, coriander, mango, avocado, olive oil and the remaining juice. Season with salt and pepper to taste. Stir gently to combine, ensuring all the ingredients are coated in the lime juice.

You can serve ceviche in a large bowl or in individual ramekins. You could also flip the ramekins onto small plates to serve. Serve with corn chips or tostadas for scooping.

A couple of drops of habanero hot sauce will lift the dish.

Modelo

Serves 4 | **Preparation time** 30 minutes | **Cooking time** 20 minutes | **Dietaries** n/a | **Difficulty** Medium

Cóctel de camarones

—

Mexican prawn cocktail

Once you've tried this Mexican prawn (shrimp) cocktail, which is enjoyed all over Mexico, you won't go back to the creamy seafood sauce–dunked prawn cocktails of years gone by! You can add oysters, clams or cooked octopus to make it a true seafood cocktail. It's a perfect hangover cure as well. The only other thing you need is some Salada crackers (original only!) and you're set.

½ brown onion, roughly chopped
3 garlic cloves
1 small thyme sprig
1 teaspoon table salt
1 bay leaf
750 g (1 lb 10 oz) small/medium raw whole prawns (shrimp), unpeeled
1 small white onion, finely chopped
2 tomatoes, deseeded and finely diced
¼ bunch coriander (cilantro), chopped, plus extra leaves to garnish
1 avocado, diced (optional)
8 large Salada (Original) crackers (or other saltine-style crackers)
2 limes, cut into wedges

SAUCE

250 ml (1 cup) tomato juice
125 ml (½ cup) tomato ketchup
125 ml (½ cup) freshly squeezed orange juice
60 ml (¼ cup) freshly squeezed lime juice (from 2 limes)
110 ml (3½ fl oz) of the prawn cooking broth (see method)
1 tablespoon olive oil
hot sauce, such as 1 tablespoon Tabasco or 1 teaspoon habanero hot sauce (see page 247 for homemade), plus extra to garnish
salt, to taste
freshly ground black pepper, to taste

Fill a medium saucepan over medium–low heat with 1.5 litres (6 cups) of water. Add the brown onion, garlic, thyme, salt and bay leaf and bring to the boil. Add the prawns and cook for 3 minutes.

Take the prawns out of the saucepan with a mesh strainer, reserving the broth in the pan as you will need it later. Set aside.

Let the prawns cool, then peel and devein, reserving the shells. Place the prawn shells into the reserved broth, bring to the boil again and cook for another 10 minutes before turning the heat off and letting it cool. Strain the broth and reserve for the sauce.

For the sauce, in a bowl, whisk together the tomato juice, ketchup, orange juice, lime juice, reserved prawn broth, olive oil and hot sauce until well combined. Add salt and pepper to taste.

Fill four cups or bowls with three layers of prawn, white onion, tomato and a little coriander. Pour the sauce over but don't fully cover the prawns. Garnish with diced avocado (if using) and extra coriander leaves. Add the hot sauce.

Place the cups on small plates and serve each portion with two whole Salada crackers and lime wedges.

Tacos, tortas y tostadas

—

Tacos, loaded rolls + tostadas

This chapter is dedicated to tacos, tortas and tostadas, collectively known as 'Vitamin T'. These are some of Mexico's most iconic dishes and are everywhere in Mexico. You can't walk 100 metres without coming across a cart or stand slinging these street-food essentials. Each deserves to shine in their own chapter, but I thought I'd include all three here as they all belong to the same colloquial Vitamin T food group (along with tamales, tlayudas and tlacoyos).

Even though most people have an idea of what a taco is, it's only recently that traditional Mexican tacos with a soft corn tortilla, filling and salsa (rather than hard-shell Tex-Mex tacos with minced/ground beef, lettuce and sour cream) have become the accepted version sold in 'Mexican restaurants' and prepared in homes around the world. This pleases me no end, as hard-shell tacos (popularised by Taco Bell in the 1960s) are more fast food than street food.

While tacos are ubiquitous the world over, tortas and tostadas are only now starting to get global attention. Tostadas are similar to tacos and just as popular as their more famous sibling in Mexico. The main difference is that while tacos are folded and soft, tostadas are flat and crunchy.

Tortas are a different kettle of fish altogether. You can think of tortas as loaded Mexican sandwiches. Like Vietnam's bánh mìs, they are a local take on a baguette, influenced by French occupation. They can be fresh or toasted.

You can hit the streets to find dedicated stalls, called taquerías, torterías and tostaderías, to enjoy them as a snack, or head to a sit-down restaurant and eat them as a snack or a full meal. If you enjoy them as a snack you'll usually have one or two, while a full meal will see you eat four or five tacos or tostadas. These are the soul of street food.

TACOS

Mexico's most famous dish. The holy trinity of the taco is: tortilla, filling, salsa.

So why are they called tacos? There are several theories. One is that taco comes from the Nahuatl word tlahco, which translates to 'half', or 'in the middle'. Another theory relates to mining. In the 18th century, a filled tortilla resembled a taco, which was the name for a paper roll of dynamite. Good story, but is it true? True or not, it is estimated that 95% of Mexico City's 22 million residents live less than 400 metres (a quarter mile) from a taquería! The latest estimate is that there re 11,000 taquerías in the capital city alone.

In my experience, people in Australia get confused between a tortilla and a taco and use their names in the wrong context. I always use the sandwich as an analogy; the tortilla is like the bread of a sandwich; a tortilla with the filling and salsa is a taco; and a place that sells tacos is a taquería, like ours in Port Adelaide – La Popular Taqueria.

Tacos are a great option when entertaining. I often organise a taquiza (taco party, see pages 89 and 260) if there is something to celebrate. Let your guests make their own tacos by placing all your dishes, including Red rice (page 225), Refried beans (page 220) and, of course, warm tortillas on a table, buffet-style.

Clockwise from top right: Tacos campechanos (page 115), Salsa tatemada (page 241), Agua de limón (page 205), Tacos de asada (page 114), Salsa taquera (page 239)

Makes 25

Preparation time 25 minutes, plus 4–24 hours marinating

Cooking time 20 minutes

Dietaries Can be gluten free

Difficulty Easy

Tacos de asada — Steak tacos

This recipe (pictured on page 113) is easy and versatile and is the dish to serve when you host a dinner party with friends. There's not much to it; just slap a marinated steak on the barbecue, slice it up, then serve with tortillas, or serve as tacos. It's a no-brainer for ensuring your party is a guaranteed hit. We generally use rump (sirloin) or flank steak for this, but you can use any cut that doesn't need to be slow-cooked. I like to cook Cebollitas cambray (page 78) when I'm on barbecue duty.

- 160 ml (5¼ fl oz) vegetable oil
- 3 tablespoons lime juice (from 2 limes)
- 3 tablespoons freshly squeezed orange juice
- 4 garlic cloves
- ½ bunch coriander (cilantro)
- 1 tablespoon onion powder
- ¼ teaspoon garlic powder
- 1 tablespoon freshly ground black pepper
- 2 kg (4 lb 8 oz) rump (sirloin) or flank steak
- salt, to taste
- 25 corn tortillas (gluten free) or wheat tortillas (shop-bought or see pages 253 or 234 for homemade), warm
- 500 g (1 lb 2 oz) Salsa tatemada (page 241), Salsa roja (page 238), Salsa verde cruda (page 242) or Salsa verde cocida (page 245)
- 1 small white onion, finely diced
- 1 bunch coriander (cilantro), chopped
- mozzarella cheese, for cheese crust (optional)

Place the oil, lime juice, orange juice, garlic, coriander, onion powder, garlic powder and pepper into a food processor or blender and process until smooth to create a marinade. Do not add salt.

Place the meat in an airtight container or a plastic sealable bag and add the marinade. Mix to make sure all the meat is well covered in the marinade. Leave to marinate for at least 4 hours or overnight. (You can prepare it the day before.)

Heat the barbecue to high – preferably coal, but gas works fine, too – and cook the steak for 6 minutes on each side (or longer if very thick). Salt while cooking. After cooking, leave to rest for 10 minutes.

Cut the rump or flank steak against the grain into 5 mm (¼ inch) strips and place on a platter. Serve with warm corn or wheat tortillas. Add a tablespoon or two of salsa, and garnish with some diced onion and coriander.

If you want to make the taco more decadent, you could add a cheese crust. It basically comes down to melting about a handful of cheese (such as mozzarella) per taco in a frying pan or on a hotplate and placing a tortilla on top. Once the cheese has stuck to the tortilla and has gone golden brown, you add the meat and toppings. You will thank me for this tip later.

Makes 8

Preparation time 15 minutes

Cooking time 20 minutes

Dietaries Gluten free

Difficulty Easy

Tacos campechanos – Mixed tacos

Campechano generally means 'from Campeche', a state in the Yucatán Peninsula, but these tacos (pictured on page 113) are not really from there, as campechano also means 'mixed'. To go off on a tangent, this probably all started with 18th-century English seafarers. They would dock at the port of Campeche and visit local bars to order a mixed spirit drink with rum, cognac and aguardiente. This was then mixed with plant root called cola de gallo or 'rooster's tail'. The English sailors brought this term – cock's-tail – back to England. This is one theory on the origin of the term cocktail. But I digress, as these drinks had no local name; they were called campechano and, over time, this term came to refer to anything that is mixed – see Cuba libre campechana (page 213).

So, long story short, a taco campechano is a mixed taco made with steak, chorizo and chicharrón. When organising your taquiza, just have some fried chorizo and pork crackling in a bowl, throw a steak on the barbecue and you're as happy as an 18th-century English sailor with a glass of rum, cognac and aguardiente.

- 1 tablespoon vegetable oil
- 1 Mexican or Spanish chorizo (about 100 g/3½ oz; ensure chorizo is gluten free if necessary)
- 300 g (10½ oz) rump (sirloin) steak, marinated (optional; see Tip)
- salt, to taste
- freshly ground black pepper, to taste
- 50 g (1¾ oz) chicharrón, or pork crackling
- Salsa taquera (page 239) or Salsa verde cruda (page 242)
- ½ small white onion, finely diced
- ¼ bunch coriander (cilantro), chopped
- 8 corn tortillas (shop-bought or see page 253 for homemade)

Heat a medium frying pan over medium heat and add the oil. If using Mexican chorizo, take it out of the casing, crumble it into the pan and cook until it is well done and almost crispy; this will take about 10 minutes. If using Spanish chorizo, cut it into small 1 cm (½ inch) cubes and fry for about 5 minutes.

When half-cooked, add the chorizo to a food processor (not a blender) and chop until it has a minced (ground) meat consistency. Fry again until it is nicely cooked – it can be a bit oily, but this is all flavour! Place the chorizo in a bowl, ready for serving – it does not need to be hot, warm is fine.

Fry the steak in the same pan as the chorizo, or cook it on the barbecue to your liking – I like it medium–rare, 2–3 minutes per side over high heat. Season with salt and pepper. Let the steak rest for 5 minutes, then cut it into 5 mm (¼ inch) thick strips. Place in a bowl to serve.

Finally, place the chicharrón, salsa, onion and coriander in separate bowls. Heat up the tortillas and keep them in a chiquihuite in a clean tea (dish) towel. Place all the bowls on the table.

Make your taco by adding a couple of strips of meat, a tablespoon of chorizo, then add your salsa. Finish with chicharrón and garnish with white onion and coriander. Delicious.

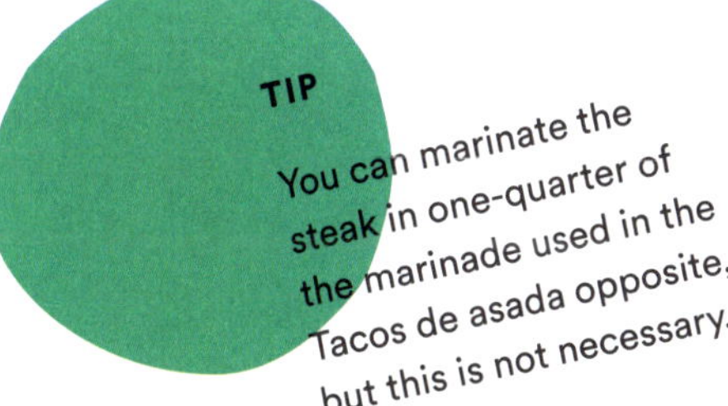

TIP

You can marinate the steak in one-quarter of the marinade used in the Tacos de asada opposite, but this is not necessary.

Makes
8

Preparation time
25 minutes

Cooking time
15 minutes

Dietaries n/a

Difficulty Easy

Tacos de pescado estilo Ensenada

—

Baja-style fish tacos

Having grown up in Mexico City, I didn't know about Baja fish tacos until I travelled for work to Baja California. That was the moment I was sold. Just before I moved to Australia, I went to visit El Tuinky, a very good friend of mine, in Ensenada and he took me to his favourite places to eat. One of them was a little stall on the street where I had the most amazing fish taco from a humble street cart that was basically just a big pot of oil and the catch of the day. I don't remember how many I had! They were cooked to perfection, the batter was light, crispy and flaky, and they had many different toppings and salsas for you to choose from.

This is one of the most popular dishes at La Popular Taqueria. People absolutely love it, and I'm always getting requests for the recipe. I'm going to give away a trade secret here: it's really easy to make (you can even prepare the sides and batter separately and keep them in the fridge until it's time to serve). With the fish, I like to use ocean jacket (or any leatherjacket), a by-catch fish in Australia that is environmentally sustainable and extremely tasty, but you can use any firm white fish. (Salmon or tuna will work too, but I prefer white fish.) Another option, if you're not into fish, is to replace the fish with peeled prawns (shrimp). For vegetarians, par-boil florets of cauliflower. To go vegan, leave out the egg and use vegan mayo.

It took me a long time to get this recipe to how I like it and remembered it – crispy. There were many iterations of batters and dustings, but I think I have nailed it.

- 1 litre (4 cups) vegetable oil
- 300 g (10½ oz) firm white fish, cut into 10 cm (4 inch) strips
- 150 g (1 cup) plain (all-purpose) flour, to coat the fish
- 8 corn tortillas (shop-bought or see page 253 for homemade)
- ¼ small red cabbage, thinly sliced
- Pico de gallo (page 246)
- ½ telegraph (long) cucumber, finely diced
- 2 limes, cut into wedges

CHIPOTLE MAYONNAISE

- 250 ml (1 cup) whole-egg mayonnaise
- 1 tablespoon tinned chipotle in adobo

FISH BATTER

- 200 g (1⅓ cups) plain (all-purpose) flour
- 2 teaspoons table salt
- 1 teaspoon baking powder
- 1 tablespoon dried Mexican oregano
- ¼ tablespoon freshly ground black pepper
- 330 ml (11¼ oz) can Mexican lager beer, cold
- 1 egg

For the chipotle mayo, blend the mayonnaise and chipotle chilli in a food processor until smooth. Place in a serving bowl.

For the batter, combine the dry ingredients in a medium bowl.

In a separate bowl, mix the cold beer and egg. Once well combined, add the dry ingredients and mix until you have a thick and smooth batter.

Heat the oil over medium heat to 180°C (350°F). I use a thermometer to test, but if piece of bread dropped in the oil browns in 15 seconds, the oil is at the correct temperature.

Dust the fish strips in plain flour and dip into the batter, one by one, so they are lightly but fully coated. Now, this is the most important bit to get them crispy: dust them again in flour, then put them straight into the oil.

Fry each strip for a couple of minutes, turning regularly, until the batter is crisp and golden. Place on a tray lined with paper towel to drain.

To build the taco, grab a warm tortilla, place some fish in the middle, add red cabbage, followed by chipotle mayonnaise, pico de gallo and cucumber. Serve with the lime wedges, squeezing the lime over the fish before digging in. Repeat with the remaining tortillas and ingredients.

I recommend building the tacos on the plate or tray you are serving on. You could also make it a build-your-own dinner by placing all the toppings in the centre of the table (make sure you serve the hot fish straight away).

Makes / serves About 12 / 4

Preparation time 20 minutes

Cooking time 20 minutes

Dietaries Can be gluten free

Difficulty Easy

Tacos de alambre de res

—

Steak on a skewer, without a skewer

Tacos de alambre de res literally translates to 'tacos with meat on a wire', or meat skewer. Not a pre-Hispanic dish, it finds its origin in the Middle East and is an adaptation of the shish kebab. Initially, meat with vegetables and bacon would be cooked over a barbecue on skewers. Over time, the skewers were ditched and it is now made in a pan. Alambre must include meat, capsicum (pepper), onion and bacon.

At my parents' local taquería, TAPSA, in Iztapalapa, Mexico City, I used to watch the taquero de la plancha – hotplate taco maker – work his magic on the plancha, adding the ingredients at the perfect time so the alambre was not overcooked or soggy. Taquerías will often have specialised taqueros, each on their own section. I like my alambre tacos with hot wheat tortillas and salsa verde cocida, salsa roja or salsa tatemada.

150 g (5½ oz) bacon slices
500 g (1 lb 2 oz) rump (sirloin) steak
1 large white onion
1 green capsicum (pepper)
1 red capsicum (pepper)
¼ teaspoon garlic powder
½ teaspoon onion powder
½ teaspoon freshly ground black pepper
1 teaspoon table salt
2 tablespoons vegetable oil
12 wheat or corn tortillas (shop-bought or see page 234 or 253 for homemade; use corn tortillas for gluten free)
Salsa verde cocida (page 245), Salsa roja (page 238) or Salsa tatemada (page 241)

Start by cutting all the meats and vegetables into even-sized strips (1 cm/½ inch wide and 5 cm/2 inches in length).

On a plate or in a bowl, add the garlic and onion powders, pepper and salt to the rump steak and set aside.

Heat the oil in a large frying pan over medium heat and fry the bacon until the fat has rendered and is crispy, 5–10 minutes. Take the bacon out of the pan and set aside in a bowl.

In the same pan, fry the vegetables over high heat for 5 minutes. Keep tossing so they don't burn. Transfer the cooked vegetables to a bowl and set aside.

Fry the steak in the same pan over high heat for another 5 minutes – the steak should now be seared. You want the meat to be medium–rare (of course!).

Add the bacon and vegetables. Mix everything well and cook until all the ingredients have heated up again. Now it's ready to serve with tortillas and salsa.

Makes / serves 16 / 4

Preparation time 10 minutes, plus 2–24 hours marinating

Cooking time 20 minutes

Dietaries Gluten free

Difficulty Easy

Tacos de pollo adobado

—

Adobo chicken tacos

A classic that will take your average chicken to another level. I prefer using thighs as they are juicier, but chicken breasts work, too. The chicken is marinated in the same marinade as Cochinita pibil (page 146), although the final flavour will be totally different. You will achieve the best results on a coal barbecue. Another way to use this recipe is to prepare a whole butterflied chicken with the marinade. Not a taco per se, but a great showstopper when you have friends around.

100 g Recado rojo (page 223)
1 kg (2 lb 4 oz) boneless, skinless chicken thighs
salt, to taste
16 corn tortillas (shop-bought or see page 253 for homemade)
300 g (10½ oz) Salsa taquera (page 239)
1 small white onion, finely diced
½ bunch coriander (cilantro), chopped
mozzarella cheese, for the cheese crust (optional)

Mix the recado rojo with the chicken in a large bowl and leave to marinate for a couple of hours. You could do this overnight.

Oil the grill of a barbecue (preferably coal) so the chicken does not stick, then heat to high. Grill the chicken for about 20 minutes, turning regularly until the meat is cooked through – you can check by cutting into the meat. Let the chicken rest for 5–10 minutes, then cut into 1 cm (½ inch) cubes.

Serve with hot tortillas. Top with a splash of salsa and finish with diced onion and coriander.

As for the Tacos de asada on page 114, you can make the tacos more decadent by adding a cheese crust. Melt about 30 g (1 oz) of cheese (such as mozzarella) per taco on a comal, hotplate or in a non-stick frying pan and place a tortilla on top. Once the cheese has stuck to the tortilla and has gone golden brown, add the chicken and toppings. Enjoy!

Makes / serves 8 / 4 | **Preparation time** 30 minutes | **Cooking time** 20 minutes | **Dietaries** Vegetarian | **Difficulty** Medium

Tacos de chile jalapeño relleno

—

Stuffed jalapeño tacos

This is quite an elaborate taco but fun to make and tasty as hell. Jalapeños are always a gamble – sometimes they are really hot, sometimes not. You can make the chillies in advance and heat them up before serving them in the taco. It's best to eat them directly after frying. I occasionally serve the stuffed chillies as they are, without the tortilla, and it makes a great starter.

SALSA

- 350 g (12 oz) ripe tomatoes
- ¼ small white onion, plus ¼ white onion, thinly sliced
- 1 garlic clove
- ¼ cinnamon stick
- 6 black peppercorns
- 1 clove
- 1 teaspoon table salt
- ½ teaspoon sugar
- 125 ml (½ cup) water
- 1 tablespoon vegetable oil

CHILLIES

- 8 large jalapeños
- 100 g (3½ oz) mozzarella, cut into batons (around 1 cm/½ inch wide and 5 cm/2 inches long)
- 2 eggs, at room temperature, separated
- 100 g (⅔ cup) all-purpose (plain) flour
- 500 ml (2 cups) vegetable oil

TO SERVE

- 8 corn tortillas (shop-bought or see page 253 for homemade)
- White rice (page 224)

Place all the salsa ingredients, except the sliced onion and oil, in a blender and process at full speed for 2 minutes until pureed. Pass through a fine-mesh strainer.

Add the 1 tablespoon of oil to a medium saucepan over medium heat and fry the sliced onion until translucent. Add the salsa and cook for 10–15 minutes over low heat until it has reduced a little. Set aside – but warm it up before serving.

On a chopping board, start by making a T-shaped opening in the side of each jalapeño with a small paring knife. (Make a small cut across the chilli near the stem, then a long cut lengthways towards the tip. When making the cut near the stem, try to cut through the seed stem, as this will make cleaning the jalapeños easier.)

Place the jalapeños in a small saucepan with water and boil them for about 5 minutes. They will change colour and become dull green. Remove the jalapeños from the heat and cool them down in a colander under cold running water. With a small paring knife or a teaspoon, remove the seeds and veins, but try not to damage the chillies.

Place the jalapeños on paper towel to drain. They need to be dry on the outside and inside, so use paper towel inside the jalapeños as well if necessary. (If they are wet, they might spatter and burn you.)

Fill the cavity in each jalapeño with a cheese baton – get as much of the cheese in as possible without stretching the chilli too much. Set the jalapeños aside.

Add the egg whites to a bowl and beat them with hand-held electric beaters, or in a stand mixer with the whisk attachment, on medium speed until they form soft peaks. Incorporate the yolks by carefully folding them in.

If you're going to serve the jalapeños immediately after frying, warm up the salsa in a small saucepan. Add the flour to a small bowl.

Heat the oil to 180°C (350°F) in a medium frying pan over medium heat. I use a thermometer to test the oil, but if a piece of bread dropped into the oil browns in 15 seconds, the oil is at the correct temperature.

The next few steps can be a bit messy. Dust each stuffed chilli in flour until it is white all over, shaking off the excess. Now, holding the chilli

at the stem, dunk it into the egg batter until it is fully covered – this layer can be quite thick. Place the chilli carefully in the oil and fry for approximately 3 minutes, flipping regularly with a spatula. The chillies need to be golden brown. They will not be crispy but rather spongy. If you get the hang of the process, you can do multiple chillies at a time. Place the fried chillies in a bowl lined with paper towel to let them drain.

Serve the stuffed jalapeños hot. Place a warm tortilla on a plate, add a scoop of white rice, the chilli on top and add some of the warm salsa. Eat immediately. ¡Buen provecho!

Loaded rolls

Tortas are loaded bread rolls or sandwiches that find their origin in the days when Mexico was occupied by the French. As author Benito Taibo says, all of Mexico's history sits between the two pieces of bread – a good torta demonstrates the desire to have the world between your hands. More than simply food, he says, it is 'a refuge, a lifeline, an identity symbol, the sum of our passions and the perfect reflection of the splendour of all our crossbreeds'.

You'll find tortas everywhere in Mexico City. When I visit my parents, I like to order mine from Tort-As. We generally eat these in the evening as a lazy dinner. One of the key ingredients is a good white bread roll; it needs to be crunchy and light, and soft in the middle. Tortas are a great way to use up your leftovers, such as roasted pork (lomo adobado) or chicken. A torta can be basic, made of simple ingredients such as ham and cheese, or complicated, like a torta de chile relleno – a stuffed poblano chilli filled with cheese, then fried. Milanesa tortas are also very popular; these are tortas made with thin pork schnitzels. If you add crispy fried chorizo, you convert it to a milchori torta. The options are infinite, and every tortería has its own specialties. Go wild, but start with the basic ingredients on the following pages and you'll soon be a pro.

Clockwise from left: Torta de lomo adobado (page 125), Cochitorta (page 126), Pepito (page 126)

Serves 1

Preparation time 5 minutes

Cooking time 5 minutes

Dietaries n/a

Difficulty Easy

Basic torta with no filling

This is a basic recipe to get you started on your torta journey, followed by a few of the classics of the genre. No need to fall back on your trusty ham and tomato sandwich after this.

1 crusty bread roll
unsalted butter
whole-egg mayonnaise
about 2 generous tablespoons warm Refried beans (page 220)
2–3 slices of tomato
¼ avocado, sliced
Chiles en escabeche (page 229)
crispy chorizo (optional)
cheese slices (optional)
salsa of your choice (optional)

Cut the bread roll in half lengthways. I never do the following step, but it is SO Mexican: remove the migajón – the soft bread in the middle of the roll – to create a cavity. (Arguments for doing this include: you can fit more into your torta, or – and this is not something I invented – the migajón makes you gain weight!)

Start by smearing the roll with a light coat of butter and toasting the bread, butter-side down, in a medium frying pan over medium heat. When toasty, add some mayo, then add the refried beans.

Now add the filling of your choice – see some of the torta examples on the following pages – then the tomato, avocado and chiles en escabeche. Cut in half.

It's optional to fry some chorizo until crispy and add as an extra topping or on the side. Other extras include slices of cheese, melted or not, and you could do a splash of salsa, if desired.

Torta de lomo adobado

—

Pork loin in adobo torta

50 g (5½ oz) Lomo adobado (page 150)
1 tablespoon vegetable oil
1 crusty bread roll
unsalted butter
whole-egg mayonnaise
about 2 generous tablespoons warm Refried beans (page 220)
2–3 slices of tomato
¼ avocado, sliced
Chiles en escabeche (page 229)

Cut the left-over lomo adobo into thin slices and fry these in the oil in a medium frying pan over medium heat for 1 minute each side. Add a tablespoon of the adobo sauce from the pork to the pan and build your torta as described in the basic torta recipe opposite. Cut in half to serve.

Torta de milanesa

—

Pork schnitzel torta

1 pork loin steak (about 150 g/5½ oz)
salt, to taste
freshly ground black pepper, to taste
garlic powder
1 egg
50 g (⅓ cup) plain (all-purpose) flour
50 g (½ cup) breadcrumbs
125 ml (½ cup) vegetable oil
1 crusty bread roll
unsalted butter
whole-egg mayonnaise
about 2 generous tablespoons warm Refried beans (page 220)
2–3 slices of tomato
¼ avocado, sliced
Chiles en escabeche (page 229)

With a meat hammer, pound the pork loin until thin, about 5 mm (¼ inch). Season with the salt, pepper and garlic powder.

Whisk the egg in a bowl and add some salt and pepper. Put the flour and breadcrumbs in separate bowls.

Dust the loin in flour, then dip it into the egg mixture and finally coat with the breadcrumbs.

Fry the pork in the oil in a large frying pan over medium heat until golden brown, about 3 minutes each side. Cut the schnitzel into 1 cm (½ inch) wide strips and build your torta as described in the basic torta recipe opposite. Cut in half to serve.

Pepito

Steak and cheese torta

1 tablespoon vegetable oil
1 minute (sizzle/cube) steak (about 100 g/3½ oz)
salt, to taste
freshly ground black pepper, to taste
1 slice manchego cheese or any other yellow cheese that melts (I use sharp cheddar)
unsalted butter
1 crusty bread roll
about 2 generous tablespoons warm Refried beans (page 220)
whole-egg mayonnaise
2–3 slices of tomato
¼ avocado, sliced
Chiles en escabeche (page 229)

Heat the oil in a frying pan over high heat and fry the steak for 1 minute on each side. Season with salt and pepper.

Add a slice of cheese on top of the steak and cook until it melts. Start building your torta as per the basic torta recipe on page 124. Once you have smeared on the beans, add the steak with cheese followed by the rest of the torta ingredients. Cut in half to serve.

Cochitorta

Cochinita pibil torta

1 crusty bread roll
100–150 g (3½–5½ oz) Cochinita pibil (page 146)
Cebolla curtida (page 228)
habanero hot sauce (shop-bought or see page 247 for homemade)

Ignore the basic torta recipe for this one. Cut the crusty roll in half and fill with a good layer of the cochinita pibil with all the juices, some cebolla curtida and habanero hot sauce. Cut in half to serve.

TOSTADAS

Tostadas are close relatives of the taco. They are flat tortillas that have been fried or toasted, which is where their name comes from – tostada meaning 'toasted'. Tostadas are less popular outside of Mexico, but in Mexico we have tostaderías, which specialise in tostadas. Tostadas are loaded with toppings, and at tostaderías you can enjoy them in many different ways, topped with everything from ceviches to refried beans to slow-cooked meats.

I will only touch the surface of taco and tostada diversity here. The rules of which sauce or topping goes with what taco or tostada can be complicated, as it is something you learn from experience. If you see my eyes roll for a special request in the restaurant, it generally means that it is a prohibited combination.

Clockwise from top: Tostadas de cueritos (page 134), Tostadas de jitomate y salsa macha (page 133), Tostadas de salpicón (page 131)

Makes / serves
450 g (1 lb) /
18 small or 10 large

Preparation time
20 minutes

Cooking time
3 minutes

Dietaries
Gluten free

Difficulty Easy

Tostadas de paté de pescado ahumado

—

Smoked fish tostadas

This dish is traditionally made with smoked marlin, and it comes from Baja California. The first time I tried it was while grey whale–watching in Bahía Todos Santos. After the tour, we had lunch at the local eatery and enjoyed grated fish ceviche and pâté de marlin. Delicious! As a marine biologist, always thinking about sustainability, I prefer not to use marlin, as it is a threatened species. So, in my version of the recipe, I use hot smoked trout, but any other hot smoked oily fish will work. I like to make this pâté for tostadas, but it is also very popular as a dip. Just add some corn chips or Ritz crackers and you're set.

150 g (5½ oz) hot smoked trout, or any other hot smoked fish, skin and bones removed (I generally get these at the fish section of the supermarket)
20 g (¾ oz) red capsicum (pepper)
50 g (1¾ oz) cream cheese
25 g (1 oz) whole-egg mayonnaise
50 ml (1½ fl oz) thickened (heavy) cream
45 g (1½ oz) tinned chipotle in adobo
2 teaspoons freshly squeezed lime juice
1 small garlic clove
18 small fried Tostadas (10 cm/4 inches in diameter), or 10 large Tostadas (15 cm/6 inches in diameter) (page 256)
black sesame seeds (optional)

Start by cleaning the fish by removing the bones and skin, if there are any. Split into two portions.

Place the capsicum on a fork and char over an open flame to release some of the sweetness. (If you have an electric stove, you can dry-char in a small frying pan.)

Place the cream cheese, mayonnaise, cream, chipotle, lime juice and garlic into a bullet blender and process until the chillies are well blended and the texture is creamy.

Add half the fish to the creamy goodness in the blender and process until smooth, 10–20 seconds.

Scrape the mixture out of the blender into a bowl using a silicone spatula, then add the rest of the fish. Mash with a fork – it needs to be slightly chunky.

For this recipe I used small tostadas, so they are more like a canapé; I made 18. If you want to use larger tostadas, it will serve about 10.

Grab a tostada and smear a generous tablespoon of pâté on top. Sprinkle with black sesame seeds to make it pop, if desired. Delish.

Makes / serves	Preparation time	Cooking time	Dietaries	Difficulty Medium
6 / 2 (for dinner) or 6 (as a starter)	45 minutes	1½ hours	Gluten free	

Tostadas de salpicón

—

Pickled beef tostadas

Salpicón de res reminds me of my mother. I would always get excited whenever she said, 'Tomorrow, we are having salpicón,' because it meant two things. First, besides enjoying salpicón for lunch, it meant we were going to also enjoy Sopa de migas (page 50), one of my favourites! Second, as I was going to help her shred the meat, I knew I would get to taste it while shredding! It is a dish made with cold, slow-cooked, pulled meat that is pickled in white vinegar. Tangy, juicy meat – yum.

It's important to remember that because this dish is served cold, it takes a bit of planning to get the meat cooked and shredded. (Tostadas de salpicón is pictured on page 129.)

500 g (1 lb 2 oz) beef flank steak or brisket
600 g (1 lb 5 oz) beef bones
1 large brown onion, quartered
10 peppercorns
½ tablespoon dried Mexican oregano
4 garlic cloves, crushed
2 bay leaves
1 teaspoon table salt
60 ml (¼ cup) olive oil
90 ml (3 fl oz) white vinegar
30 g (1 cup) coriander (cilantro) leaves
3 radishes, thinly sliced
100 g (3½ oz) tomatoes, diced
50 g (1¾ oz) queso fresco, crumbled (in Australia you can substitute La Casa del Formaggio brand's Homestyle Fresh Cheese, otherwise use Indian paneer cheese)
6 fried Tostadas (page 256)
1 avocado, sliced
Chiles en escabeche (page 229; optional)

Place the flank steak and bones in a saucepan with 2 litres (8 cups) of water. Add the onion, peppercorns, oregano, garlic, bay leaves and salt and bring to the boil over medium–low heat. Simmer, half-covered, for 1½ hours. Check the meat to see if it is tender, otherwise cook a bit longer. You can do the same in a pressure cooker and cook for 30 minutes.

Remove the flank steak and keep the stock for Sopa de migas (page 50). Discard the bones.

Let the flank steak cool until you are able to touch it. In a large bowl, pull it to shreds with your hands, then add the oil, vinegar and salt and pepper to taste. Mix well. Leave to rest for 10 minutes.

Add the coriander, radish, tomato and crumbled cheese. Toss gently to coat everything in the meat dressing.

Allow the salpicón mixture to marinate in the refrigerator for at least 20 minutes, stirring occasionally. After marinating, taste and adjust the seasoning if needed.

To assemble, spread a layer of the salpicón mixture onto each tostada. Top with avocado and, if you like a bit of heat, add chiles en escabeche. Serve immediately, as they will get soggy if you leave them too long! You can also place all the toppings in the centre of the table and each person can build the tostadas themselves.

Makes / serves 8 / 4

Preparation time 20 minutes

Cooking time Nil, if you have tostadas and refried beans

Dietaries Gluten free, vegan

Difficulty Easy

Tostadas de jitomate y salsa macha

—

Tomato tostadas with salsa macha

This tostada heroes tomatoes and salsa macha. I love the combination of the crunch of the beans with the sweetness of the tomato and salsa. Ripe tomatoes are absolutely key. I like to use small heirloom tomatoes but, if you can't find them, use cherry tomatoes. I made this recipe for 12 cm (4½ inch) tostadas, but you can make the tostadas smaller, or cut the tortillas in half before baking to make canapés. (Tostadas de jitomate y salsa macha is pictured on page 129.)

- 8 baked Tostadas (page 256)
- 100 g frisée lettuce (curly endive), or other small-leafed lettuce mixture
- 300 g (10½ oz) Refried beans, made using black beans (page 220), warm
- 150 g (5½ oz) Salsa macha (page 244)
- 16 cherry tomatoes (about 350 g/ 12 oz), quartered
- ½ red onion, thinly sliced

There are a couple of things you need to do before assembling the tostada. Make eight tostadas (my tortillas are 15 cm/6 inches for this recipe – they will shrink while baking). Make them thin if you can. Tear the lettuce into small leaves about 5 cm (2 inches) long. Prepare the refried beans, and mix the salsa macha so it has some chunky bits.

To assemble, grab a tostada and smear with a generous tablespoon of refried beans, then add a layer of lettuce leaves – to make it look pretty. Top with the quarters of two tomatoes and add some of the sliced red onion. Drizzle with a tablespoon of salsa macha – don't forget the chunky bits.

Serve on a platter or individual plates. Eat immediately or the tostadas will become soggy.

Makes / serves
350 g (12 oz) / 4

Preparation time
30 minutes, plus overnight chilling

Cooking time
1 hour

Dietaries
Gluten free

Difficulty Medium

Tostadas de cueritos

—

Pickled pork skin tostadas

It was a good day when my abuelito (grandfather) took me to la tiendita (the corner store) to buy supplies. At the store, there was always a jar full of cueritos on the counter – my grandfather knew I loved it, which is why he took me along. He'd always ask, 'Do you want some cueritos?' The question was obviously rhetorical, because the answer was always the same: 'YES!' The storeperson would serve them in a plastic bag with plenty of Valentina sauce and a toothpick. We'd then walk back home, and I'd be happily sharing cueritos with my beloved abuelito.

This might look like a challenging dish, but tostadas de cueritos (pictured on page 129) are totally worth the time and effort. Essentially crispy flat tortillas topped with pickled pork skin and other garnishes, they are absolutely delicious! The pork has a similar texture to jellyfish but with a crunch.

Pork skin is not the most common cut at butchers in Adelaide, so I generally get my pork skins from Asian supermarkets. Valentina sauce is a very common sauce in Mexico (basically a vinegar-based dry chilli sauce). If you can't find it, you could use Tapatío or Huichol sauce.

Cueritos will keep for up to 6 months in a jar in the fridge, so if you are going to make them, make heaps! (The recipe can be easily doubled or tripled.) Don't forget they need to rest at least overnight in the fridge before they're ready.

CUERITOS
500 g (1 lb 2 oz) pork skin (about 5 mm/¼ inch thick), clean with no fat
5 teaspoons table salt
500 ml (2 cups) white vinegar
½ white onion, thinly sliced
1 tablespoon cumin seeds
1 tablespoon peppercorns
1 tablespoon dried oregano
1 tablespoon whole allspice
3 bay leaves
2 garlic cloves, smashed

TOSTADAS
8 fried Tostadas (page 256)
350 g (12 oz) cueritos (see left)
250 g (9 oz) iceberg lettuce, thinly sliced
50 g (1¾ oz) thinly sliced white onion
50 g (1¾ oz) finely diced tomatoes, no seeds
⅓ bunch coriander (cilantro), chopped
250 g (9 oz) Refried beans (page 220), warm
150 ml (5 fl oz) thickened (heavy) cream
250 g (9 oz) ricotta salata, grated
salt, to taste
freshly ground black pepper, to taste
Valentina sauce
extra-virgin olive oil
2 avocados, sliced, to garnish
2 limes, cut into wedges

For the cueritos, wash the pork skin under cold water, then cut it into squares of about 5 cm (2 inches). With a long, sharp, thin knife, remove all the fat. The clean pork skin should be about ½ cm (¼ inch) thick.

Place the pork skin in a medium saucepan with water to cover. Add 2 teaspoons of the salt and bring to the boil over medium–low heat. When it reaches the boil, lower the heat and simmer for 45 minutes until the skin is translucent and tender.

While the pork is cooking, make the pickling liquid. In a medium saucepan combine 1 litre (4 cups) of water, the vinegar, the remaining salt, the onion, spices, bay leaves and garlic. Bring to the boil over high heat. Reduce the heat to low and simmer for 10 minutes.

Remove the saucepan from the heat and transfer the skin to the pickling liquid using a slotted spoon. Let the mixture cool down for at least an hour.

Transfer the cueritos with the pickling liquid to a jar or container and rest overnight in the fridge. (You can store cueritos for up to 6 months in the fridge.)

For the tostadas, slice the cueritos into 3–5 mm (⅛–¼ inch) thick strips.

In a small bowl, combine the lettuce, onion, tomato and coriander.

To assemble, spread a layer (about 30 g/1 oz) of refried beans on each tostada – do this just before serving or the tostadas will become soggy.

Add a layer of the cueritos, add a handful of the lettuce mix, then drizzle with cream and sprinkle some grated cheese over the top. Finish with a few drops of Valentina sauce and garnish with olive oil and avocado.

Place the tostadas on a plate with a wedge of lime and serve immediately. Tostadas can be served as a starter or as a snack. I sometimes like to snack on cueritos with potato chips (crisps) and drops of Valentina.

Platos fuertes

—

Mains

Platos fuertes means 'strong plate' or 'main'. It's difficult to classify some dishes as a main or a starter, as they can be both. For example, I'll enjoy enchiladas for breakfast with a steak on top for good measure, but they are also a lunch or dinner staple. However, guisados (see page 158) are proper mains and are usually stews served with rice, beans and tortillas.

Then again, a guisado is not always a stew; some guisados can be used as toppings or fillings for sopes, gorditas or tostadas, which are antojitos (snacks) and garnachas. It's all a bit fluid and adds to the sometimes 'modular' way Mexican food is prepared.

Strong plate or main, this chapter is my way of introducing you to some of the larger, heavier dishes that aren't that well known outside of Mexico. If you want to know how to make authentic Enchiladas (page 170), Mole con pollo (page 165) and Cochinita pibil (page 146), you'll discover how in the following pages.

Serves 4 | **Preparation time** 30 minutes | **Cooking time** 35 minutes | **Dietaries** n/a | **Difficulty** Medium

Albóndigas – Traditional Mexican meatballs

In Spanish, albóndigas simply means 'meatballs'. If you're used to Italian meatballs, this dish comes with a warning due to the spice kick you get with the smoky chipotle chilli (dried and smoked jalapeño chillies). Albóndigas is an everyday dish, not fancy but very tasty. You commonly see this on the daily special for lunch – the main meal in Mexico. The meatballs are generally made with spearmint, but this is not always available, so for this recipe we used regular mint.

Albóndigas are generally served with rice and corn tortillas, and they are at their best when you make your own tortillas. This is a great winter warmer dish.

MEATBALLS

50 g (1¾ oz) stale bread roll (1 day old is fine)
½ cup (125 ml) full-cream (whole) milk
4 whole allspice
2 garlic cloves
8 large mint leaves
1 tablespoon table salt
500 g (1 lb 2 oz) regular minced (ground) beef (not super lean)
1 large egg
2 hard-boiled eggs

SAUCE

750 g (1 lb 10 oz) ripe tomatoes, cut into chunks
½ white onion, cut into chunks
2 garlic cloves
100 g (3½ oz) tinned chipotle in adobo
salt, to taste
1 tablespoon vegetable oil
250 ml (1 cup) vegetable, beef or chicken stock (see page 221 for homemade)

TO SERVE

White rice (page 224)
corn tortillas (shop-bought or see page 253 for homemade)

Start by soaking the bread for the meatballs with the milk in a bowl until soft.

For the sauce, add the tomato, onion, garlic, chillies and salt to a blender or food processor and process until smooth.

Place a large cast-iron pot on the stovetop, add the oil and set the heat to medium. Add the sauce and stock and bring to a simmer, then cook for about 10 minutes. Make sure the sauce does not get too dry – add water if needed.

While the sauce is simmering, make the meatballs. Place the allspice, garlic and mint in a molcajete or mortar and pestle with the salt and pound to a paste.

Place the beef in a large bowl and add the spice paste and soaked bread (do not include the milk in the bowl). Lightly beat the large raw egg in a cup and add this to the mixture. Mix all the ingredients with your hands until even.

Peel the boiled eggs and cut each one into eight cubes.

Grab a portion of the meatball mixture and make a small patty. Place a piece of egg in the middle and form a meatball about the size of a golf ball. Three to four meatballs per person is the goal. (I generally have a few egg pieces left at the end.) Add the meatballs to the simmering sauce as you make them, then cook for about 30 minutes.

Place the albóndigas in a large dish (or serve straight from the pan) and serve with white rice and warm corn tortillas.

Makes / serves 8 / 4 **Preparation time** 30 minutes **Cooking time** 20 minutes **Dietaries** n/a **Difficulty** Medium

Chile güero relleno de picadillo
—
Stuffed banana chilli with picadillo

For this dish, I use picadillo as a filling in a chile güero, or blond chilli. In Australia, they are called banana chillies and are very mild. This is a hassle-free dish you can prepare in advance. Everything is cooked before you place the chillies in the oven, so they just need to be warmed up.

8 banana chillies
vegetable oil, for greasing
800 g (1 lb 12 oz) Picadillo (page 164)

TO SERVE
White rice (page 224)
Refried beans (page 220)
corn tortillas (shop-bought or see page 253 for homemade)

Remove the skin from the chillies in the same way as for the poblano chillies on page 231.

Once peeled, place the chillies on a chopping board and make an opening along the side of the chilli using a small paring knife. To do this, make a small cut near the stem of the chilli, then make a long cut lengthways towards the tip, about three-quarters along the length of the chilli. When making the cut near the stem, try to cut through the seed stem without damaging the flesh.

Remove the seed stem and seeds – holding the chilli under cold water might help.

Place the empty chillies, open-side up, on a lightly oiled baking tray.

Preheat the oven to 160°C (325°F).

Fill each chilli with the picadillo, overfilling the chillies a little so they are nice and plump. Make sure the chillies are placed snugly next to each other on the tray so the filling does not fall out. Bake for approximately 20 minutes, until they are warm.

Serve the chillies as a main or a starter. As a main, serve with white rice, refried beans and corn tortillas.

Makes / serves 1 litre (4 cups) / 4 | **Preparation time** 20 minutes | **Cooking time** 30 minutes | **Dietaries** Gluten free | **Difficulty** Easy

Carne en su jugo — Beef in a tomatillo broth

This is one of my husband, Kor's, all-time favourite dishes. My sister, Maru, introduced me to it, which struck me as quite strange at the time as she wasn't much of a cook when we were growing up. Maru made this dish for a big crowd at my brother-in-law's holiday house, and I really enjoyed all the flavours; and I guess it tasted even better because she made it. I was impressed. Nice one, sis.

Carne en su jugo literally translates to 'meat in its own juices'. It hails from Jalisco, one of the western states of Mexico. I am no historian, but it seems to be quite a recent dish. It finds its origin with a street vendor in Guadalajara in 1968.

SALSA

250 g (9 oz) tomatillos, fresh or tinned
3 serrano or jalapeño chillies
½ white onion
handful of coriander (cilantro)
1 garlic clove
½ teaspoon dried Mexican oregano
½ teaspoon ground cumin

STEW

100 g (3½ oz) bacon, cut into small strips (ensure bacon is gluten free if necessary)
1 tablespoon vegetable oil
1 brown onion, diced
4 spring onion (scallions), trimmed to 15 cm (6 inches)
500 g (1 lb 2 oz) minute (sizzle/cube) steak, cut into 1 cm (½ inch) strips
500 ml (2 cups) beef stock (ensure stock is gluten free if necessary)
salt, to taste

TO SERVE

300 g (10½ oz) cooked pinto beans (see page 218)
½ white onion, finely diced
⅓ bunch coriander (cilantro), chopped
8 radishes, thinly sliced
corn tortillas (shop-bought or see page 253 for homemade)
2 limes, cut into wedges
habanero hot sauce (shop-bought or see page 247 for homemade)

For the salsa, bring 500 ml (2 cups) of water to the boil in a small saucepan. Add the tomatillos, chillies, white onion, coriander and garlic. Boil for about 5 minutes.

Drain in a colander and add the ingredients to a blender, along with the oregano and cumin. Blend until smooth, then set aside in a bowl.

For the stew base, fry the bacon in the oil in a medium saucepan over medium heat until crispy. Remove the bacon and set aside in a bowl.

In the same saucepan, fry the diced brown onion until translucent. Add the spring onion and steak. Cook for a couple of minutes until the steak changes colour from red to brown. Add the salsa and beef stock and simmer for approximately 30 minutes. Season with salt.

Serve carne en su jugo in a large bowl. First, add the broth with the meat, then add a generous scoop of pinto beans. Sprinkle with diced white onion and coriander and garnish with the sliced radish. Serve with a basket of fresh tortillas and lime wedges on the side. You will also need some hot sauce – I like habanero, but any hot sauce will do.

To eat, squeeze the lime into the broth and add some habanero hot sauce. Grab a tortilla and fill it with some of the meat and beans. Enjoy!

Serves 6–8

Preparation time 30 minutes, plus 4 hours resting

Cooking time 5–7 hours

Dietaries Gluten free

Difficulty Medium

Cochinita pibil – Yucatán-style pulled pork

Cochinita pibil is an all-time favourite. You can easily cook this dish anywhere in the world, and it was the first dish I cooked after arriving in Australia. It always reminds me of the Yucatán Peninsula, where I worked as a marine biologist, and also of my friends Lucia and Tar. I travelled with them through Europe for several months as a babysitter. They are my kind of people; they love to eat and are not shy of trying weird things. Back then they lived in Paris and were connoisseurs of French cuisine. They showed me around and took me to exciting places to eat and drink. They always said you have to try this or that. I remember trying andouillette, a pork intestine sausage. Tar was sure I was going to love it, because I eat and finish most things, but I couldn't finish that intestine sausage! This trip was also the first time I tried Vietnamese food, at a little restaurant in Paris. I will never forget that experience – it was a revelation.

It was during this trip that I made cochinita pibil at a dinner party with a group of friends, and everyone loved it. Sadly, Tar passed away a few years ago. So when I make this, it brings back happy memories of Tar, Lucia and Paris.

Cochinita is generally eaten for Sunday breakfast. You will find it at markets or stalls in the main squares of villages around Yucatán and Quintana Roo. We would get up super early if we wanted to grab these tacos for breakfast, as the stall would always run out. The pork is slow-cooked in banana leaves overnight at a very low temperature. It is traditionally cooked in a pib, which is the Mayan word for an underground earth oven. The trick to a good cochinita is to keep it moist, then serve on a tortilla or bread roll (see Cochitorta on page 126) with cebolla curtida and habanero hot sauce. Slow-cooked pork, cebolla curtida and habanero hot sauce really is the holy trinity of taco fillings. This is a great dish for a big dinner party, as you can make it the day before and reheat when the party kicks off.

2 kg (4 lb 8 oz) skin-on pork shoulder
3 teaspoons table salt
150 g (5½ oz) Recado rojo (page 223)
2–3 banana leaves

TO SERVE
corn tortillas (shop-bought or see page 253 for homemade)
Cebolla curtida (page 228)
habanero hot sauce (shop-bought or see page 247 for homemade)

Place the pork in a large bowl. Rub the salt, then the recado rojo, into the meat. Cover with plastic wrap and leave to marinate for at least 4 hours or overnight.

Preheat the oven to 150°C (300°F). Heat the banana leaves over an open fire – I generally use the largest burner on my stove, but you could also do it on a barbecue. The leaves should warm up, but not burn. The leaves will change colour and become flexible – you will see the waxy cover melt.

Line a cast-iron pot with most of the banana leaves, leaving enough room to close the pot. Place the marinated meat on the leaves and spoon the rest of the marinade onto the meat. Cover the pork with the remaining leaf and seal the pot with a lid or foil so the moisture doesn't escape.

Place in the oven for 5 hours. Check the meat to see if it is falling apart. If not, leave in the oven for another couple of hours.

When ready, shred the pork using a couple of forks. I find the fat the most delicious part of the dish, so don't throw it out. And make sure you leave the pork in its juices.

Place the cochinita in a bowl – or leave it in the pot you cooked it in – with some tongs, and let your guests help themselves.

To eat: grab a tortilla and place some of the pork in it, then top with some cebolla curtida and finish with some habanero hot sauce. Don't let the tacos get cold!

Leftovers are excellent in a crispy bread roll (see Cochitorta, page 126).

Makes / serves
1.5 kg (3 lb 5 oz) / 6

Preparation time
30 minutes, plus at least 2 hours marinating

Cooking time
About 6 hours

Dietaries
Gluten free

Difficulty Medium

Barbacoa de cola de canguro — Kangaroo tail barbacoa

I might have told a little white lie. While I mentioned you can find all these recipes in Mexico, I can guarantee you won't find this Australian twist on barbacoa. My kangaroo-tail version continues the tradition of barbacoa having many different regional takes. Kangaroo tail is not the easiest meat to find but, as it's a gelatinous meat ideal for slow-cooking, you can replace it with lamb neck and leg, osso buco or short ribs. You might think the word barbacoa refers to a barbecue, but it's actually a pit style of cooking that is generally done underground. Goat or mutton are more traditional barbacoa meats.

On our last visit to Oaxaca City, we went on a day trip, and on my list of restaurants to visit was Maíz Cocina Tradicional. We arrived at 1.55 pm, and at 2 pm the barbacoa would be unearthed. One of the guests had the honour of pulling out the blessed bottle of mezcal that was buried in the underground oven with the meat, and a round of shots was served. Imagine, hot 100-proof mezcal in the early afternoon – quite a hit to the system! But what a way to enjoy a barbacoa. Mimi, the owner, was really friendly and explained the whole process but did not share the secret recipe. Here is my version. This recipe will take a bit of planning as there is some marinating to do, and, if cooked in the oven, it will take about 6 hours.

5 guajillo chillies
3 ancho chillies
2 morita chillies
1 cinnamon stick
4 teaspoons sesame seeds
½ teaspoon black peppercorns
1½ teaspoons dried Mexican oregano
1½ teaspoons thyme
2 garlic cloves
1 tablespoon white vinegar
2 kg (4 lb 8 oz) kangaroo tail, an alternative is 1 kg (2 lb 4 oz) lamb neck plus 1 kg (2 lb 4 oz) lamb leg
300 g (10½ oz) dried chickpeas
1 carrot, cut into 1 cm (½ inch) chunks
2 banana leaves, halved

TO SERVE
½ bunch coriander (cilantro), to garnish
1 white onion, finely diced, to garnish
6 limes, halved
Salsa verde cocida (page 245)
corn tortillas (shop-bought or see page 253 for homemade)
White rice (page 224)

Start by charring the chillies, one by one, on a comal or hotplate or in a dry non-stick frying pan. The chillies are ready when they change colour – this will take about 30–60 seconds, depending on the chilli type.

Add the chillies to a small saucepan with 500 ml (2 cups) of water and bring to the boil. Turn off the heat and leave to steep for 5 minutes.

Toast the cinnamon and sesame seeds in a dry frying pan. They are ready when the sesame seeds start to pop.

Place the chillies with their water, toasted cinnamon and seeds, peppercorns, oregano, thyme, garlic and vinegar in a blender and process until smooth.

Marinate the meat in this barbacoa mix for at least 2 hours (or overnight for the best result).

Preheat the oven to 150°C (300°F).

You will need a large cast-iron pot, with a lid, that will fit a steamer basket inside. Before placing the basket in the pot, add the chickpeas and carrot to the pot together with 1 litre (4 cups) of water. Now insert the basket.

Place one of the banana leaves on the basket, breaking it in pieces if you have to, and add the marinated

meat with all the sauce. Leave nothing behind.

Cover the meat with the rest of the banana leaves, tucking it in so it makes a parcel. Now place a sheet of foil over the pot, carefully place the lid on top, and seal the edges with the foil. Cook in the oven for at least 6 hours.

Take out the banana leaf parcel and place it in a bowl. The meat should be falling apart. Take the basket out and check the broth. Add some water if necessary, but it should be an intense broth.

Place the coriander, diced onion, cut limes and salsa verde on the table. Prepare a basket full of tortillas – you probably need four each.

Serve in a large soup bowl. Start by adding a scoop of white rice, then a handful of meat, followed by a generous scoop of the barbacoa broth with chickpeas.

Add the onion, coriander and lime to the broth, then eat with a spoon. Make tacos with the meat, adding onion, coriander, salsa verde and lime juice. ¡Provecho!

Makes / serves 1.5 kg (3 lb 5 oz) / 6

Preparation time 30 minutes, plus overnight marinating

Cooking time About 2½ hours

Dietaries Gluten free

Difficulty Medium

Lomo adobado

—

Pork loin in adobo

At family gatherings during the Christmas holidays in Mexico, there was always a big table of turkey, bacalao a la vizcaína (salted cod), romeritos and this lomo adobado. It might seem a relatively simple recipe, but it's difficult to cook right. It dries out easily like turkey, so use a meat thermometer so you don't overcook it. Adobo is a sort of marinade, generally thicker in consistency. This adobo is made with two chillies: guajillo and morita. My advice is to make more meat than you need, because you'll want to make Torta de lomo adobado (page 125) the next day.

8 guajillo chillies, deseeded
4 morita chillies, deseeded
8 garlic cloves
1½ teaspoons dried Mexican oregano
1 teaspoon dried thyme
1 teaspoon cumin seeds
½ teaspoon black peppercorns
1 heaped tablespoon table salt
80 ml (⅓ cup) apple cider vinegar
500 ml (2 cups) freshly squeezed orange juice
1 pork loin, about 2 kg (4 lb 8 oz)

TO SERVE
Red rice (page 225)
cooked black beans (see page 218)

Start by charring the chillies, one by one, on a comal or hotplate or in a dry non-stick frying pan. The chillies are ready when they change colour – this will take about 30–40 seconds, depending on the chilli type.

Place the chillies in a small saucepan and add enough water to just cover them. Bring to the boil, then simmer for 10–15 minutes – they need to become soft. Drain the chillies and reserve 1 cup (250 ml) of the cooking water.

Place the garlic, herbs, spices, salt and reserved cooking water in a blender and process on high speed until liquified. Add the chillies, vinegar and orange juice. Blend until you have a smooth sauce. If your blender is not powerful enough, you may need to strain the sauce to remove the larger pieces.

Place the pork in a large snaplock bag and add 1 cup (250 ml) of the sauce. Seal the bag and marinate overnight. Store the left-over sauce in a sealed container in the fridge until needed the next day.

A couple of hours before you cook it, remove the pork from the fridge.

Preheat the oven to 175°C (350°F).

Place the pork and its marinade, and the left-over sauce, in a large cast-iron pot (it should fit snugly) or deep baking tray. Place in the oven and cover with foil or the lid. Roast for 1 hour, then uncover and baste the meat with the liquid. Continue to cook, basting every 10 minutes, until cooked to medium–rare, around 2 hours total cooking time. Take care not to overcook or the meat will become dry. You can use a temperature probe to test if the meat is cooked; it should be 63°C (145°F) for medium–rare.

Take the loin out of the oven and allow to rest for 20 minutes.

Serve the loin on a platter and carve it at the table. Collect the juices and sauce and place them in a bowl. The loin goes well with red rice and black beans.

Left-over lomo is excellent for making tortas the next day (see page 125)!

Serves 4

Preparation time 20 minutes

Cooking time 40 minutes

Dietaries Gluten free, vegetarian

Difficulty Medium

Chile relleno

—

Stuffed poblano chilli

I decided to include this simple but flavour-packed chile relleno recipe in this book because one of my girlfriends, Karla, loved to eat this when she was pregnant with her first baby.

Recently, I asked her, 'What recipe makes you think of me?' and she said 'chile relleno'. I was convinced she was going to say Enmoladas (page 173), because I used to make them every year for her birthday.

Karla's baby boy is no longer a baby, and he stands at 1.9 metres (6 feet 2 inches) tall! I guess my chile relleno helped!

SALSA

750 (1 lb 10 oz) ripe tomatoes, cut into chunks
½ white onion
2 garlic cloves
½ cinnamon stick
12 black peppercorns
2 cloves
2 teaspoons table salt
1 teaspoon sugar
250 ml (1 cup) water
2 tablespoons vegetable oil

CHILLIES

4 poblano chillies, whole with stem, toasted and skin off (see page 231), or you can use tinned
160 g (5½ oz) queso oaxaca or mozzarella

TO SERVE

1 corn cob, roasted (see page 76), kernels sliced off the cob
White rice (page 224)
corn tortillas (shop-bought or see page 253 for homemade)
cooked black beans (see page 218)

To make the salsa, working in batches, place all the salsa ingredients, except the oil, in a blender and process at full speed for 2 minutes. Pass the salsa through a fine-mesh strainer.

Add the oil to a medium saucepan over medium heat. When the oil is hot, add the salsa and bring to the boil, then immediately lower the heat to a slow simmer and cook for 10 minutes. Set aside and warm up before serving.

Preheat the oven to 180°C (350°F).

Place the chillies in a lightly oiled baking dish. Fill each chilli with one-quarter of the cheese and cover the dish with foil. Place the dish in the oven for 15 minutes.

To assemble, place the stuffed chillies on a warm plate, add a generous scoop of tomato salsa on top, and a scoop of white rice on the side. Garnish with the corn kernels.

Serve with white rice, a basket of tortillas and a bowl of black beans.

Serves 4

Preparation time 15 minutes

Cooking time 15 minutes

Dietaries Can be gluten free

Difficulty Easy

Camarones al ajillo – Garlic chilli prawns

This packs a huge flavour punch for such a basic recipe. To get a tad technical, the guajillo chillies add heat and depth of flavour, while the intense garlic aroma complements the prawns (shrimp) with a layer of complexity. Truth be told, I have no idea where this dish originates from, but I have fond memories of eating it at the beach – with white rice, refried beans and freshly made tortillas – from before I can remember.

30 ml (1 fl oz) olive oil
6 garlic cloves, minced
4 guajillo chillies, deseeded and stems removed, thinly sliced
salt, to taste
freshly ground black pepper, to taste
juice of 2 limes
400 g (14 oz) large prawns (shrimp), peeled and deveined
30 ml (1 fl oz) dry white wine
1 teaspoon sweet paprika

TO SERVE

White rice (page 224)
corn or wheat tortillas (shop-bought or see pages 253 and 234 for homemade; use corn tortillas for gluten free)

Start by making the ajillo – the garlic and chilli oil. Heat the olive oil in a large frying pan over medium heat. Add the garlic and cook, stirring as it burns easily, until translucent, about 1–2 minutes. Add the sliced chillies and keep stirring – the oil will start changing colour. Fry and stir until fragrant, 10–15 seconds. Add salt and pepper to taste, then add the lime juice. Mix well.

Add the prawns to the pan and cook for about 2 minutes per side until they turn pink and opaque. Stir occasionally to ensure even cooking. Only flip once.

Add the wine and paprika. Season with salt and pepper to taste. Stir everything together and cook for a further 1–2 minutes.

Remove the pan from the heat and place the mixture on a plate. Serve immediately.

Serve the camarones al ajillo hot, either as a standalone dish or as a filling for warm tortillas. I recommend serving with white rice. There will be a fair bit of reddish oil in the pan and this is all pure flavour, so mix it through the rice. It is delicious.

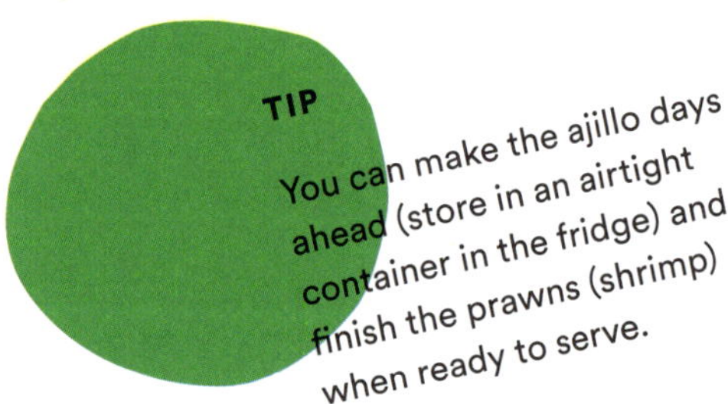

TIP

You can make the ajillo days ahead (store in an airtight container in the fridge) and finish the prawns (shrimp) when ready to serve.

Serves 6–8

Preparation time 30 minutes

Cooking time 1 hour

Dietaries Gluten free

Difficulty Medium

Pescado tikin xik – Yucatán-style achiote grilled fish in banana leaves

When living in Puerto Morelos, we would go to La Laguna Manatí for special occasions. This was about an hour's drive north (just outside Cancún). We would get a table at a rustic restaurant on the side of a mangrove lagoon and eat pescado tikin xik, a Mayan dish that literally translates to 'dry fish'. There, you chose your fish and they prepared it for you using the traditional tikin xik method. Some claim that the OG tikin xik comes from Isla Mujeres, a small island just across from Cancún. Locally, the marinade is made with sour oranges, but this recipe uses a mix of orange juice and vinegar.

This is a dish to share, as it's fun to make and will impress. It will also take a fair bit of planning. You'll need a large coal barbecue (gas will not give you the same flavour and heat) and a large barbecue grilling basket to cook the fish in. Finally, you need a whole fish, with scales on, that has been butterflied. Depending on where you live, the fish will be different. Choose a fresh fish (not frozen) and ask your fishmonger to butterfly it for you (the head needs to be split, too). You want to cook the fish with its scales on, as these protect the meat from burning. Most recipes remove the spine, but I like to leave it in as it adds flavour, and it is easier to remove without losing meat after it's cooked. Choose a fish that has firm meat; I like snapper or nannygai.

1 large fish, butterflied, scales on (I like to use snapper or nannygai in Adelaide, but sea bass or snapper will work, too)
60 ml (¼ cup) vegetable oil
3 banana leaves
4 teaspoons table salt
2 teaspoons freshly ground black pepper
250 g (9 oz) Recado rojo (page 223)
1 red onion, sliced
1 large tomato, sliced

TO SERVE

corn tortillas (shop-bought or see page 253 for homemade)
Refried beans (page 220)
White rice (page 224; optional)
4 limes, halved
habanero hot sauce (shop-bought or see page 247 for homemade)

Place the fish on a flat surface – your fish will already be butterflied so the spine will still be attached to one side of the fish.

With a sharp knife, slice the spine from the attached side to separate it from the fish, but leave it attached near the top, so you can fold it open and fold it back after marinating, like a triptych.

Oil the barbecue basket lightly to prevent it from sticking. Place a banana leaf or two on one side of the basket so it covers the whole side.

Place the fish, scales-side down, on top of the leaves. Make shallow cuts in the thicker parts of the fish, as this will help it to cook evenly. Add salt and pepper and rub them into the fish.

With a brush, baste the fish and spine with the recado rojo – you don't have to use it all; the fish just needs a good coating.

Fold the spine back and place the vegetables evenly over the fish.

On a cutting board, cut the vein out of a banana leaf, then tear into 2 cm (¾ inch) strips in the direction of the grain. These strips will be placed in a criss-cross pattern over the fish to prevent the vegetables from falling out and sticking to the basket (see photographs opposite).

Close the basket, making sure the fish is well secured. You should be able to flip it without anything falling out. The fish can be stored this way for a couple of hours until you are ready to grill.

Light the barbecue well ahead of time – about an hour before – with plenty of coals. You want the coals to be white, but still burning hot.

01

02

03

04

Place the basket with the fish on the grill, scales-side down. Cook for 10–20 minutes, but don't let the banana leaves on the scales side get too burnt. Flip the basket and grill on the open side with the vegetables. Cook for 5–10 minutes until the vegetables and fish start charring – you want a bit of char on the fish. Check if the fish is cooked by inserting the tip of a small knife into the thickest part.

Place the whole fish on a large plate in the middle of the table. Serve with warm corn tortillas, refried beans and maybe some white rice. Add a bowl of lime wedges and habanero hot sauce to finish.

The idea is that everyone makes their own tikin xik tacos. A cold beer is essential.

Serves 4 | **Preparation time** 30 minutes | **Cooking time** 20 minutes | **Dietaries** Gluten free | **Difficulty** Medium

Camarones zarandeados

—

Grilled marinated prawns

In 1995, when I was a student, I volunteered with a couple of friends, Guille and Dení, at the Isla Isabel National Park in Nayarit, which is a nesting area for seabirds in the Pacific Ocean. This was part of a program to eradicate feral cats and mice from this beautiful island. It was also where I had pescado (fish) zarandeado for the first time, prepared for us by local fishermen.

Camarones zarandeados, and any zarandeado, comes from Nayarit, in the north of Mexico. It originates from the Nahuatlacas people, who would cook fish on a mangrove wood fire. Zaranda comes from the way of cooking the fish, or prawns (shrimp) in this recipe. The fish is held in a grilling basket, and the flipping movement is called zarandear in the north.

Camarones zarandeados need to be cooked on the barbecue. With modern barbecues it is not necessary to use a basket if you are using prawns, but if you want to replace the prawns with fish or octopus, then a basket is recommended, as it makes flipping so much easier.

We recently made a batch meant for four people, but the two of us ate it all – it's too tasty to resist.

1 kg (2 lb 4 oz) large raw prawns (shrimp), in their shells
juice of 1 lime

MARINADE
120 g (4¼ oz) whole-egg mayonnaise
30 g (1 oz) American mustard (ensure mustard is gluten free if necessary)
¼ teaspoon ground cumin
1½ teaspoons dried Mexican oregano
1 tablespoon olive oil
100 ml (3½ fl oz) Valentina or Huichol hot sauce

TO SERVE
corn or wheat tortillas (shop-bought or see page 253 or 234 for homemade; use corn tortillas for gluten free)
White rice (page 224)
Refried beans (page 220)
Valentina or Huichol sauce
2 limes, halved

Add all the marinade ingredients to a bullet blender or small mixer. Blend until you have a smooth cream. Place the creamy goodness in a bowl.

Using a large, sharp, serrated knife (like a bread knife), butterfly the prawns by cutting through the back and the head, then opening them out. The easiest method is to place a prawn on its side on a chopping board then, pushing the prawn down with your hand, use the other hand to cut horizontally with the knife through the back and head, but not all the way through. Make sure the two halves remain attached.

Remove the black vein and any sandy bits, but keep the yellow-coloured bits around the head as this is all flavour. Blot the prawns dry with some paper towel and place on a large tray.

Using a basting brush, coat both sides of the prawns with the marinade.

Preheat the barbecue for 15 minutes if using gas. If using coal, light it around 1 hour before grilling.

Make sure your barbecue is hot, then grill the prawns for 1–2 minutes on the meat side, then for about 3 minutes on the shell side. The shells should be crunchy – some dark spots on the shells are perfect.

Serve the prawns with some corn or wheat tortillas, white rice, refried beans, spicy Valentina or Huichol sauce. If the prawn shells are crunchy, I eat the whole thing, shell and tail, but add some lime juice first.

GUISADOS

Stews

I am not sure there is a proper translation for guisados. They can be stews, but this is not always the case. Guisados are dishes generally served in cazuelas (clay cooking pots). They are daily, affordable meals. You find guisados at fondas where you have la comida del dia, or 'menu of the day', which is generally served around 2–3 pm. Guisados can be festive or plain and are made in bulk so they are ready to go. It's not uncommon to see 20–30 guisados on offer at a popular restaurant. On our last trip to Mexico, we went to see our friend Raúl in Zacatlán de las Manzanas, and he took us to his favourite place. There were at least 10 clay pots filled with guisados, which made choosing very difficult! It's also common to serve guisados at dinner parties known as taquizas (see pages 89 and 260), where everyone can serve themselves in a buffet-style set-up. The number of dishes served will depend on the size of the party.

Guisados can be served in multiple ways: with rice, beans and a stack of tortillas; as fillings for tacos or stuffed chillies; and as toppings for tostadas, gorditas and sopes.

Chicharrón en salsa serde (page 160)

Serves 4

Preparation time 15 minutes

Cooking time 1 hour

Dietaries Gluten free

Difficulty Difficult

Chicharrón en salsa serde

—

Pork crackling in salsa verde

This is a great dish (pictured on page 159) to make if you have left-over salsa verde cocida and good pork crackling with meat. If you can't find crackling with meat, it becomes quite a challenging dish, but it's worth the effort! Making pork crackling is a very messy job and you will get spattered, so I recommend doing this outside in an area you can clean easily. I like to use a camping stove or portable induction hob.

Below is the recipe for making your own meaty chicharrón, but if you don't feel comfortable, feel free to use 500 g (1 lb 2 oz) of meatless crackling, which is much easier to find at Asian stores. I have done this many times in the past.

750 g (1 lb 10 oz) pork belly, cut into 2 cm (¾ in) slices
½ brown onion
2 garlic cloves
2 bay leaves
1 teaspoon black peppercorns
3 teaspoons table salt
about 500 g (1 lb 2 oz) lard
1 tablespoon vegetable oil
500 g (1 lb 2 oz) Salsa verde cocida (page 245)

TO SERVE

Refried beans (page 220)
corn tortillas (shop-bought or see page 253 for homemade)
white onion, sliced (optional)
4 sprigs of coriander (cilantro; optional)

Add 2 litres (8 cups) of water to a medium saucepan over medium heat. Add the pork, onion, garlic, bay leaves, peppercorns and salt and bring to the boil. Reduce the heat and let simmer for 25–30 minutes.

Remove the boiled meat from the water and dry it really well. Make regular perpendicular cuts – about 2 cm (¾ inch) apart – in the meaty bits of the pork pieces, but don't cut into the fat under the skin.

The next part is messy and potentially dangerous if care is not taken. As mentioned before, do this outside. Add the lard to a large cast-iron pan and heat to 140°C (275°F), using a thermometer. Carefully add the meat to the pan using long-handled tongs. Because the meat has water in it, it will spatter and this can burn you! I place a grease-spatter screen on top, with a paper towel on top of that, but it is still a messy job. Grease will be everywhere.

Let the meat fry for about 20 minutes until the skin is crispy. The spattering will reduce as the meat loses its moisture. Turn off the heat, remove the meat and place it in a baking tray lined with paper towel. Your chicharrón is ready. I know you won't be able to resist, as it's delicious, so try a sneaky bite.

Cut the chicharrón into 3–4 cm (1¼–1½ inch) chunks and set aside.

Place the oil in a large frying pan and heat up the salsa verde, adding some water if necessary. Add the pork and cook for another 10–15 minutes.

Serve the chicharrón with refried beans and a basket of corn tortillas. Top with onion slices and coriander sprigs (if using). You can also serve the fried chicharrón (without the salsa verde) as a snack with some guacamole.

Serves 4 | **Preparation time** 30 minutes | **Cooking time** 20 minutes | **Dietaries** Gluten free, vegetarian | **Difficulty** Medium

Rajas con crema

—

Poblano chilli in cream

Rajas con crema is my kind of comfort food; simple and tasty. This is a traditional dish from the central region of Mexico and is a staple of any taquiza. If you prefer a spicier version, you can leave some of the poblano chilli seeds and veins intact when slicing. Also, you can add cubed boiled potatoes or corn when you add the rajas to the pan.

Fresh poblanos are becoming easier to find in Australian supermarkets, and you can always replace them with tinned chillies if you can't get hold of the fresh stuff.

5 poblano chillies, roasted and peeled (see page 231), or use tinned
2 tablespoons vegetable oil
1 large onion, thinly sliced
250 ml (1 cup) thickened (heavy) cream
salt, to taste
freshly ground black pepper, to taste
100 g (3½ oz) grated mozzarella

TO SERVE
corn tortillas (shop-bought or see page 253 for homemade)
Red rice (page 225)

Cut the tops off the roasted and peeled poblano chillies and remove the seeds and veins. Slice the chillies lengthways into 5 mm (¼ inch) strips and set aside. If using tinned poblano chillies, they are already peeled, so just give them a good rinse and cut them the same way.

Heat the vegetable oil in a large frying pan over medium heat. Add the onion and saute until the onion becomes translucent and starts to caramelise, about 7 minutes.

Add the sliced poblano chillies to the pan. Stir everything together and cook for another 2–3 minutes.

Reduce the heat to low and pour in the cream. Stir gently to combine all the ingredients. Let the mixture simmer for about 5 minutes, allowing the flavours to meld together. Season with salt and pepper to taste.

Add the mozzarella over the rajas con crema. Stir until the cheese melts and the sauce becomes creamy.

Remove the pan from the heat.

You can enjoy rajas con crema with tortillas and red rice. It is also a delicious side dish with grilled meat.

Serves 4–6

Preparation time 15 minutes

Cooking time 40 minutes

Dietaries Gluten free

Difficulty Easy

Bistec en salsa de chile pasilla

—

Steak in pasilla sauce

This is a typical stew you would find at a fonda, where simple meals are served. It is fairly stress-free to make and is full of flavour. Even though the sauce base includes chillies, it is not a spicy dish.

This recipe – as with most of the recipes from my mum – were handed down by my abuelita (grandmother) Josefina. These recipes for daily meals are simple to make. I am very proud to have them in the book.

1 ripe roma (plum) tomato
400 g (14 oz) tomatillos, fresh or tinned
½ small brown onion, quartered
2 garlic cloves
10 pasilla chillies, deseeded
5 black peppercorns
1 clove
⅛ teaspoon cumin seeds
½ teaspoon dried Mexican oregano
1 teaspoon table salt
2 tablespoons vegetable oil
600 g (1 lb 5 oz) steak, such as minute (sizzle/cube), cut into 1 cm (½ inch) strips
salt, to taste
400 g (14 oz) all-purpose potatoes (I like brushed Dutch cream), peeled and cut into 2 cm (¾ inch) chunks
180 g (6½ oz) tinned nopales

TO SERVE

White rice (page 224)
cooked black or pinto beans (see page 218)
corn tortillas (shop-bought or see page 253 for homemade)

Place the whole tomato, tomatillos, onion and garlic in a medium saucepan over medium heat and cover with water. Bring to the boil and cook for 7–8 minutes only – it's important that the tomatillos don't fall apart. Drain and place the vegetables in a blender.

Add the chillies to a small saucepan over medium heat, cover with water and let them simmer for 5–6 minutes until soft. Drain the chillies, reserving the boiling liquid.

Add the cooked chillies, spices, oregano and salt to the blender with the vegetables and blend. Add some of the chilli boiling liquid if the mix is too dry. It should become a smooth thickened sauce.

Heat a large frying pan over high heat, add the oil and sear the cut steak for a couple of minutes on each side – the meat just needs to change colour. Season the steak with salt to taste. Once the steak has turned brown, reduce the heat to medium–low, add the potato and cook for another 10 minutes.

Add the sauce and some more chilli cooking liquid if necessary.

Cook until the potato is done, probably another 10 minutes. Add the nopales at the end, as these are already cooked.

Serve bistec en salsa de chile pasilla with some white rice, black beans and corn tortillas. This is an excellent dish if you are organising a taquiza.

Makes / serves 1.75 kg (3 lb 12 oz) / 6–8

Preparation time 30 minutes

Cooking time 40 minutes

Dietaries Gluten free

Difficulty Easy

Picadillo

—

Minced meat stew

Everyone has that one dish they absolutely hated for no reason when they were younger – this is that dish for me. I have no idea why I disliked this dish so much when I was little, as it's absolutely delicious. Picadillo is traditionally found at a fonda. It's easy and cheap to make, and every family has their own version. Picadillo comes from the word picar, which means 'chopping', and it's basically a minced (ground) meat dish, with some finely chopped vegetables for good measure. Picadillo can be eaten as is, with some rice and beans, but you can use it as a stuffing for chillies (see Chile güero relleno de picadillo, page 142) or as a topping for sopes, tostadas and gorditas. This recipe makes a large amount by design, to ensure you have plenty of leftovers.

2 tablespoons vegetable oil
1 brown onion, finely chopped
700 g (1 lb 9 oz) minced (ground) beef
400 g (14 oz) all-purpose potatoes (I like brushed Dutch cream), finely diced
2 carrots, finely diced
100 g (⅔ cup) frozen peas
3 teaspoons table salt

SAUCE

1 tablespoon vegetable oil
1 ancho chilli
500 g (1 lb 2 oz) ripe tomatoes
2 garlic cloves
½ small brown onion
⅓ teaspoon cumin seeds
½ teaspoon dried Mexican oregano
4 whole allspice

TO SERVE

White rice (page 224) or Red rice (page 225)
cooked black beans (see page 218)
corn tortillas (shop-bought or see page 253 for homemade)

For the sauce, heat the oil in a large cast-iron pan over medium heat and fry the ancho chilli for 1 minute. Place the chilli, the rest of the sauce ingredients and 250 ml (1 cup) of water in a large blender and process until smooth.

Heat the 2 tablespoons of vegetable oil for the picadillo in the same cast-iron pan over medium heat, then fry the onion for 2 minutes. Add the beef and break it down really well until it is crumbly. Cook for 3 minutes until the colour changes, then add the diced potato and carrot and the salt. Cook for 5 minutes, then add the picadillo sauce and simmer for 15–20 minutes. Finish by adding the frozen peas.

Serve the picadillo with white or red rice, black beans and a stack of corn tortillas.

Makes / serves 1.5 litres (6 cups) mole / 4

Preparation time 20 minutes

Cooking time 1½ hours

Dietaries n/a

Difficulty Medium

Mole con pollo – Chicken mole

Mole is a celebratory dish. You'll find it on birthday and wedding menus, so of course it was on the menu for my wedding with Kor! Mole translates to 'sauce', and there are many, many moles, with poblano being the most famous. One of the first questions we ask a foreigner in Mexico is: have you tried mole yet?! Did you like it? Your answer is important, so it's best to try before you go.

Making mole paste is complicated and involves hours of charring, grinding and cooking, hence most people don't make their own. They go to the market and buy the paste and finish the sauce at home. I learned how to make mole from scratch in Oaxaca, but for this book I will show you how to make a mole negro using a bought paste – it's still a complex process. You might like to boil the chicken leg quarters before making the mole, as you can use the stock for making the mole.

I made this recipe based on the size of a standard jar of mole negro, which is about 500 g (1 lb 2 oz). This might be too much mole for you, but you can freeze the leftovers. A chicken mole is generally served with rice and tortillas.

4 chicken leg quarters, boiled (see page 222)
2 tablespoons sesame seeds

MOLE
½ brown onion, roughly chopped
2 garlic cloves
500 g (1 lb 2 oz) tomatoes, quartered
700 ml (24 fl oz) chicken stock (see page 221 for homemade) or vegetable stock
90 g (3 oz) Mexican chocolate (1 tablet)
500 g (1 lb 2 oz) mole poblano negro paste, you can use oaxaqueño, too

TO SERVE
Red rice (page 225)
corn tortillas (shop-bought or see page 253 for homemade)

For the mole, start by charring the onion and garlic in a dry frying pan over medium heat – or directly over a flame, which is how I like to do it.

Add all the mole ingredients, except the mole paste, in batches to a blender and process on high speed until smooth. Set aside.

Add the mole paste to a large saucepan over medium–low heat and cook for 10–15 minutes, stirring constantly – you don't want it to burn.

At this point, STOP. Look. And admire the mixture, the colour and texture and smell the flavours. (This sauce is a collective invention that has been perfected over the centuries; it's a gift from my culture to the world.)

Add the blended mole mixture to the mole paste in the pan over low heat – watch how it changes colour and texture. Cook for about 30 minutes. Keep scraping the bottom of the saucepan with a wooden spoon, so it does not burn.

When the sauce is silky, with a runny batter-like consistency, turn off the heat. You can make the mole a day or two in advance if that is more convenient.

Boil the chicken leg quarters according to the Pollo cocido recipe on page 222.

In a small dry frying pan over medium heat, toast the sesame seeds until golden brown. This will take about a minute.

The best way to serve mole con pollo is with red rice and corn tortillas. Start with a scoop of rice, then place the warm chicken on the plate and cover completely with the warmed mole. Sprinkle it with the toasted sesame seeds.

If you have left-over mole, you can either use it for Enmoladas (page 173) or you could make breakfast – Huevos con mole (page 42).

Serves 8

Preparation time 30 minutes

Cooking time 3½ hours

Dietaries Gluten free

Difficulty Medium

Entomatado de res — Slow-cooked short rib in tomatillo

This dish is a pure celebration of one of my favourite ingredients – tomatillo! I used to cook entomatado de res at dinner parties in Puerto Morelos. Everyone loved it, especially my dear friend Melina. She suggested we include the entomatado de res recipe in the book, as it's a dish that we are both very fond of; it's perfect for entertaining and creating memories.

In Mexico City, tomatillos are actually called tomates, and the red tomatoes are called jitomate. Tomatillos are very hard to get in Australia, and I think this has to do with the fact that nobody knows how to use them. My guess is that people put them in their salads, and they are horrible that way. Tomatillos are meant for saucing, either raw or cooked, and the entomatado is a great example of this. I like using short ribs, but osso buco works well, too. Any meat with a bone that needs to be slow-cooked does the trick.

2 tablespoons vegetable oil
1.6 kg (3 lb 8 oz) beef short ribs, cut into 10 cm (4 inch) chunks (let your butcher do this!)
1.2 kg (2 lb 12 oz) tomatillos, fresh or tinned
2 brown onions, cut into long, thin strips (julienned)
4 garlic cloves
2 teaspoons dried Mexican oregano
1 teaspoon cumin seeds
3 teaspoons table salt
1 long red chilli

TO SERVE

cooked black beans (see page 218)
corn tortillas (shop-bought or see page 253 for homemade)

You will need a large cast-iron pan or enamelled cast-iron casserole dish with a lid to make this recipe. Preheat the oven to 150°C (300°F).

Add the oil to the cast-iron pan over medium heat. Do this on your front burners, as there will be some active cooking here.

Using tongs, grab a few of the short rib pieces and cover the bottom of the pan – you will probably fit three or four chunks – and brown the meat for about 10 minutes. Turn the chunks until they are nice and brown – this will give the dish a lot of flavour. Once browned, place the ribs in a bowl and repeat with the rest of the meat.

Once everything is nice and brown, take the pan off the heat. Add the ribs and the remaining ingredients, cover with the lid or foil, and place in the oven. After 2½ hours, remove the lid and cook for another 30 minutes. After 3 hours you should have a rich sauce with meat that is falling off the bone – if the meat is still tough, cook for another 30 minutes.

You could either serve the entomatado on a big plate in the centre of the table, or serve individually. The best way to eat entomatado is with black beans and corn tortillas. You could use red rice, too, but in my opinion just beans is the way to go.

Put a bit of everything in your tortilla and you'll have an amazing taco; it will be sweet, sour, salty and sticky – delicious.

Entomatado can be made a day or two in advance and kept refrigerated. Just remove from the fridge 30 minutes before reheating in a 160°C (325°F) oven for 30 minutes.

Serves 6

Preparation time 20 minutes

Cooking time 1½ hours

Dietaries Gluten free

Difficulty Medium

Carne de puerco con calabacitas — Pork with zucchini

This is a dish that many Mexicans associate with family and growing up – at least I do. This is my favourite recipe from my mother; she makes it exceptionally well and uses pork ribs. Ask your butcher to cut the ribs into 5 cm (2 inch) chunks – you want the ribs to be meaty and not too fat. You can make this dish a day in advance and reheat it just before serving. Perfect for a taquiza.

1 kg (2 lb 4 oz) pork ribs, cut into 5 cm (2 inch) chunks
2 garlic cloves
3 teaspoons table salt
1 small brown onion, diced
600 g (1 lb 5 oz) tomatoes, finely diced
400 g (14 oz) zucchini (courgettes), diced

TO SERVE

White rice (page 224)
corn tortillas (shop-bought or see page 253 for homemade)

Add the pork, 500 ml (2 cups) of water, the garlic and 1 teaspoon of the salt to a large cast-iron pan over medium heat. Bring to a gentle boil and cook for about 1 hour, or until the water evaporates and the meat starts to fry in its own fat. Fry until the meat is golden brown. Turn off the heat.

Remove the pork from the pan – retaining the fat in the pan – and set aside in a bowl.

In the same pan with the rendered fat, fry the onion until translucent. Add the tomato and zucchini and cook for 3–4 minutes. Season with the remaining salt and return the meat to the pan. Cook for another 10 minutes.

Serve carne de puerco con calabacitas with white rice and a stack of corn tortillas.

ENCHILADAS

Enchiladas are folded corn tortillas covered in salsas generally made with chilli. Enchiladas can be basic – just some tortillas with sauce – or more complex, with fillings and cheese. The tortillas are first shallow-fried on each side to make them foldable and prevent them from becoming soggy. There are hundreds of different enchiladas and you will find local specialties across Mexico. Enchiladas get their name from the Spanish word enchilar, which means 'adding chilli'. The origin of the dish is pre-Hispanic. In the Florentine codex of the 16th century, created by a Spanish friar, it is referred to as chillapitzalli, which is a combination of chilli and tlapitzalli, a flauta or 'flute', therefore a 'chilli flute'.

Most enchiladas are filled with shredded chicken, but you can use queso panela or haloumi if you prefer vegetarian. Left-over Jamaica flowers (see page 202) are a great vegan substitute – but it's best to fry them with some onion first. Replace the shredded chicken in the recipes that follow with your preferred filling.

In this section are three recipes made with unique sauces: avocado, mole and Swiss. More straightforward enchiladas would be made with Salsa roja (page 238) or Salsa verde cocida (page 245), so feel free to mix things up.

Left to right: Aguacatadas (page 172), Enmoladas (page 173)

Makes / serves	Preparation time	Cooking time	Dietaries	Difficulty Easy
12 / 4	20 minutes	20 minutes	Gluten free	

Aguacatadas – Avocado enchiladas

If you like avocados (and let's face it, who doesn't!) you will love aguacatadas (pictured on page 171): special cold sauce enchiladas made with an avocado-based salsa. My mum used to make this on days when she was short on time, as they are super easy to make and don't require much preparation.

- 3 jalapeños
- 4 tomatillos, fresh or tinned
- ½ white onion
- 1 garlic clove
- ¼ bunch coriander (cilantro), including stalks
- 2 avocados
- 1½ teaspoons table salt
- 350 g (12 oz) chicken, boiled and shredded (see page 222)
- 60 ml (¼ cup) vegetable oil
- 12 corn tortillas (shop-bought or see page 253 for homemade)
- 100 g (3½ oz) queso fresco, crumbled (in Australia you can substitute La Casa del Formaggio brand's Homestyle Fresh Cheese, otherwise use Indian paneer cheese)

Bring a small saucepan with 625 ml (2½ cups) of water to the boil over medium heat and add the jalapeños, tomatillos, onion and garlic. Cook until the chilli skins burst – this will take approximately 10 minutes from when the water starts boiling. Drain the vegetables and reserve the cooking water. Cool for 10 minutes.

Transfer the blanched vegetables, along with the reserved cooking water, to a blender and add the coriander, avocado and salt. Blend until you have a smooth green sauce – it should not be runny but creamy. You might have to add more water to get the right consistency.

Take the chicken out of the fridge 30 minutes before you're ready to serve. When it's room temperature, you're ready to build your enchiladas.

Add the oil to a small frying pan over medium heat and fry the tortillas, one at a time, for 5–10 seconds on each side. This process will heat up the tortillas and make them fold without breaking. The oil will also prevent the tortillas from becoming soggy.

Place a warm tortilla on a plate or chopping board and fill with a handful of warm shredded chicken. Don't overfill, as you want the enchilada to close and make a nice roll. Place the enchilada on a plate with the fold down so it does not unfold. Finish all 12 tortillas, placing them next to each other so they support each other and hold their shape. Begin plating immediately.

On a flat, medium-sized plate, pour about one-sixth of the avocado sauce, then place three rolled-up tortillas with the chicken side by side. Pour a small quantity of avocado sauce across the centre of the enchiladas and sprinkle some cheese over the sauce. Repeat with the remaining ingredients and serve.

Makes / serves
12 / 4

Preparation time
20 minutes

Cooking time
10 minutes

Dietaries n/a

Difficulty Easy

Enmoladas

—

Mole enchiladas

Enmoladas (pictured on page 171) are enchiladas made with mole. These enchiladas are perfect for lovers of rich and complex moles, and can be made without any filling or by replacing the chicken with queso fresco or other fresh cheese.

600 ml (21 fl oz) mole negro (make the mole in Mole con pollo on page 165)
60 ml (¼ cup) vegetable oil
12 tortillas (shop-bought or see page 253 for homemade)
350 g (12 oz) chicken, boiled and shredded (see page 222), warm
150 ml (5 fl oz) thickened (heavy) cream
100 g (3½ oz) queso fresco (in Australia you can substitute La Casa del Formaggio brand's Homestyle Fresh Cheese, otherwise use Indian paneer cheese)
½ white onion, thinly sliced
coriander (cilantro) leaves (optional)
sesame seeds, toasted (optional)

Heat the mole in a medium saucepan over low heat – it does not need to boil. It needs to be a pouring consistency, but not too runny, so add some water if necessary.

Add the oil to a small frying pan over medium heat and fry the tortillas, one at a time, for about 5–10 seconds on each side. This process will heat up the tortillas and make them fold without breaking. The oil will also prevent tortillas from becoming soggy.

To fill the enmoladas, place a warm tortilla on a plate or chopping board and fill with a handful of warm shredded chicken. Don't overfill, as you want the enchilada to close and make a nice roll. Place the enchilada on a warm plate with the fold down so it does not unfold. Finish all 12 tortillas, placing them next to each other so they keep their shape and heat. Begin plating immediately.

On a warm plate, place three rolled tortillas with chicken side by side. Pour the mole over the tortillas, then some cream. Garnish with crumbled cheese, the white onion and coriander leaves or sesame seeds, if desired. Repeat with the remaining ingredients and serve.

Makes / serves 12 / 4

Preparation time 20 minutes

Cooking time 15 minutes

Dietaries Gluten free

Difficulty Easy

Enchiladas suizas – Swiss enchiladas

There are multiple theories about the origin of this dish. One goes like this: a Swiss visitor at a famous restaurant in Mexico City – Sanborns de los Azulejos – found his enchilada order too spicy. He was a regular so, to please him, the restaurant added some cream to the salsa with cheese on top, to reduce the spice, then grilled (broiled) them in the oven. And enchiladas suizas was born! Is this true? Who knows! All I know is that I love these enchiladas. When I was a little girl we used to go for dinner at Sanborns, which is a massive franchise now. There, I always ordered them with a vanilla milkshake. It was a very heavy dinner but an absolute treat!

- 500 g (1 lb 2 oz) Salsa verde cocida (page 245)
- 125 ml (½ cup) cooking cream
- 12 corn tortillas (shop-bought or see page 253 for homemade)
- 60 ml (¼ cup) vegetable oil
- 300 g (10½ oz) chicken, boiled and shredded (see page 222)
- 120 g (4 oz) grated mozzarella

Place the salsa verde in a small saucepan over low heat and add the cream. Warm the sauce until it starts to simmer – it doesn't need to boil.

Heat the oil in a small frying pan over medium heat and fry the tortillas, one at a time, for about 5–10 seconds on each side. This process will heat up the tortillas and make them fold without breaking. The oil will also prevent tortillas from becoming soggy.

Enchiladas suizas can be plated individually on a deep plate (three each) or in a large tray. Make sure the plates are ovenproof.

To fill the enchiladas, place a warm tortilla on a warm plate or chopping board and fill with a handful of warm shredded chicken. Don't overfill, as you want the enchilada to close and make a nice roll. Place the enchilada on the heatproof plate or tray with the fold down so it does not unfold.

Cover the enchiladas with the creamy salsa verde, then cover with cheese.

Place the plate or tray under a hot grill (broiler) and cook the enchiladas for approximately 5 minutes. The cheese needs to be melted and you want some brown spots to appear.

Ready to serve! If using a tray, place it in the middle of the table.

Dulce

—

Sweet

Mexico is a nation of sweet tooths. We love all things related to confectionery, desserts and pastries, including paletas (ice blocks; see page 194) and pan dulce (sweet breads), as well as one of the best known Mexican cakes, Pastel tres leches (page 186). When enjoying a menu of the day at a fonda, you are generally served a simple dessert to finish your meal. Flan, such as Flan de queso (page 180), and gelatina (jello) are classic examples.

If you've never seen gelatina before, they are like the jelly of your childhood but taken to a bombastic new level. They come in all shapes and colours, from floral bursts to multilayered cups, and are as stunning as they are delicious.

Paletas are a colourful example of how creative Mexicans can be with seemingly simple foods. Unlike ice creams and ice blocks from other parts of the world, Mexico's take features bold flavours and a hit of chilli. Paletas are generally not eaten as dessert, but rather are a snack that cools you in the afternoon heat.

While Mexico is a nation of sweet tooths, I am one of the few who is adverse to most desserts and sweet treats. I still have my favourites. The ones I can't resist are in this chapter.

Serves 8–12

Preparation time 30 minutes

Cooking time 75 minutes

Dietaries Gluten free, vegetarian

Difficulty Medium

Flan de queso — Cheese flan

This is a deliciously rich dessert that your friends will not only thank you for but will forever request you make! I get complaints every time I take it off the menu at La Popular Taqueria, so be careful who you choose to serve this to, as you might be stuck on flan duties for a very long time! In Mexico, a flan is typically served at a fonda or a casual diner, usually as part of the economical menu – the comida corrida.

150 g (5½ oz) caster (superfine) sugar
250 g (9 oz) cream cheese, at room temperature
340 ml (11½ fl oz) tinned evaporated milk
400 ml (14 fl oz) tinned condensed milk
5 eggs, at room temperature
seeds scraped from ½ vanilla bean, or ½ teaspoon vanilla bean paste
½ teaspoon ground cinnamon
½ teaspoon table salt

I generally use a round Pyrex pie dish (24 cm/9½ inches in diameter) as a mould. It is transparent and makes coating with burnt sugar easier. You will also need a roasting tin that the mould fits inside, in order to create a bain-marie.

Preheat the oven to 180°C (350°F).

Place the sugar and 80 ml (⅓ cup) of water in a heavy-based saucepan over medium–high heat. Bring to the boil and cook the sugar until it starts to change colour. Reduce the heat to medium–low and keep cooking until the sugar is light brown to brown; this can take 10–15 minutes. Be careful – the sugar will be about 180°C (350°F), and you can burn yourself. You have to be careful not to burn the sugar, so stay vigilant. When the sugar starts smoking, it's ready. Have a couple of oven mitts ready and your mould on a flat and secure surface.

When the sugar is ready, quickly pour it into the mould and, with oven mitts on, distribute the caramel over the bottom and two-thirds of the way up the side of the mould. The caramel will dissolve into syrup when the flan is ready and will make unmoulding easy. Set the mould aside.

Boil 1.5 litres (6 cups) of water in a kettle.

Add all the remaining ingredients to a blender. Blend on the lowest speed for 1 minute, until the mixture is smooth but not too frothy. Pour it into the mould and cover with foil.

Place the mould in the roasting tin. Place the tin with the mould inside on a middle shelf in the oven, then pour the hot water into the tray until it reaches two-thirds of the way up the outside of the mould. Cook for 1 hour.

When ready, with your mitts on, take the tin filled with water and the mould out of the oven and check if the flan is cooked. Jiggle the mould softly – it should be wobbly. If the middle is still runny, return to the oven for another 10 minutes.

Take the mould out of the tin and place on a wire rack to cool – note that the flan is very fragile at this stage. When cool, run a paring knife around the edge of the flan – which will make unmoulding easier later – then place in the fridge.

To unmould the flan, you need a plate that is larger than the mould, preferably with a raised edge.

Place the plate upside down on top of the mould. Holding both the plate and mould very securely, flip them both upside down so the flan lands on the plate. Do not wear your Sunday best at this stage, as you might splash it with flan goodness! Collect the syrup from the mould and place it in a little jug.

With a long, thin knife, cut the flan into slices. Clean the knife between cuts so it keeps the flan pretty. Serve the slices on dessert plates and finish with a drizzle of syrup.

Makes /serves 15–20 / 4–6 | **Preparation time** 15 minutes | **Cooking time** 30 minutes | **Dietaries** Vegetarian | **Difficulty** Medium

Churros con chocolate

—

Churros with chocolate dip

Everyone loves churros. They were brought to Mexico or, more correctly, Latin America, by the Spanish in the 16th century, but it is believed that Portuguese merchants first learned about churros on their trips to China. Anyway, Mexicans now see them as an integral part of their culture. You can find churros on carts at the plazas or in fancy restaurants. When we visited Coyoacán, we were impressed by the size of the churros. Massive deep-fryers with enormous presses would produce giant, metres-long circular churros! The skilled cook would get the oil in a swirl and pump the churro mix directly into the hot oil. By keeping the swirl in the oil, a snail-shaped round churro forms.

Churro batter is really thick and needs to be pressed out of a piping bag with a star-shaped nozzle, so you need a good one! Cheap ones will burst.

Churros are also excellent with Chocolate caliente mexicano (page 206) or atole (see page 184).

CHURROS

160 g (5½ oz) plain (all-purpose) flour
½ teaspoon baking powder
60 g (2 oz) unsalted butter
½ teaspoon table salt
2 eggs, whisked in a bowl
60 g (2 oz) caster (superfine) sugar
1 teaspoon ground cinnamon
vegetable oil, for frying

CHOCOLATE DIP

50 g (1¾ oz) caster (superfine) sugar
90 g (3 oz) Mexican chocolate (1 tablet)
90 ml (3 fl oz) double (thick) cream

In a large bowl, combine the flour and baking powder.

In a medium saucepan, heat 250 ml (1 cup) of water, the butter and salt. Once the mixture starts to boil, turn the heat off and add all the flour mixture at once, mixing really well with a wooden spoon. Let cool for approximately 3 minutes – it needs to be warm but not too hot.

Add the whisked eggs and incorporate until you have a smooth, slightly sticky dough. When adding the eggs, you might think at first that it's going wrong, but don't worry. It's all good, just keep going.

Fit star-shaped nozzles or pastry tips (I have used #5 or #7) to a piping bag, then add the warm dough. Remove the air bubbles by twisting the top of the bag and compacting the dough. Set aside.

Combine the sugar and cinnamon on a large flat tray.

This is a good moment to make your dip. It's easy to make: just add 50 ml (1¾ fl oz) of water and the sugar to a small saucepan over low heat and bring to a simmer. Let the sugar dissolve, then add the chocolate tablet. Mix continuously with a small whisk to dissolve the chocolate; this will take a couple of minutes.

Remove from the heat and let cool for a couple of minutes, then stir in the cream. Mix well until you have a smooth, dark sauce. Your chocolate dip is ready. Set aside.

Place a saucepan large enough to fit a couple of churros inside on the stove. (You can also use a deep-fryer.) Add the oil (at least 3–4 cm/1¼–1½ inches deep) and heat over medium heat to 180°C (350°F). I use a thermometer to test the oil, but if a piece of bread dropped into the oil browns in 15 seconds, the oil is the correct temperature.

Now it's time to pipe the churros. When using the #5 nozzle, my churros are 20 g (¾ oz) when wet, and long and thin (about 10 cm/4 inches long); with the larger nozzle (#7), they are 35 g (1¼ oz). First pipe out a couple of practice churros onto baking paper, to get the feel of the pressure required. You could make all your churros this way, then transfer to the oil, or you can pipe them directly

into the oil, which is a bit more tricky but yields a prettier churro.

Fry the churros for 2–3 minutes until golden brown, turning them a couple of times. Place them on paper towel to drain.

Transfer the still-warm churros to the sugar-cinnamon tray and coat them with the mix – I sprinkle it on. Take them out with care. They are ready to serve.

Always serve churros warm! If the chocolate mix is cold, warm it up – but make sure it's not too hot, or it might split.

Makes / serves 1 litre (4 cups) of atole and 8 regañadas / 4

Preparation time 30 minutes

Cooking time 20 minutes

Dietaries Can be vegetarian

Difficulty Easy

Atole de vainilla con regañadas

—

Vanilla corn drink with sugar biscuits

Atole is a pre-Hispanic drink, originally made with masa and water. Following the arrival of the Spanish, people started adding milk, cane sugar and spices. Atoles can be sweet, savoury or even sour. They are very rich, so they almost count as a meal. In Mexico City, you'll find people on every corner selling tamales and atole in the mornings. You notice them on cold days thanks to the steam rising from the tamales and the atole pot. I particularly love atole in winter.

Tamales and atole are a must for celebrations as well, especially Christenings. As I mentioned, the base of an atole is masa combined with water or milk and fruits, seeds and spices added for flavour. This mix of flavours depends on the region and its flora. It's a rich and energetic kickstarter for the morning, with plenty of calories for the day ahead. If you add Mexican chocolate, you'll have a champurrado.

Regañadas are basic biscuits from Oaxaca. On our last trip to Mexico, we went to Oaxaca City and rented a house close to the city centre, near a place called La Atolería, a traditional bakery where they specialise in atoles. You can order a flight of atoles (a series of different atoles in small cups), which I did, and they came with a regañada. So, when I returned to Adelaide I decided to make atole – of course – but the regañadas was the challenge, as I had never made them before. This is my take.

REGAÑADAS

¼ teaspoon table salt
250 g (1⅔ cups) plain (all-purpose) flour, plus extra for dusting
75 g (2½ oz) lard or ghee
100 g (3½ oz) white (granulated) sugar
2 tablespoons lard or vegetable oil

ATOLE

1 litre (4 cups) full-cream (whole) milk
100 g (3½ oz) white (granulated) sugar
2 cinnamon sticks
seeds scraped from ¼ vanilla bean, or ¼ teaspoon vanilla bean paste
300 g (10½ oz) Masa (page 250)
Optional: To make it a champurrado, add 90 g (3¼ oz), or 1 tablet, of Mexican chocolate

For the regañadas, preheat the oven to 200°C (400°F) and line a baking tray (or two) with baking paper.

Combine the salt and 100 ml (3½ fl oz) of water in a bowl.

Place the flour on a clean flat work surface and heap it into a volcano shape. Add the water and salt mixture and the lard to the centre and incorporate them into the flour with clean hands until you have a smooth dough, adding water if necessary.

Take portions of the dough and form little balls about the size of golf balls. Set aside.

Clean your work surface and dust it with extra flour. Flatten the balls on your dusted surface and sprinkle with more flour. Roll into flat (about 1 mm/1⁄32 inch) circular shapes of 15–18 cm (6–7 inch) diameter.

Spread the white sugar on a flat round plate and set aside.

Brush the top surface of each regañada with lard or vegetable oil, then press the brushed side onto the sugar-covered plate – just press ever so slightly, making sure the sugar sticks evenly to the biscuits.

Place the regañadas on the lined baking trays with the sugar side facing up. Bake for 10–12 minutes, but keep an eye on the process as these biscuits burn easily. They need to be blistered and golden brown, and parts of the sugar should be melted. If they go dark, they will be bitter.

Let them cool on the tray. You can keep regañadas for a few days in a sealed container, but they are best when eaten on the day they are made.

For the atole, add half the milk, the sugar, cinnamon and vanilla to a medium saucepan over low heat.

Add the other half of the milk to a blender, and add the masa. Blend until smooth, then add to the saucepan with the warming milk mixture. Let it come to the boil, then reduce the heat to the lowest setting to keep warm (but not boiling). Mix continuously, making sure the atole doesn't stick to the bottom of the pan. Taste and adjust the sweetness with more sugar, if necessary. Remove the cinnamon sticks.

Atole is served warm in a nice mug. Place the regañadas on a decorative plate and enjoy.

Serves 8–12

Preparation time 30 minutes, plus 1–1½ hours cooling/soaking

Cooking time 30 minutes

Dietaries Vegetarian

Difficulty Medium

Pastel tres leches

—

Three milk cake

Pastel tres leches, or three milk cake, is a quintessential Latin American cake. Its origins are not very clear and, as with Australians and New Zealanders arguing over the origins of pavlova, it is claimed by many countries as their own.

This cake is a celebration. In Mexico, there are shops that only sell one thing: pastel tres leches. It is hard to find in Australia and, when you do, it is generally not that good. The 'secret' of this cake is the sponge, which you can enjoy on its own in the morning with coffee.

Diana was the first chef I had at La Popular, and she's one of my best friends here in Australia. I made this cake for one of her milestone birthdays, but I made it extra large. The party wasn't going to be that big, but I knew how much she loved my cake, so it was baked several layers high. When the party ended, the cake was half finished. That meant cake for days – but it only lasted two. She ate it all! I made the same cake for her next milestone birthday, but this time I made two: one for the party and one just for her!

For this recipe, I recommend using two mixers if you have them – a stand mixer to whip the egg whites and hand-held electric beaters to mix the yolks (though one mixer is fine, too). You also need a lot of bowls for this recipe.

You can make the cake a day or two in advance, but whip the cream just before serving.

SPONGE CAKE

5 eggs, separated, at room temperature
60 ml (¼ cup) vegetable oil, plus extra for greasing
¼ teaspoon vanilla bean paste
120 g (4¼ oz) caster (superfine) sugar
120 g (4¼ oz) plain (all-purpose) flour sifted
½ teaspoon baking powder
¼ teaspoon fine salt

THREE MILKS

300 ml (10½ fl oz) full-cream (whole) milk
400 ml (14 fl oz) tinned condensed milk
340 ml (11½ fl oz) tinned evaporated milk
¼ teaspoon vanilla bean paste

TO SERVE

300 ml (10½ fl oz) whipping cream
40 g (1½ oz) caster (superfine) sugar
125 g blackberries, or any other fruit of choice (berries, mango, cherries and plums are all good)

Preheat the oven to 175°C (350°F).

Prepare a 23 cm (9 inch) non-stick springform cake tin. Take the base out of the tin and cut a circular sheet of baking paper to fit the base. Lightly oil the base and reassemble the tin. Make sure the side of the tin is not oily, as the cake will use it to rise. Place the round sheet of baking paper in the bottom of the tin.

Place the egg yolks in a medium bowl, along with the oil, vanilla bean paste and 60 g (2 oz) of the sugar. Set aside.

Place the flour, baking powder and salt in a separate bowl and mix well. Sift and set aside.

Place the egg whites in the bowl of a stand mixer fitted with a whisk and start mixing slowly for 30 seconds. Increase the speed to full over a further 30 seconds, gradually adding the remaining 60 g (2 oz) of sugar. Once you reach full speed, keep mixing for another 1½ minutes. The egg white mixture should be firm, forming peaks, but not too stiff. Set aside.

Now start mixing the yolk mixture with hand-held electric beaters. Do this for 3 minutes at full speed. The final consistency should be like pancake batter.

Add the yolk mixture and flour mixture, in small batches at a time, to the bowl with the egg white mixture and incorporate using a silicone spatula. Do this with care, as we don't want to lose the air in the mix – this is what makes the cake spongy. Once all is incorporated, pour the batter into the prepared cake tin and spread it evenly with the spatula.

Bake in the oven for 30 minutes, then test with a toothpick or cake tester. It should come out clean after being inserted into the centre, and the cake should be golden brown and about double the size.

Place the tin on a wire rack and let cool for at least 30 minutes. The cake will lose a bit of height, but that is okay.

Once the cake has cooled, loosen it from the side of the tin using a bamboo skewer or a cake tester. Unmould the cake and place it face-down on the cooling rack. Peel the baking paper off.

Mix the three milks together with the vanilla bean paste in a bowl. Put one-third of the mixture in a nice little jug for plating.

Place the cooled sponge cake on a deep plate and, using a fork, make little holes in the top. Pour the remaining two-thirds of the milk mixture over the cake, then keep basting with the mixture. Allow it to soak for 30 minutes to 1 hour.

Just before serving, whip the cream with the sugar in the stand mixer fitted with a whisk. I mix for about a minute – the first 20 seconds at medium–high speed, then I slow it down for the remainder of the time. Whipped cream can become buttery and feel fatty if you whisk it too long, so be careful.

Cover the cake with the cream and decorate with the fruit. Serve with the reserved three-milk mixture in the jug.

ENTRAD

Makes 8–10

Preparation time 2–3 days

Cooking time Nil

Dietaries Gluten free, vegetarian

Difficulty Easy

Calaveritas

—

Sugar skulls

Calaveritas (pictured on page 207) might seem out of place in this book, or slightly morbid to those outside of Mexico, but they are so fun to make and are an important part of our culture. We make calaveritas for Día de Muertos (the Day of the Dead) on 1 and 2 November, and place them on Day of the Dead altars. The sugar skulls are made to remember the dead and are given to friends and family, particularly children. Calaveritas are a nice touch for a dinner party. They can be a lot of work if you want to decorate them with loads of detail, but they are a fun activity for kids during the holidays approaching Día de Muertos. I like to place them on the side of a dessert, such as Helado de chocolate (page 190).

250 g (2 cups) icing (confectioners') sugar
1 teaspoon corn syrup
½ egg white
1 teaspoon freshly squeezed lime juice
edible paint or markers

Start by sifting the sugar into a bowl, then add the corn syrup, egg white and lime juice. Mix into a soft 'dough', starting with a spoon and finishing with your hands.

Form the dough into little balls about 3 cm (1¼ inches) in diameter, then mould them into skulls. You do this by placing the ball on a flat surface. Squeeze the sides of the ball with your thumb and index finger, slightly pressing it down, making the ball flatter at the bottom and with indentations, to resemble the hollow part between the cheeks and the jaw. Then, using a small round object or your little finger, create indents for the eyes. With a fork, make long indentations for the teeth.

Place the skulls on a baking tray lined with baking paper and let them dry for a couple of days. You want the skulls to be hard on the outside and softer on the inside.

If you want to paint or colour the skulls, they need to be solid so they don't fall apart and so the colour doesn 't run.

Now comes the fun part: painting or colouring. I generally do both. I paint the larger surfaces with edible paint, using a small brush, then draw the details with an edible paint marker.

Sugar skulls are best kept in an airtight container at room temperature for 2 weeks. But, being full of sugar, they will last for ages.

Makes / serves 1.5 litres (52 fl oz) / 8

Preparation time 30 minutes, plus chilling and freezing

Cooking time Nil

Dietaries Vegetarian

Difficulty Difficult

Helado de chocolate — Mexican chocolate ice cream

Chocolate is the hero of this dessert. Mexican chocolate is different from what you find in Europe and elsewhere. We don't process it too much – it is basically cocoa beans with sugar and cinnamon, ground to a paste. Helado de chocolate is luscious and delicious, a perfect finish to a dinner party. You will need an ice-cream maker for this. If you don't have one, you might be in luck and have a neighbour who can lend it to you. Hot tip: Always be nice to your neighbours; you never know when you will need to borrow their ice-cream maker!

600 ml (21 fl oz) thickened (heavy) cream
30 g (1 oz) unsweetened cocoa powder
160 g (5½ oz) Mexican chocolate tablets, chopped into chunks, plus an extra chopped ¼ tablet to garnish
250 ml (1 cup) full-cream (whole) milk
115 g (½ cup) caster (superfine) sugar
1 cinnamon stick
pinch of salt
pinch of instant coffee granules
6 large egg yolks
1 teaspoon vanilla bean paste
ice bath

Heat half the cream in a small saucepan over low heat. While heating, whisk in the cocoa powder and bring to a simmer. Whisk until the cocoa is well incorporated; this will take 3–5 minutes. Remove the saucepan from the heat and stir in the Mexican chocolate pieces until completely melted and incorporated.

Pass the mixture through a fine-mesh strainer into a large metal bowl. Add the remaining cream and stir to incorporate. Place in the fridge to chill. When cold, place the bowl on a bench with a fine-mesh strainer on top and promptly move to the next step.

Place the milk, sugar, cinnamon, salt and coffee granules in a saucepan over low heat and heat until steamy (not boiling), stirring to incorporate the spices and dissolve the sugar.

Place the egg yolks in a medium saucepan with no heat. Slowly pour the heated milk with spices into the pan with the egg yolks, whisking continuously to temper the eggs. Once well mixed, turn the heat to medium and, using a wooden spoon, stir the milk and egg mixture constantly, scraping the bottom as you stir, until the mixture thickens.

To test if it's ready, stir the mixture with your wooden spoon and do a finger test. Trace a line across the back of the spoon with your fingertip. If the line remains visible, the sauce is ready to go.

Remove the saucepan from the heat and immediately pour the mixture into the bowl through the sieve, then stir into the cream mixture.

Add the vanilla and stir it in. Let the mixture cool by transferring the bowl into an ice bath for 5 minutes, then chill in the fridge until completely cold, covered with plastic wrap to avoid it drying out. This might take a couple of hours or overnight.

Churn the mixture in an ice-cream maker until creamy. Transfer to a container with a lid and store in the freezer. The ice cream will keep for a couple of weeks.

Before serving, remove the ice cream from the freezer and let stand for 10–15 minutes. This will make the ice cream scoopable.

Serve in a nice bowl and sprinkle with the extra chopped Mexican chocolate. This is a great way to show your friends the difference in the flavour of raw chocolate.

Clockwise from bottom left: Helado de mango (page 192), Helado de mango con Chamoy and Tajín (page 192), Helado de chocolate (opposite)

Makes / serves 1.5 litres (52 fl oz) / 6

Preparation time 20 minutes

Cooking time Nil

Dietaries Gluten free, vegan

Difficulty Easy

Helado de mango – Mango sorbet

This is your go-to recipe (pictured on page 191) when it's mango season, and the fruits are cheap(er) and sweet(er). It 's very simple but delicious. You will need an ice-cream maker to make the sorbet. I like to add Chamoy, a sweet chilli syrup that is so Mexican in its flavour profile – sweet, sour, salty and spicy – though it's originally from China. It goes well with mango sorbet, or any fruit, really.

1 kg (2 lb 4 oz) ripe mangoes (about 3 large)
260 ml (9¼ fl oz) corn syrup
250 ml (1 cup) agave syrup (if you don't have this, use more corn syrup)
3 tablespoons freshly squeezed lime juice (about 2 limes)
½ teaspoon table salt
Chamoy (optional)
Tajín

Peel the mangoes and remove all the flesh from the seed. Place the flesh in a blender and add the two syrups. Blend for 1 minute – start slow and ramp up to a higher speed. It should have a thick, smoothie-like consistency.

Pass the mixture through a fine-mesh strainer into a large bowl, using a spatula to press the fruit through the strainer. Add the lime juice and salt. Place the bowl in the fridge to cool for a couple of hours.

Transfer the mixture to an ice-cream maker and churn until ready. It should have an ice-cream texture. Transfer to a container with a lid and store in the freezer for up to 2 months.

Before serving, remove the sorbet from the freezer and let it stand for 10–15 minutes. This will make it easier to scoop. Put a couple of scoops in a nice bowl or glass, drizzle with Chamoy (if using) and sprinkle with some Tajín.

Makes About 15

Preparation time 30 minutes

Cooking time 25 minutes

Dietaries Can be vegetarian

Difficulty Medium

Puerquitos de piloncillo

—

Pig-shaped raw sugar biscuits

The name of this slightly chewy cookie (pictured on page 207) comes from its swine-like shape. They are also known as marranito, cochinito or cerdito; all these names refer to its unique shape. They are also sometimes called chichimbré, which probably hails from gingerbread, as the textures are similar.

Originally made with pork lard, puerquitos de piloncillo are simple cookies made with raw sugar, or piloncillo. Piloncillo is not the same as granulated raw sugar (and nor is panela); it is unprocessed, boiled-down sugar-cane juice that has been poured into cone-shaped moulds. It is a style of sugar found throughout Latin America

You will need cookie cutters for these. I have my pig-shaped ones, but any shape will work – just don't make them too small.

- 200 g (7 oz) piloncillo (Mexican brown sugar) or panela
- 1 teaspoon ground cloves
- 1 cinnamon stick
- 375 g (2½ cups) plain (all-purpose) flour
- 125 g (4½ oz) wholemeal (whole-wheat) flour
- 7.5 g bicarbonate of soda (baking soda)
- 7.5 (¼ oz) baking powder
- 50 g (1¾ oz) lard or ghee
- 1 egg, well whisked

Firstly, make a syrup with the piloncillo. Add the piloncillo, 250 ml (1 cup) of water, the ground cloves and cinnamon stick to a small saucepan and cook for approximately 10 minutes over low heat, or until the sugar has completely dissolved. Strain the mixture and let cool until it is lukewarm.

Preheat the oven to 220°C (425°F).

Mix the two flours in a bowl, then pour the flour mixture onto a clean work surface and heap it into a volcano shape. Add the syrup, bicarbonate of soda and baking powder to the flour and mix using clean hands. Knead until you have a dough that is firm but not too hard. Add the lard or ghee and mix until you have a smooth dough.

Roll out the dough evenly to a 1 cm (½ inch) thickness. Cut the dough with the cookie cutter and place the cookies on a baking tray lined with baking paper (you might need two). Brush the cookies with the egg wash, then bake for 10–15 minutes.

Puerquitos are best served at room temperature and should be slightly chewy. I enjoy one with a morning coffee or with a cup of tea after dinner.

PALETAS

Ice blocks

Wherever you go in Mexico, you will find paleterías in town squares selling paletas, which are ice blocks (popsicles) made with water or cream. At some paleterías you will find an infinite number of flavours, but the most common paletas are made with fresh fruit.

They were originally invented in the US but quickly made their way to Mexico in the 1940s. The village of Tocumbo in the state of Michoacán is the probable origin of the Mexican paleta, and one of the most famous paletería franchises is named after that state.

To make paletas you will ideally have large ice-block moulds, but smaller moulds will also work. You can make paletas days in advance of your dinner party, and they will last for a couple of weeks in the freezer. Don't store them much longer than that, though, as they will lose moisture. Make a mix of colourful paletas to impress your friends.

Paletas de aguacate

—

Avocado ice blocks

Makes About 1 litre (35 fl oz) / 8–10 paletas

Preparation time 20 minutes, plus freezing

Cooking time 5 minutes

Dietaries Gluten free

Difficulty Easy

- 500 ml (2 cups) full-cream (whole) milk
- 210 g (7½ oz) caster (superfine) sugar
- 1 teaspoon gelatine powder
- 2 avocados, cut into 2 cm (¾ inch) cubes
- juice of ½ lime

Add the milk, sugar and gelatine powder to a small saucepan and bring to the boil over low heat. Let simmer until it thickens a little – this will take about 5 minutes. Remove the saucepan from the heat and let cool.

The next step is to blanch the avocados. Bring about 2 litres (8 cups) of water to the boil in a medium saucepan or in a kettle.

Place the avocado cubes in a colander or sieve over the sink, then pour the boiling water over them. The cubes will change colour to bright green.

Transfer the avocado, along with the milk mixture and lime juice, to a blender and process until smooth.

Fill the moulds with the avocado mixture. Place the moulds in the freezer and cool until the cream reaches a slurry consistency, approximately 30 minutes.

Add the sticks and freeze overnight.

UNMOULDING, STORING AND SERVING PALETAS

Unmoulding can be challenging. You can briefly place the paleta mould in lukewarm water to let the outside of the ice block (popsicle) melt slightly, then pull out the ice blocks. But don't do this for too long, as they might get soft.

To store the paletas, wrap them in strips of freezer film or plastic sheets as wide as the paleta; this way they will not stick together and dry out. Place them back in the freezer to harden.

Once you are ready to serve, you can place the paletas on a cold plate with crushed ice so they will last.

If you dip paletas de mango in a bowl of Tajín, you will get a 'next level' paleta. Chamoy, a tangy sweet chilli syrup, will also make fruit paletas taste awesome and very Mexican.

Paletas de chocolate mexicano

—

Mexican chocolate ice blocks

Makes About 1 litre (35 fl oz) / 8–10 paletas

Preparation time 30 minutes, plus chilling and freezing

Cooking time 10 minutes

Dietaries Vegetarian

Difficulty Easy

250 ml (1 cup) thickened (heavy) cream
450 ml (16 fl oz) full-cream (whole) milk
100 g (3½ oz) caster (superfine) sugar
2 teaspoons unsweetened cocoa powder
1 cinnamon stick
½ teaspoon table salt
135 g (4¾ oz) Mexican chocolate

Place the cream, milk, sugar, cocoa, cinnamon and salt in a medium saucepan over low heat. Bring to a slow boil and simmer for 5 minutes. Add 100 g (3½ oz) of the Mexican chocolate to the mix and stir to dissolve. Strain the mixture and chill in the fridge for at least 1 hour.

Break the remaining chocolate into little pieces and place in a bowl.

Fill the ice block moulds with the chilled mixture, leaving enough space to add the chocolate pieces. Don't add them yet, though.

Place the moulds in the freezer and cool until the cream reaches a slurry consistency, approximately 30 minutes.

Fill the moulds with the remaining chocolate pieces. Add the sticks, then freeze overnight, at least.

Paletas de mango

—

Mango ice blocks

Makes About 1.5 litres (52 fl oz) / 12–15 paletas

Preparation time 30 minutes, plus freezing

Cooking time 10 minutes

Dietaries Gluten free, vegan

Difficulty Easy

1 kg (2 lb 4 oz) ripe mangoes (about 3 large)
400 g (14 oz) caster (superfine) sugar
250 ml (1 cup) water
50 ml (1¾ fl oz) freshly squeezed lime juice
½ teaspoon table salt
Tajín

Place all the ingredients, except the Tajín, in a blender and blitz until you have a smooth consistency. Pour the mixture into the moulds.

Place the moulds in the freezer and cool until the cream reaches a slurry consistency, approximately 30 minutes.

Add the sticks and freeze overnight. Put some Tajín on a plate or bowl and dip the paletas in it just before serving.

Bebidas

—

Drinks

In Mexico, as with food, drinks are never just drinks. We take our drinks very seriously. Most have a history dating back to pre-Hispanic times, including arguably the most famous: hot chocolate. There is so much more to explore than a mug of warm cocoa. Atole (see page 184) is a warm, thick, corn-based drink that is best enjoyed with a tamal as the perfect breakfast on a cold morning. Then there are cold drinks, such as tejate, pozol, bupu, tascalate, popo and tejuino. In addition, every region of Mexico has its own drinks – sweet, sour, fermented or savoury. Some, mostly pre-Hispanic, are culturally important, as they play a significant role in a community's identity. However, the recipes in this chapter are the more familiar drinks I grew up with in Mexico City and are not necessarily pre-Hispanic; I would need more cultural understanding before sharing the recipes for pre-Hispanic regional drinks.

Probably the most quintessential Mexican drink is agua fresca, or cool water, which has pre-Hispanic origins. These drinks are made with seasonal fruits, flowers, grains and sugar, and are the common go-to at any fonda or taquería. But, as they are generally easy to make, they are also great to enjoy at home. There are, of course, the more modern drinks that are famous the world over, particularly the agave-based spirits, tequila and mezcal. But these are not the only Mexican spirits, and raicilla, sotol and charanda are equally delicious. In more recent times, these drinks have been made into cocktails and are now staples of bars, restaurants and parties all over the world, thanks to cocktails such as the Paloma (page 212) and Margarita (page 209). Finally, there are the ubiquitous Mexican lagers that are some of the most famous global beers. You can also do tasty things with them as a cocktail base (see Michelada on page 208).

Makes / serves
2 litres (8 cups) / 8

Preparation time
5 minutes, plus
15 minutes resting

Cooking time
10 minutes

Dietaries Gluten free, vegan

Difficulty Easy

Agua de jamaica – Hibiscus water

Agua de jamaica, also known as hibiscus water or hibiscus iced tea, is found all over Mexico and is a go-to at any economy restaurant or fonda. I don't understand why it hasn't caught on everywhere: it's so simple, fresh and delicious. You can make it as sweet or as sour as you want – go sugar-free if you like your drinks on the sour side.

35 g (1¼ oz) dried Jamaica flowers (rosella), plus extra to garnish, if desired
200 g (7 oz) white (granulated) sugar
ice cubes

Place 2 litres (8 cups) of water in a large saucepan over high heat and bring to the boil. Add the Jamaica flowers, reduce the heat to medium–low and let simmer for 10 minutes. Turn the heat off and leave the flowers to rest for 15 minutes.

Pass the liquid into a jug through a fine-mesh strainer, pressing to squeeze as much liquid from the flowers as you can. Discard the flowers or keep to use as a vegan meat substitute (see page 23). Add the sugar and stir until dissolved, then set aside to cool.

Serve in a large glass with ice cubes, garnished with extra dried Jamaica flowers, if you like.

Agua de jamaica will keep for a week in the fridge.

TIP

I normally make a concentrate – about 600 ml (21 fl oz) – with three times the solids in the same amount of water, then freeze the concentrate in snaplock bags for future use. Melt the contents of one bag into 1.25 litres (5 cups) of water, and you have a cool agua de jamaica. The frozen concentrate will keep for up to 6 months in the freezer.

From left: Agua de horchata (page 204), Agua de jamaica (opposite), Agua de limón (page 205)

Makes / serves 2 litres (8 cups) / 8

Preparation time 10 minutes, plus overnight soaking

Cooking time Nil

Dietaries Gluten free, vegetarian

Difficulty Easy

Agua de horchata

—

Horchata

This rice drink (pictured on page 202) is so iconic that indie darlings Vampire Weekend even wrote a song about it!

So what is horchata? A lot of people assume it tastes like rice pudding due to the rice, cinnamon and condensed milk, but it really doesn't. It's the exact opposite of the gluggy rice pudding of your childhood. It's actually super refreshing due to the soaked raw rice and condensed milk. Agua de horchata is very common at cocinas economicas and fondas, where they serve comida corrida, an inexpensive set meal, for lunch. Here, you often see a jug of horchata in the middle of the table.

Hot tip: a good blender is essential, as the rice is going to be blitzed to milk.

220 g (7¾ oz) white rice (I generally use jasmine)
1 cinnamon stick
400 ml (14 fl oz) tinned condensed milk
200 g (7 oz) white (granulated) sugar
ice cubes

Place the rice in a container with a lid and add 500 ml (2 cups) of water, together with the cinnamon stick. Leave to soak overnight.

The next day, place the soaked rice mix in a blender with the condensed milk, sugar, and 1 litre (4 cups) of water and blend to a smooth liquid – start mixing on slow speed and gradually increase to full speed. The grains of rice should be completely ground.

Strain the liquid into a jug (ideally with a lid that seals) through a fine-mesh strainer. Store the jug in the fridge.

Horchata should be served really cold on ice and, if you can, with a paper straw.

Before serving, you have to shake the jug until the solids at the bottom have completely dissolved – use a large spoon if your jug has no seal. It is normal for your horchata to be a little grainy.

Horchata keeps in the fridge for up to 2 days.

Makes / serves	Preparation time	Cooking time	Dietaries	Difficulty
2 litres (8 cups) / 8	5 minutes	Nil	Gluten free, vegan	Easy

Agua de limón
—
Fresh lemonade

This just might be the simplest of all drink recipes. Agua de limón (pictured on page 205) is a like a lemonade but made with limes – just because we're Mexican and love limes. We also love to add a scoop of chia seeds, but this is optional.

250 ml (1 cup) freshly squeezed lime juice (about 6–8 limes)
300 g (10½ oz) white (granulated) sugar
1 teaspoon chia seeds (optional)
ice cubes

Combine the lime juice, sugar, 1.7 litres (59 fl oz) of water and the chia seeds (if using) in a jug. Mix well. Done. This will keep for a week in the fridge.

A second way to make this is more controversial. Cut the lime (skin on) into chunks, then add all the ingredients, except the chia seeds, to a blender and process for 30 seconds. Strain. This blitzed lemonade needs to be drunk the same day, as it will become bitter after a couple of hours. The taste of this lemonade is slightly different.

Either way, serve with some ice on a summery day. Very simple. Very delicious.

Makes / serves 1 litre (4 cups) / 4

Preparation time 5 minutes

Cooking time 10 minutes

Dietaries Vegetarian

Difficulty Easy

Chocolate caliente mexicano

—

Mexican hot chocolate

Mexican hot chocolate tastes slightly different from your everyday hot chocolate, thanks to the addition of spices and the use of unprocessed cacao beans. Mexican chocolate does not come in a powder as most other drinking chocolates do, but rather the beans and spices are processed into solid tablets.

The first people to make a warm chocolate are probably the Olmecs (1200–400 BCE), the drink being reserved for warriors and royalty only. Hot chocolate was originally drunk with water, but milk was used as a substitute post-colonisation. Personally, I still like to drink it with water; this way it tastes more chocolatey and less creamy. In Mexico, chocolate milk is served frothy and foamy; to achieve this, you use a wooden milk frother called a molinillo. If you don't have one, use a balloon whisk or stick blender. This hot chocolate is great to serve with Churros con chocolate (page 182) or Puerquitos de piloncillo (page 193 and pictured opposite).

1 litre (4 cups) full-cream (whole) milk (you can also use water)
140 g (5 oz) Mexican chocolate

Add the milk to a medium saucepan over high heat. When it comes to the boil, reduce the heat to medium and add the chocolate. Stir frequently until the chocolate completely dissolves. Froth the milk, if desired. Serve hot.

Clockwise from top left: Calaveritas (page 189), Chocolate caliente mexicano (opposite), Puerquitos de piloncillo (page 193)

Serves 1

Preparation time 3 minutes

Cooking time Nil

Dietaries n/a

Difficulty Easy

Michelada

If you're partial to a bloody Mary or two, you will love this michelada (pictured on page 211). In essence, it's a tomato juice–based cocktail served with a cold beer. Win win. There is some debate around the name, though, as michelada is sometimes called chelada in Mexico City, but elsewhere chelada generally refers to a beer with lime juice and salt. Whatever you call it, this is a summer classic.

Normally this drink is made with clamato – a blend of tomato juice and clam broth, with some spices blended in – but it is hard to get in Australia, so I use plain tomato juice. However, you could top the drink with a shucked oyster to get a similar effect! It is also fun to rim the glass with Chamoy and Tajín, which will make the drink spicier.

lime wedge
flaky salt, for rimming the glass
Chamoy or Tajín, for rimming the glass (optional)
ice cubes (optional)
2 dashes Maggi sauce
2 dashes Worcestershire sauce
2 dashes Tabasco sauce (add more if you like it spicy)
60 ml (¼ cup) tomato juice
45 ml (1½ fl oz) freshly squeezed lime juice
1 cold Mexican lager

Rim a tall beer glass with salt flakes by rubbing a lime wedge around the rim, then dipping the rim of the glass in salt spread on a small plate (plus a little Chamoy or Tajín if you like).

Fill one-third of the glass with ice cubes (if using). Add all the sauces and juices.

Serve with a cold beer. Pour the beer into the glass and enjoy.

For a chelada, just rim the glass with salt, and add ice and lime juice.

Serves 1

Preparation time 4 minutes

Cooking time Nil

Dietaries Gluten free, vegan

Difficulty Easy

Margarita

Truth be told, I never drank a margarita in Mexico, let alone made one. It's more of a tourist drink. We didn't even originally serve it at La Popular Taqueria but after getting a glut of requests for it, we got to work on creating our take on the famous party drink. This recipe (pictured on page 211) is the result of much trial and error (and many hangovers). I recommend making enough margarita mix for 10 or more drinks, depending on the size of your party (just multiply the below recipe by 10 for a party of 10). Mix 100 ml (3½ fl oz) of margarita mix per serve in your cocktail shaker, and you're ready to go.

lime wedge, plus extra to garnish
sea salt flakes, for rimming the glass
ice cubes
45 ml (1½ fl oz) quality tequila
30 ml (1 fl oz) freshly squeezed lime juice
15 ml (½ fl oz) triple sec or Cointreau
dash of agave syrup or sugar syrup
habanero hot sauce (shop-bought or see page 247 for homemade), or a wedge of jalapeño (optional)

Rim a glass with salt flakes by rubbing a lime wedge around the rim, then dipping the rim of the glass in salt spread on a small plate. Fill the glass with ice cubes.

Add the tequila, lime juice, triple sec and syrup in a cocktail shaker.

Add a generous scoop of ice cubes, place the lid on the shaker and mix for about 20–30 seconds. The ice will dilute and cool the mixture. If you shake it for too long, you'll end up with too much liquid and a weak marg.

Strain the mixture into the glass (or glasses) and garnish with an extra wedge of lime. To spice things up, add a dash of habanero hot sauce or bash a wedge of jalapeño in the shaker before adding the liquids.

From left: Paloma (page 212), Cuba libre campechana (page 213), Michelada (page 208), Margarita (page 209)

CERVEZA

Serves 1

Preparation time 3 minutes

Cooking time Nil

Dietaries Gluten free, vegan

Difficulty Easy

Paloma

—

Grapefruit tequila long drink

Margarita is the most popular cocktail in Mexico, right? Wrong. So wrong. That title goes to paloma (pictured on page 210), a grapefruit-tequila drink that is finally getting its place in the sun. The key to a good paloma? Sourcing delicious grapefruit soda that isn't too sweet. Trust me, the quality of your grapefruit soda makes a huge difference. Don't go cheap with your tequila either (for this drink and in general!) – it needs to be 100% blue agave.

orange or grapefruit wedge, plus a slice to garnish
Tajín, for rimming the glass and to garnish
ice cubes
60 ml (¼ cup) quality tequila
15 ml (½ fl oz) grapefruit cordial (optional)
90 ml (3 fl oz) quality grapefruit soda (not too sweet)

Rim a long glass with Tajín by rubbing a grapefruit wedge around the rim, then dipping the rim in Tajín spread out on a small plate.

Fill the glass two-thirds full with ice cubes. Add the tequila and grapefruit cordial (if using), then pour in the grapefruit soda until the glass is almost full. Garnish with a slice of grapefruit and sprinkle with extra Tajín. Add a paper straw for drinking.

Serves 1

Preparation time 3 minutes

Cooking time Nil

Dietaries Gluten free, vegan

Difficulty Easy

Cuba libre campechana

—

Mixed Cuba libre

After beer, mixed Cuba libre (pictured on page 210) is the most common alcoholic drink in Mexico. Its origin story goes all the way back to the 1900s, where an American captain poured Coca-Cola into a glass of white Bacardi with some lime juice, and greeted his fellow Cuban soldiers with 'Por Cuba Libre' ('To a free Cuba'). A legendary drink was born. To make the Cuba libre less sweet, Mexicans like to add sparkling water, making it a campechana, or mixed drink (read more about the history/story on page 115).

ice cubes
60 ml (¼ cup) white rum
1 regular can of cola
sparkling water
1 thick slice of lime

Add ice to a long glass, then add the rum. Fill the glass, half and half, with cola and sparkling water. Squeeze some lime juice in and drop the lime slice into the glass, or place it on the side of the glass, as garnish. ¡Salud!

Lo básico

—

Essentials

In this chapter, you will find the building blocks of Mexican cooking – recurring recipes with crucial ingredients that you will use in many different combinations. We're talking beans, rice, tortillas, soups and stocks. If you think I've forgotten salsas, don't stress – they've got a section of their own within this chapter (see page 236).

In many cases, it's best to think of a Mexican meal like a modular dish: a combination of masa with salsa, beans and a protein to build something unique. Once you start to understand the how and the why, you can rearrange these dishes to make your own combinations (and these will most likely be combinations that already exist in Mexico).

For many of these basic recipes, I make more than I need and keep the rest in the fridge or freezer to save for another meal. The freezer is your reliable old friend in the kitchen. You'll count on it to store your salsas, beans, proteins, stocks, soups and much, much more. Just remember to label and date the containers, and you'll soon have a freezer's worth of delicious Mexican food a mere thaw and reheat away.

Makes 1 kg (2 lb 4 oz) drained cooked beans

Preparation time 5 minutes

Cooking time 2 hours

Dietaries Gluten free, vegan

Difficulty Easy

Frijoles de la olla — Cooked pot beans

Beans are an indispensable ingredient in Mexican cooking; they are in every household and are included in most meals. I never tire of eating them, as there are hundreds of varieties and hundreds of uses. You can have them for breakfast, lunch and dinner and still want more. The first step is always the same: boil them. Then you are free to do whatever you want for things like soups and refried beans.

This is a general recipe that is more of a guide for most types of beans, such as black, bayo and pinto. I have given options for cooking on the stovetop and in a pressure cooker.

Remember, there are many types of beans out there, and they don't all behave the same way! The age, type and quality of the beans influence the cooking time. When you reach the end of the boil, check to see if the beans are fully cooked. If you're making refried beans, it might be preferable to cook them a bit longer so they will mash more easily. It is best to soak the dried beans overnight so they cook evenly. But to be honest, when I am in a rush I skip this step.

500 g (1 lb 2 oz) dried beans (any type), soaked overnight if you have time
2 garlic cloves, crushed
5 epazote leaves (optional)
½ small onion, cut into chunks
2 teaspoons table salt

TO SERVE

1 small white onion, finely diced
¼ bunch coriander (cilantro) or epazote, finely chopped

If you are cooking the beans on the stovetop, add the beans, garlic, epazote (if using) and onion to a large saucepan. Add 1.5 litres (6 cups) of water and cook at a rolling boil for approximately 10 minutes. Lower the heat and simmer for 1½ hours. Add the salt and adjust to taste.

To prepare in a pressure cooker, add the beans, garlic, epazote (if using) and onion to the pressure cooker. Add 1.5 litres (6 cups) of water and bring to the boil. Once the pressure cooker starts hissing, leave to cook for 20 minutes. Once ready, turn off the heat and let the pan cool until the pressure is gone. Add the salt and cool to room temperature.

Keep the beans in their liquid and heat them up in a pan when ready to serve.

Place the beans with some of the cooking liquid in a bowl and garnish with some diced onion and coriander (or epazote if you can find it).

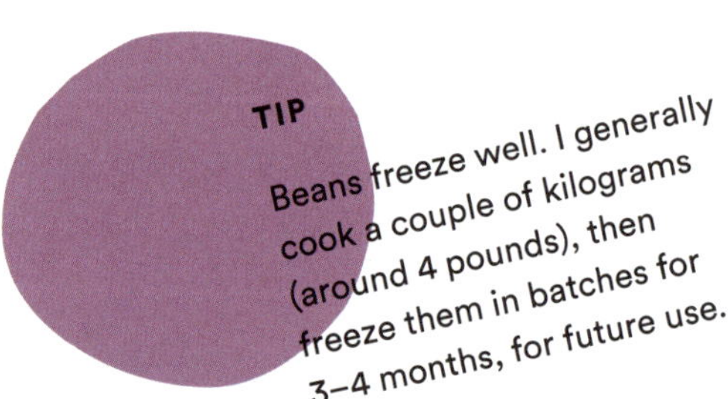

TIP

Beans freeze well. I generally cook a couple of kilograms (around 4 pounds), then freeze them in batches for 3–4 months, for future use.

Clockwise from top right: Refried beans (page 220), Cooked pot beans (opposite), Corn chips (page 252), Salsa roja (page 238)

Makes 500 g (1 lb 2 oz)

Preparation time 5 minutes

Cooking time 10 minutes

Dietaries Gluten free, can be vegetarian

Difficulty Easy

Frijoles refritos – Refried beans

Refried beans (pictured on page 219) have a million uses – they're even delicious as a side! They are the secret weapon of dishes such as Panuchos (page 99) and Molletes (page 41), and are a must-use topping for tostadas, sopes and tortas. For refried beans, black turtle or bayo are the most common beans to use but other varieties work, too. I prefer to fry my beans in lard, but vegetable oil is fine. Consistency is important. You want it spreadable but not too thick. Refried beans dry out very quickly, so add water if necessary.

- 70 g (2½ oz) lard or 100 ml (3½ fl oz) vegetable oil
- 500 g (1 lb 2 oz) Cooked pot beans (page 218) – with some of their boiling liquid as needed
- salt, to taste
- 50 g (1¾ oz) queso fresco (in Australia you can substitute La Casa del Formaggio brand's Homestyle Fresh Cheese, otherwise use Indian paneer cheese), to serve (optional)

Heat the lard or oil in a medium frying pan over medium heat. Add the cooked beans and salt and bring to a slow simmer. While simmering, mash the beans with a potato masher. Another way to mash them is to blend the beans with some water in a bullet blender before adding to the frying pan – this will give a smoother and finer texture.

Cook for 10 minutes, stirring occasionally, until the beans are smooth and heated through. If the refried beans are too thick, add a bit of the reserved cooking water to the pan and stir to combine. If they are too runny, cook them for a little longer. Taste, and adjust the seasoning if needed.

Place the beans in a bowl or on the side of a plate and maybe garnish with some crumbled queso fresco. You can also serve them as a side with Huevos rancheros (page 32), use them for Panuchos (page 99) or as a starter with some corn chips.

Makes 2 litres (8 cups)	**Preparation time** 20 minutes	**Cooking time** 2–6 hours	**Dietaries** Gluten free	**Difficulty** Easy

Caldo de pollo — Chicken stock

Nothing beats the aroma of homemade chicken stock as it drifts through the house. It's not only comforting, it's an integral base for so many Mexican dishes. A good stock will lift your dish significantly. If you don't have the time, you can substitute with a quality shop-bought stock, but making your own is so much better. And, if you're going to boil chicken for Enchiladas suizas (page 174), Mole con pollo (page 165) or Caldo de pollo estilo Yucatán (page 58), why not make a stock, too? I like to add my veggie and chicken scraps to my stock. No waste and more taste.

- 1 large chicken (about 2 kg/4 lb 8 oz)
- 1 tablespoon vegetable oil
- 5 garlic cloves
- 1 carrot, cut into chunks
- 1 celery stalk (okay if there are some leaves on the stalk)
- ½ small brown onion, halved
- 1 teaspoon dried Mexican oregano
- 2 teaspoons black peppercorns
- 1 tablespoon table salt

Start by breaking down the chicken, taking off the leg quarters, wings and breasts. This way it's easier to fit a whole chicken in a stockpot, and it will release more flavour.

Heat the oil in a large stockpot over medium heat, and fry the garlic and vegetables for a couple of minutes. Add 3 litres (12 cups) of water, the oregano, pepper and salt, and finally the chicken. While cooking, a greyish foam will form on the surface. Remove this with a ladle when it forms.

The chicken will be cooked after an hour. Take it out of the pot and harvest the meat you need for your other dishes.

Return the frame, bones (see Tip), skin and any leftovers into the pot and boil for a couple of hours over low heat. The longer you cook, the richer it will become. Add more water if needed and season with salt if necessary.

Let the stock cool down and drain all the solids. The stock is now ready for use.

Stock can be frozen for up to 6 months stored in freezer bags or sealed containers. I like to store it in 500 ml (2 cup) portions. Don't forget to label with the date.

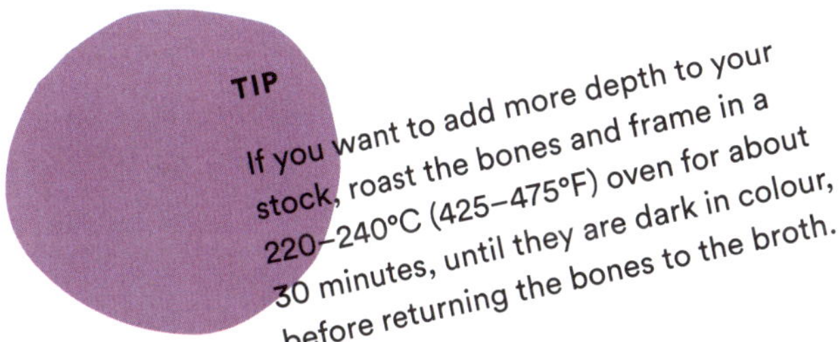

TIP

If you want to add more depth to your stock, roast the bones and frame in a 220–240°C (425–475°F) oven for about 30 minutes, until they are dark in colour, before returning the bones to the broth.

Makes 350 g (12 oz) and about 400 ml (14 fl oz) broth

Preparation time 5 minutes

Cooking time 20–30 minutes

Dietaries Gluten free

Difficulty Easy

Pollo cocido – Boiled chicken

If your dish needs boiled, shredded chicken – or boiled chicken leg quarters – here's a recipe, but make sure you use the left-over liquid as it's your passport to brothy goodness. Use it for cooking Red rice (page 225) or making soups. Again, no waste here. You could add an additional chicken frame or chicken necks for more depth. This recipe is for two chicken breasts; just multiply to get the necessary quantity.

If you feel particularly lazy or are running out of time, buy a fresh barbecued (rotisserie) chicken at the supermarket and pull the breast to shreds. Snack on the rest while you do this. This shortcut does not work for the leg quarters.

2 skinless chicken breasts or 2 skin-on chicken leg quarters (about 500 g/1 lb 2 oz)
½ small brown onion
1 garlic clove
1 teaspoon black peppercorns
1½ teaspoons table salt, plus extra if needed

Add all the ingredients to a medium saucepan and cover the chicken with water (for two breasts this is about 500 ml/2 cups). Cook the chicken breast for 20 minutes – leg quarters will take approximately 30 minutes. While cooking, a greyish foam will form on the surface. Remove this with a ladle when it forms.

After 20 minutes, take the meat out of the broth and serve, or allow to cool for shredding (see Tip). Taste and season your broth with extra salt if necessary, then strain. The broth from two breasts is enough to use for the Red rice recipe (page 225). If you're not going to use the broth, store in the freezer for up to 6 months.

TIP

If you need to shred the chicken, do this when it is still warm – cold chicken is much harder to pull apart.

Makes 250 g (9 oz) **Preparation time** 5 minutes **Cooking time** Nil **Dietaries** Gluten free, vegan **Difficulty** Easy

Recado rojo
—
Achiote marinade

This marinade is my all-rounder. It has many uses and never lets me down. I use it as a base for Cochinita pibil (page 146), adobo chicken (see page 119) and Pescado tikin xik (page 154). Achiote has a very earthy flavour and makes an excellent marinade when mixed with orange juice. They use sour oranges in the Yucatán Peninsula, but you can't find these in Australia. I add vinegar for a similar result.

100 g (3½ oz) achiote paste
100 ml (3½ fl oz) freshly squeezed orange juice
2 garlic cloves
2 tablespoons white vinegar
½ teaspoon dried Mexican oregano
¼ teaspoon cumin seeds

Place all the ingredients in a blender and process until smooth. It should be quite thick. That's it! You don't have to do anything else but enjoy the fruits of your (very minor) labour!

I like to make a large amount of marinade and keep portions in the freezer for up to 6 months.

Makes About 1 kg (2 lb 4 oz)

Preparation time 2 minutes, plus at least 10 minutes resting

Cooking time 20 minutes

Dietaries Gluten free, can be vegetarian

Difficulty Easy

Arroz blanco — White rice

Everyone knows how to make rice: chuck it in a rice cooker with water, hit a button and wait. But that's not the Mexican way. We like to fry the rice before it is boiled, to give a slightly different flavour and feel for when it's used as a side for most guisados (stews). Given how ubiquitous rice is in Mexican cooking, it might be a surprise to learn that rice didn't arrive in the Americas until it was brought to the continent by the Spanish. Once we got our hands on it, we made it our own. (Arroz blanco is pictured on page 140.)

- 50 ml (1¾ fl oz) vegetable oil
- 400 g (2 cups) jasmine rice
- 660 ml (22½ fl oz) chicken stock (see page 221 for homemade) or vegetable stock
- 1 teaspoon table salt
- 40 g (¼ cup) diced carrot
- 50 g (⅓ cup) frozen peas

Heat the oil in a medium saucepan over medium–high heat. Add the rice and fry slowly, stirring frequently, until the rice turns pale and lightly golden, about 5–10 minutes.

Mix the stock together with the salt, carrot and peas. Set aside.

In the process of frying, the rice's texture will change. It will be hard to move around at first, but when the rice has reached the right point it will have the texture of sand and will be easy to stir.

At this point, add the stock mixture and cook, uncovered, until it boils.

Reduce the heat to low, cover the saucepan with a lid and continue cooking for 8 minutes. The broth should be absorbed by the rice now, and little air holes should appear on the surface. Remove from the heat and let stand, covered, for at least another 10 minutes. Serve as a side.

Leftovers can be kept in the fridge for 3–4 days. Simply reheat in a small saucepan over low heat.

Makes 700 g (1 lb 9 oz)

Preparation time 10 minutes, plus at least 10 minutes resting

Cooking time 25 minutes

Dietaries Gluten free, can be vegetarian

Difficulty Easy

Arroz rojo — Red rice

This is one of those simple dishes that is quintessentially Latin American, as you'll find similar flavours across Central and South America. Basically, it's just rice cooked in a tomato sauce with carrots and peas. You might think this sounds a little pedestrian, but this is a recipe that packs so much flavour – which is why you'll find it dished up all over Mexico. It is delicious with a fried egg on top for breakfast or lunch. (Arroz rojo is pictured on page 227.) If you are in a rush, this rice on its own is a more than satisfying meal.

100 g (3½ oz) tinned tomatoes
½ small onion
1 garlic clove
350 ml (12 fl oz) chicken stock (see page 221 for homemade) or vegetable stock
½ teaspoon table salt
40 g (¼ cup) finely diced carrot
50 g (⅓ cup) frozen peas
2 tablespoons vegetable oil
200 g (1 cup) jasmine rice

Place the tomatoes, onion and garlic in a blender or food processor. Puree until smooth and set aside.

Mix the stock together with the salt, carrot and peas and set aside.

Heat the oil in a medium saucepan over medium–high heat. Add the rice and fry slowly, stirring frequently, until the rice turns pale white and lightly golden, about 5–10 minutes.

The texture of the rice will change. First it will be hard to move around and, when the rice has reached the right point, it will feel more like sand and will be easy to stir.

Add the pureed tomatoes to the rice and cook for 2 more minutes. Scrape the bottom of the saucepan frequently to prevent it from sticking.

Add the stock mixture and cook, uncovered, until it boils. Reduce the heat to low, cover the saucepan with a lid and continue cooking for 15 minutes. The broth should be absorbed by the rice now, and little air holes should appear on the surface. Remove from the heat and let stand, covered, for at least another 10 minutes.

Serve as a side. If you have a decorative saucepan, leave the rice in the pan to serve, otherwise transfer to a bowl.

Leftovers can be kept in the fridge for 3–4 days. Simply reheat in a small saucepan over low heat.

From left: Chiles en escabeche (page 229), Cebolla curtida (page 228), Red rice (page 225)

Makes 400 g (14 oz)

Preparation time 5 minutes, plus 2 hours pickling

Cooking time Nil

Dietaries Gluten free, vegan

Difficulty Easy

Cebolla curtida

–

Pickled red onions

Condiments don't get much easier to make than cebolla curtida (pictured on page 226). This is the perfect example of minimum effort, maximum taste. It's not really a salsa, but it serves the same function. This recipe comes with no heat, but it's common to serve with thinly sliced habaneros. One habanero with seeds should be enough for a batch. Cebolla curtida is must-have if cooking Cochinita pibil (page 146) or Cochitorta (page 126).

60 ml (¼ cup) freshly squeezed orange juice
60 ml (¼ cup) white vinegar or freshly squeezed lime juice
salt, to taste
2 red onions, thinly sliced using a mandoline
1 habanero (optional)

———

Mix the orange juice and vinegar with the salt in a medium bowl.

Add the onion to the liquid and let it sit for a couple of hours.

Serve in a nice bowl with some small tongs or a fork, perfect for cochinita pibil or a cochitorta.

The onions will keep in the fridge in a sealed container for a couple of weeks.

Makes About 2 kg (4 lb 8 oz)

Preparation time 30 minutes

Cooking time 15 minutes

Dietaries Gluten free, vegan

Difficulty Medium

Chiles en escabeche — Pickled jalapeños

The traditional method of preserving food in Mexico is called escabeche; it was introduced to the Americas by the Spanish. It's pretty much impossible to find someone in Mexico who doesn't love pickled jalapeños. We eat them straight out of the jar as a snack and use them as a condiment for tacos, quesadillas and tortas. For an easy but delicious breakfast, I like to add pickles to quesadillas with some smashed avocado. And I add heaps to my tortas to give them a kick. Many Mexican restaurants will bring a small serve of escabeche to the table as an appetiser.

There are many variations. You can swap out the vegetables: some people add potatoes, others replace the cauliflower with broccoli; you can even add green beans or nopal. But there is one non-negotiable: you cannot – I repeat cannot – leave out the chilli!

This recipe (pictured on page 226) will make a lot, but if you're going to the trouble of making chiles en escabeche, it's best to load up.

100 ml (3½ fl oz) olive oil
6 garlic cloves
1 onion, cut into wedges
500 g (1 lb 2 oz) jalapeños, quartered lengthways
3 carrots, peeled and cut into rounds
¼ cauliflower, cut into small florets
300 g (10½ oz) zucchini (courgette), sliced
500 ml (2 cups) white vinegar
35 g (¼ cup) salt
2 teaspoons white (granulated) sugar
2 tablespoons peppercorns
5 dried bay leaves
8 whole cloves
about 6–8 × 500 ml (2 cup) sterilised jars with lids (see Tip)

You will need a large saucepan or stockpot (about 4 litres/4 quarts) for making escabeche. Heat the oil in the saucepan over high heat until hot.

Fry the garlic and onion for 3 minutes. Remove from the saucepan and transfer to a bowl.

Fry the jalapeños, carrot and cauliflower for 3 minutes. Add the zucchini and cook for another 2 minutes (the chillies and veggies just need to be sauteed).

Add the vinegar, salt, sugar, fried onion, garlic and spices to the vegetable mix and cook for 3 minutes with the lid on. Reduce the heat to a slow simmer. Cook for another 3 minutes, then turn the heat off.

Fill the sterilised jars when the mix is still boiling hot. Secure the lids and cool upside down. They will keep unopened for a year in a cool, dark place. After opening, store in the fridge for up to 1 month.

Serve chiles en escabeche in a small bowl. That's it, nothing fancy.

TIP

To sterilise jars, wash them and their lids in the dishwasher on the hottest cycle.

Makes 8

Preparation time 5 minutes

Cooking time 15 minutes

Dietaries Vegan

Difficulty Easy

Chiles toreados

—

Blistered chillies

Chiles toreados literally means 'bull-fought chillies', so look out, as they are fierce and pack a punch! Is this a salsa? Not really, but I like to use chiles toreados as a condiment. They can serve a similar function to a salsa; they add depth to a dish. I love to make these when hosting a barbecue. Place them on a grill and cook until the skin blisters and the flesh is cooked. They are delicious eaten with barbecued meat or in a tortilla with beans.

8 jalapeño or serrano chillies
1 tablespoon olive oil
1 tablespoon dark soy sauce
pinch of salt
1 lime

Heat the barbecue grill to medium–low. Punch a small hole in the chillies (so they don't explode while cooking). Cook the whole chillies on the grill until fully cooked through; this will take 10–15 minutes. Place in a bowl, add the oil, soy sauce and salt, and squeeze the lime over them.

Place the chillies on the table as a condiment. They are best served warm. I love to eat this with carne asada or in a tortilla with some beans. Delicious.

Makes 4 | **Preparation time** 25 minutes | **Cooking time** 2 minutes | **Dietaries** Gluten free, vegan | **Difficulty** Easy | **Makes** 400 g (14 oz)

Roasting poblano chillies

—

This is not really a dish but a step needed to cook with poblano chillies (or other larger fresh chillies, like banana chillies). The skins of poblanos are not pleasant to eat and need to be removed. Tinned chillies come pre-charred and are ready to go, but give them a good rinse first. Use poblano chillies for Rajas con crema (page 161) and Crema de chile poblano (page 52).

4 poblano chillies
1 large airtight container or snaplock bag

On a barbecue or on a gas stove, char and blister the raw chillies over an open flame for a couple of minutes. Make sure all the corners of the chillies are burnt.

Place the hot chillies in a sealed container or plastic bag, and leave them there for about 20 minutes.

Place the chillies in a bowl and peel the skin off. They should be fairly easy to peel. If not, you haven't charred them for long enough.

Keep the stem in if you're going to stuff the chilli, but remove it if you're going to use the chilli for sauce or a stew.

Makes 350 g (12 oz)

Preparation time 30 minutes, plus 20 hours drying

Cooking time Nil

Dietaries Gluten free

Difficulty Easy

Machaca – Dried shredded beef

If you ask someone like me, who has never lived north of Mexico City, to name something traditional from the north, we would answer, 'machaca'. Similar to beef jerky, machaca has been pounded to tiny shreds. The only preservative used for machaca is salt, and it's a traditional way to preserve meats in the arid northern Mexican states.

I remember sneaking into the kitchen with my sister to grab a little bag of machaca to eat with lime. We knew we shouldn't, but it was just too tempting! Mum always scolded us for our kitchen raids, as it was an expensive, almost luxury, item. Sorry, Mum.

I've included this in this chapter, as it's not really something you would eat by itself; it enhances other dishes. Machaca con huevo (page 44) is probably the best known example, but you can find it sprucing up tacos and burritos.

If you can't get machaca, you could try beef jerky, but it needs to be seasoned with just salt. I like to make it myself; it's a bit of work, but it is satisfying. You will need an electric food dehydrator and lean meat, such as topside (top round).

1 kg (2 lb 4 oz) topside (top round) steak, or minute (sizzle/cube) steak
35 g (¼ cup) salt

Cut the meat into even 5 mm (¼ inch) slices. Save time and ask your friendly butcher to do this for you on their meat slicer.

If you haven't got access to a friendly butcher and need to slice at home, wrap the meat in plastic wrap and snap-freeze for about 15 minutes until it is slightly frozen, then slice with a very sharp large knife. Then cut slices into manageable bits that will fit in the food drier.

Lay out the meat on a chopping board and sprinkle it generously with salt on both sides (the amount in this recipe allows for a bit of spillage).

Place the meat on trays and set the dehydrator to 65°C (140°F) for 1 kg (2 lb 4 oz) of meat. I use three levels of the drier; this gives it sufficient space to let the air flow. Let it dry for approximately 20 hours. Check the meat now and then, as you want the beef to be dry and not chewy.

Now the meat is dry, but it is not machaca yet. Traditionally, you would tear the meat into small pieces, then pound in a molcajete or mortar and pestle until you have the consistency of fibres. You can also use the spiked side of a meat hammer to achieve this, but my go-to method is a bullet blender; it's really quick and gets the job done.

Machaca keeps in a sealed container in the fridge for about a week and for 3–4 months vacuum-sealed in the freezer.

Right: Dried beef before it is ground to machaca.

Below, left to right: Machaca con huevo (page 44), Machaca (opposite)

Makes About 20 **Preparation time** 1½ hours **Cooking time** 20 minutes **Dietaries** Can be vegetarian **Difficulty** Medium

Tortillas y gorditas de harina de trigo

—

Wheat tortillas and gorditas

There is a Mexican saying that goes, 'Es de sabios errar', which means 'Wise people make mistakes'. With this in mind, it's time for a confession. There was a time when I thought burritos were an American invention! Embarrassing, I know. This all changed when I travelled north in the early '90s and had some asada burritos in La Paz, Baja California, in a place called Super Burro. This was my first taste of traditional burritos, which are much different from the mega burritos full of rice and beans that you get at chain restaurants. Those things are definitely not Mexican.

Back in Adelaide, my friend Karina, who is from Chihuahua, would tell me how burritos are part of her state's culture. Recently, Karina visited the restaurant with two surprises: her mother, Rosquita (who had come to visit her from Chihuahua), and a beautiful new baby. I love babies, and I adore mothers who know how to cook. So, as far as visits go, this was a good one! We spent the night talking about food – while eating tacos, of course! They invited us to eat at their house, and Rosquita taught me how to make flour tortillas, perfect for burritos. She also taught me that if you make them thicker and smaller in diameter you get gorditas – 'little fatties' – which you can fill with guisados, similar to the gorditas made of masa (see page 258). This was so wonderful.

It's always an incredible honour to have someone share their family recipes with you. So here is a special northern Mexican recipe from Karina and Rosquita: wheat flour tortillas and gorditas (little fatties).

- 200 g (7 oz) lard or ghee, at room temperature
- 1 kg (6⅔ cups) plain (all-purpose) flour, plus extra for dusting
- ½ teaspoon baking powder
- 30 g (1 oz) salt
- 500 ml (2 cups) boiling water

Start by whipping or whisking the lard in a large bowl so it becomes creamy and glistening white.

Sift the flour and baking powder into the bowl, and add the salt. Pour most of the water in (reserve about 50 ml/1¾ fl oz). Knead the dough thoroughly until it is smooth – start in the bowl, then move to a clean work surface.

Now, place the dough on a flat surface dusted with some flour and keep kneading. Use the remaining water to get the dough to the right consistency – it needs to be easily pliable. Make a ball, put it back in the bowl, cover with a lid or plastic wrap and let it rest for 30–45 minutes (you can also store the dough in the fridge, wrapped in plastic wrap for later use; it will keep for a couple of days).

After resting, knead again, then divide the dough into small portions, about 30 g (1 oz) each, and form them into balls just slightly smaller than a ping pong ball. If you want to make burritos, make the balls double the size (50–60 g/1¾–2¼ oz). Rub the balls with a little bit of lard/ghee, and leave them to rest for 15 minutes more.

Place some flour on a flat surface and roll each ball out with a rolling pin to about 5 mm (¼ inch). If you want to make burritos, roll them to about 2 mm (1⁄16 inch). Stack the tortillas together.

Heat a comal, hotplate or non-stick frying pan over medium heat and cook the tortillas for a couple of minutes on each side, or for about 1 minute for burritos. Flip them regularly – if they puff up, you should be very happy. Keep them warm in a chiquihuite.

Serve the tortillas in the chiquihuite. The best way to eat them is as a taco with grilled marinated steak, maybe some beans, avocado slices and salsa.

If making gorditas, you need to cut them in half through the side to make a pocket. Put some Refried beans (page 220) inside, with some meat, or guisado filling, and salsa. You can add cheese, too.

If you want to make the tortillas for later use – they will keep for a couple of days in an airtight container – make sure you cool them down first; so don't place them in the chiquihuite but place them on a bench after cooking. Once cold, they won't stick to each other. When ready to use, reheat on a hot comal, hotplate or in a non-stick frying pan and place in a chiquihuite.

SALSAS

Salsa might simply mean 'sauce', but salsa isn't a simple subject. The world of salsas is more complex and diverse than you think. A common mistake is to think there is only one master salsa. Sometimes I hear people proudly proclaim that they can perfect salsa, as if there is just one version and one recipe. I then wonder, which salsa? There are so many! Cooked, uncooked, with fresh chillies, with dry chillies, a combo of both, with fried or roasted veggies or chillies – you name it, it exists! We love our salsas in Mexico; life wouldn't be the same without our beloved sauces!

There are thousands of salsa recipes, and the ones I've included in this chapter are just an example of what you can do. I'm sure other Mexican cooks will have an opinion (good or bad) about the salsas I've included. This is fine. It's part of our culture to debate salsa! Since Mexico is such a large country, there are probably 130 million opinions on salsa, and they are all valid. Salsa is one of the cornerstones of the holy trinity of a taco – and a good salsa can rescue a failed filling or a not-so-great tortilla.

Once you discover the different salsa-making techniques, you realise that, even though they all look very similar, they are different. Some are hot, some are not, some are charred, some are boiled, some are liquified, some are chunky, some are simple and some are complex. Each little tweak gives a different flavour or texture, and there are infinite iterations. Feel free to make your own version – try different chillies, mix things up, use a blender or a molcajete (see page 17).

There are pretty much two types of salsas: table salsas, which are condiments for dishes, such as tacos; and cooking salsas, which are used as part of a dish, including enchiladas and chilaquiles. Some salsas, such as Salsa roja (page 238) and Salsa verde cocida (page 245), are both. Okay, now it's getting confusing. Before I make your head spin, let's get into the recipes and then you can discover the wonderful world of salsas the best way possible – by making them!

A note on using tomatoes: most will do, but ripe roma (plum) tomatoes are a universal go-to.

Makes 750 g (1 lb 10 oz)

Preparation time 10 minutes

Cooking time 20 minutes

Dietaries Gluten free, vegan

Difficulty Easy

Salsa roja

—

Red salsa

This is a basic salsa recipe (pictured on page 219) that is the key to unlocking so many great dishes. Everyone has their own spin on salsa roja. You can play around with the quantities and some of the ingredients to suit your taste. Salsa roja literally means 'red sauce', so ripe tomatoes are key. The number of chillies depends on how hot you want it and how spicy the chillies are, so start with half the recommended amount and add more until your heat radar tells you to stop. Salsa roja is used in many dishes and can be made a day or two in advance.

400 g (14 oz) ripe roma (plum) tomatoes
3 jalapeños
½ white onion
2 garlic cloves
handful of coriander (cilantro)
2 teaspoons table salt

Place the whole tomatoes, jalapeños, onion and garlic in a saucepan with water to cover (although they will float) and bring to the boil.

Lower the heat and boil for 15 minutes. Transfer the vegetables to a bowl and leave for a couple of minutes to cool down.

Add the cooked vegetables, coriander and salt to a blender or food processor. If it does not fit, do it in batches.

Blend slowly, gradually increasing the speed, until you have the salsa to your liking. For a table salsa you might want it chunky, but if you are going to use it with Chilaquiles (page 30) or enchiladas (see page 170) you might want to blend a bit longer.

Transfer the salsa to a medium saucepan over medium heat and cook the salsa for 5 minutes – this will make the salsa more intense in colour and flavour. Taste and adjust the seasoning with salt.

If you have left-over salsa, give it a boil (see Tip).

TIP

It is good practice to place left-over salsa in a small saucepan and bring to the boil before you store it in the fridge. This will sterilise the salsa, and it will keep longer. I generally keep a salsa for up to 1 week in the fridge and 3–4 months in the freezer.

Makes 500 g (1 lb 2 oz)
Preparation time 10 minutes
Cooking time 15 minutes
Dietaries Gluten free, vegan
Difficulty Easy

Salsa taquera — Taqueria-style salsa

If you've been to Mexico, you probably remember a spicy red salsa found at taquerías all over the country. This is it. Salsa taquera (pictured on page 113) can be really spicy due to the árbol chillies, but you can adjust the heat. The mix of tomatoes and tomatillos means it's more tangy than a Salsa roja (opposite). This salsa is very good with chicken or Tacos campechanos (page 115).

1 guajillo chilli, deseeded
4 dried árbol chillies
200 g (7 oz) tomatillos
250 g (9 oz) roma (plum) tomatoes
2 garlic cloves
1 brown onion, quartered
2 tablespoons white vinegar
2 teaspoons table salt

Place the chillies, tomatillos, tomatoes, garlic and onion in a saucepan. Cover with water by about 1 cm (½ inch) and boil until the tomatoes are soft, about 15 minutes.

Drain the ingredients and reserve 170 ml (⅔ cup) of the liquid.

Destem the chillies and add all the ingredients to a food processor or blender with the reserved cooking liquid, the vinegar and salt. Blitz until you have a smooth consistency.

After using, give the salsa a short boil (see Tip opposite).

Makes 750 g (1 lb 10 oz) | **Preparation time** 5 minutes | **Cooking time** 15 minutes | **Dietaries** Gluten free, can be vegan | **Difficulty** Easy

Salsa roja yucateca – Yucatán-style tomato salsa

The star of this salsa is habanero chillies. For a number of years, I lived in Quintana Roo in the Yucatán Peninsula, where you splash this salsa on pretty much anything that is edible. I love its simplicity. It's so flavoursome, and the taste and aroma remind me of living in the beautiful Yucatán Peninsula. You can make it spicy or mild – just adjust the number of chillies. This salsa (pictured on page 243) is a little bit thick, not too runny, and great with other dishes from the Yucatán Peninsula, such as Panuchos (page 99) and Huevos motuleños (page 38).

400 g (14 oz) ripe roma (plum) tomatoes (or tinned tomatoes)
½ white onion
35 g (1¼ oz) lard or 50 ml (1½ fl oz) vegetable oil (use vegetable oil for vegan)
1 teaspoon table salt
1–2 habanero chillies, whole

Add the tomatoes and onion to a blender or food processor and blitz until smooth.

Add the lard to a small saucepan over medium heat. Add the blended mixture and salt, and cook together with the whole habaneros for 15 minutes.

If you like your salsa mild, don't let the habanero burst – cook it on low heat to be safe. I love spicy food, so I let my chillies burst with gusto.

After using, give the salsa a short boil (see Tip on page 238). Store in a sealed container in the fridge for up to 1 week, or freeze for 3–4 months.

Makes 750 g (1 lb 10 oz) | **Preparation time** 10 minutes | **Cooking time** 15 minutes | **Dietaries** Gluten free, vegan | **Difficulty** Easy

Salsa tatemada – Charred tomato salsa

This is similar to Salsa roja (page 238) but with a big difference: salsa roja's ingredients are boiled while tatemada's (which translates to 'blackened') are charred. Again, the number of chillies depends on how hot you want it. This salsa (pictured on page 243) is generally more chunky than boiled salsa roja. I love it; the flavours are deep and smoky, and the chunky texture is perfect over Tacos de asada (page 114) or over fried eggs. You can serve the salsa as a starter or as a snack with corn chips, pork crackling or fresh cheese.

400 g (14 oz) ripe tomatoes
3 jalapeños
½ white onion, plus extra diced onion to serve
2 garlic cloves
1 teaspoon table salt
handful of coriander (cilantro), chopped, plus extra to serve

Preheat a comal, hotplate or heavy-based frying pan to medium heat (you can also do this on a barbecue).

Place the tomatoes, jalapeños, onion and garlic in the frying pan (no oil!). The garlic and onion will be ready before the tomatoes, so remove them from the pan first. Continue to char the vegetables for 10–15 minutes, turning occasionally, until they are blackened and soft.

In a molcajete or mortar and pestle, mash the garlic and salt until you have a soft paste. Add the onion and continue mashing until it's incorporated. Add the tomatoes, one by one, and smash them until everything is mixed in. Add the coriander and mix well.

If you need a smooth salsa, blend the cooked vegetables, coriander and salt in a food processor. Blend slowly and increase the speed until you have the salsa to your liking. Taste and adjust the seasoning with salt.

If you made the salsa in a molcajete, serve it in that. Add some diced onion and coriander on top.

This salsa will not last long and should be eaten fresh. If there is any left-over salsa, give it a quick boil (see Tip on page 238).

Makes 300 g (10½ oz)

Preparation time 15 minutes

Cooking time Nil

Dietaries Gluten free, vegan

Difficulty Easy

Salsa verde cruda
—
Raw tomatillo salsa

I absolutely love this salsa; it really showcases the sweetness and sourness of tomatillos. I make it whenever I get fresh tomatillos, and I love to make a taco with chicharrón with this salsa on top: simple and delicious. Unfortunately, if you can't get fresh tomatillos, you won't be able to make it, as tinned tomatillos aren't the same (instead, see Salsa verde cocida on page 245, for which you can use tinned tomatillos). Grow your own tomatillos if you can. I like this salsa spicy, but you can make it as hot or as mild as you like. This salsa also goes on tacos, similar to the cooked version of this salsa. Use it for sopes or quesadillas, Barbacoa de cola de canguro (page 148) or Tacos de asada (page 114).

250 g (9 oz) fresh tomatillos
½ white onion, quartered
1 small garlic clove
2 jalapeños or serrano chillies
¼ bunch coriander (cilantro)
1 teaspoon table salt
½ avocado (optional)

Place the tomatillos, onion, garlic, chillies and coriander in a food processor or blender, and blend until smooth (add some water if it's not blending well). Taste and add salt if necessary.

You can add some diced avocado to the finished salsa to give it some structure, if needed.

Serve in a bowl with a spoon. This salsa will not last, and leftovers need to be boiled to become salsa verde cocida (see Tip on page 238).

Once boiled, store in a sealed container in the fridge for up to a week and the freezer for 3–4 months.

Clockwise from top: Salsa macha (page 244), Salsa roja yucateca (page 240), Salsa verde cruda (opposite), Salsa tatemada (page 241)

Makes 300 g (10½ oz)

Preparation time 15 minutes

Cooking time 30 minutes

Dietaries Gluten free, vegan

Difficulty Medium

Salsa macha – Crispy chilli oil

This isn't your everyday Mexican salsa; it's more Chinese crispy chilli oil. Chunky with bits of chilli, sesame seeds, peanuts and pepitas (pumpkin seeds) mixed in, it's an excellent condiment for so many foods, Mexican and non-Mexican alike. Salsa macha takes me back to the state of Veracruz, where this salsa originated. You'll find it on every table there. In the cities of Xalapa and Coatepec, where it's called salsa de chile seco, it skips the nuts and sesame seeds. They even send your box of pizza with a container of salsa de chile seco! Nowadays, you find different spins of this condiment all around Mexico, such is the love for this spicy oil. Salsa macha comes with a spice warning, which is why I love it! Salsa macha is perfect to put on a sope with refried beans, fresh cheese and onion; on your quesadillas; on tostadas; or just with refried beans and corn chips.

240 ml (8 fl oz) olive oil
11 árbol chillies
1 guajillo chilli
2 morita chillies
40 g (1½ oz) raw peanuts
40 g (1½ oz) pepitas (pumpkin seeds)
2 garlic cloves
3 teaspoons roasted sesame seeds
2 teaspoons table salt

Heat the oil in a small frying pan over medium–low heat until it is around 165°C (325°F). I use a thermometer, but if a piece of bread dropped in the oil browns in about 25 seconds, the oil is the correct temperature.

Fry the chillies. I recommend frying them in batches by type. Be careful, as chillies burn easily – keep turning them until they change colour but are not black (árbol 45 seconds, guajillo 2 minutes, morita 1 minute). Burnt chillies will make the salsa bitter.

Take the chillies out and set them aside on a plate. When they cool down, they will be brittle – that means they are perfect.

In the same oil, fry the peanuts until golden, about 2 minutes. Set them aside, then add the pepitas and fry until golden and crispy, or until they start to burst, about 30 seconds. Take them out of the pan and set them aside as well. Turn off the heat and add the garlic, then let the oil cool down.

In a molcajete or mortar and pestle, add half the fried peanuts, half the fried pepitas and half the sesame seeds and mash them until you get medium-sized bits. Set aside.

Once the pan is cool enough to touch, place the remaining ingredients (including the whole peanuts, pepitas and sesame seeds), together with the salt, in a food processor or blender. Pulse until everything starts to break down. You don't want to overblend; it needs to be a chunky sauce. Mix it with the mashed sesame seeds, peanuts and pepitas.

Serve in a small bowl, but give the salsa a good stir before you use it as the solids sink to the bottom.

Store the salsa in a jar with a lid at room temperature for up to 4 weeks.

Makes About 1 kg (2 lb 4 oz)

Preparation time 10 minutes

Cooking time 12 minutes

Dietaries Gluten free, vegan

Difficulty Easy

Salsa verde cocida – Cooked green salsa

This is another super simple salsa that is ubiquitous all over Mexico. Similar to Salsa verde cruda (page 242) but with one major difference: it's cooked. You can use fresh or tinned tomatillos for this salsa. This salsa goes well with steak and chicken tacos and Enchiladas suizas (page 174).

800 g (1 lb 12 oz) fresh tomatillos (or tinned, drained)
1 white onion, quartered
2 garlic cloves
5 serrano or 2 jalapeño chillies (you want them spicy!)
1 teaspoon cumin seeds
3 teaspoons table salt
⅓ bunch coriander (cilantro)

Place the tomatillos, onion, garlic, chillies and cumin in a medium saucepan. Cover with water by about 1 cm (½ inch) and boil until the tomatillos are soft, 10–12 minutes.

Gently pass the ingredients through a fine-mesh strainer, and reserve 500 ml (2 cups) of the liquid.

Place all the ingredients, including the salt and coriander, in a food processor or blender with 250 ml (1 cup) of the reserved cooking liquid.

Blend slowly for a chunky texture (the seeds are still whole and small bits of skin) or blend fast and hard for an even, smooth sauce (you might want to add more cooking liquid to help achieve a smooth sauce).

Serve in a bowl with a spoon.

If you have left-over salsa, give it a quick boil (see Tip on page 238).

Makes 500 g (1 lb 2 oz) | **Preparation time** 10 minutes | **Cooking time** Nil | **Dietaries** Gluten free, vegan | **Difficulty** Easy

Pico de gallo

—

This is a classic. But its inclusion in the salsa section might be a tad controversial. I have listed it under salsas as it serves a similar function, but it is technically not a salsa! I believe salsa is a sauce in the true sense of the word, so it needs to be a liquid. But this is a contentious topic even in Mexico!

I have a large group of friends in Mexico who always get together when Kor and I visit. We have a chat group and I asked an important question for this book: 'Is pico de gallo a sauce or topping?' Oh my god, why did I ask? Everyone had their own opinion. After two or three days of arguing, we couldn't agree on anything. I decided to place it in the salsas section – even though it goes against my beliefs, as it's a topping and not a salsa – because there is no topping section! Whatever side of the salsa fence you sit on, pico de gallo (pictured on page 80) is super easy to make. Sometimes called salsa bandera ('Mexican flag salsa') in northern Mexico, it packs a punch and lifts a dish. You could add a bit of green chilli, such as jalapeño or serrano, for that extra kick of heat. Serve pico de gallo as a starter or a snack with corn chips. It is your key topping for dishes such as Molletes (page 41) and Tacos de pescado estilo Ensenada (page 116).

- 2 ripe roma (plum) tomatoes, finely chopped
- 2 small white onions, finely chopped
- ½ bunch roughly chopped coriander (cilantro)
- salt, to taste
- freshly ground black pepper, to taste

Combine the tomato, onion and coriander in a medium bowl. Add salt and pepper to taste. That's it! You don't need to do anything else.

Pico de gallo is best eaten fresh, but at a pinch it could be stored in the fridge for 24 hours.

Makes 150 g (5½ oz)

Preparation time 10 minutes

Cooking time About 40 minutes

Dietaries Gluten free, vegan

Difficulty Easy

Salsa de habanero tatemada

—

Habanero hot sauce

Here it is, Mexico's hottest salsa. Despite its heat, it's an integral part of Yucatán cuisine, commonly used as a condiment for dishes such as Cochinita pibil (page 146), Panuchos (page 99), Ceviche de pescado con mango y aguacate (page 104) and Chicken stock (page 221). In Mexico, most habanero sauces are made with green or orange habaneros. Funnily enough, in Australia I can only get fresh red habaneros. The thing about habaneros is that they are not only hot, they are also very fragrant. In Yucatán, this sauce is made with the juice of sour oranges, but I can't find these in Australia, so I mix normal OJ with vinegar (you can also use lime juice).

For me, and many others, this salsa is highly addictive. It burns your mouth, but you just keep adding more despite the fire engulfing your tastebuds. If you make this hot sauce, make plenty as it bottles well. This recipe is for approximately one jar or bottle, so just multiply for as many sauces you want to bottle. It will keep for 12–18 months if pasteurised. It also makes a great gift.

Warning: Make sure you make the sauce in a ventilated place, as the blending will make your eyes tear up and might make breathing a tad difficult.

100 g (3½ oz) red habaneros
2 tablespoons freshly squeezed orange juice
50 ml (1¾ fl oz) white vinegar
1 teaspoon table salt

Preheat a comal, hotplate or heavy-based frying pan to medium heat (you can also use a barbecue).

Place the habaneros on the hotplate or in the frying pan (no oil!) and let the chillies char, turning them until they are half-blackened and soft. This will take about 10 minutes, but keep checking and take them out as soon as they are ready.

Remove the stems and place the chillies in a food processor or blender with the rest of the ingredients. Close the lid and blend until the sauce is smooth. Depending on your preference, you can keep it thick to use as a paste or add some water to make it runny.

Place in a small bowl or sauce bottle. It will keep for a couple of weeks in the fridge.

For long-term storage (12–18 months), jar or bottle the sauce in sterilised containers (see Tip on page 229) and pasteurise it by placing the capped bottles or jars in a saucepan with cold water, fully submerged, then boiling for 30 minutes.

MAÍZ Y MASA

Corn and dough

Corn is the foundation of Mexico's culinary history. Believe it or not, corn is a grass, *Zea mays*, native to Mexico. Based on archaeological excavations in the Tehuacān Valley, it is estimated that its cultivation and domestication started around 7000 years ago, although findings at other sites suggest it's 10,000 years. For perspective, the pyramid of Giza is 'only' 4600 years old.

Primitive corn looked very different from the corn we know and love today; the cobs were small with irregular shapes. Genetic research has revealed that corn's wild ancestors are four species of teocintle (a species of grass), which is also part of the *Zea* genus. Through selective breeding and replanting kernels from larger cobs, corn has now evolved into hundreds of varieties worldwide, and there are 40–65 varieties in Mexico alone. Corn can be many colours, most commonly white, yellow and blue, but red, green and black varieties also exist.

Before the Spanish arrived, corn was grown in small plots called milpas, using a permaculture method (still used today) where corn, chillies, beans, pumpkins and herbs are grown together. Women are believed to have played an important role in the harvesting and selection of seeds, both for consumption and planting. The word milpa comes from the Nahuatl words milli ('parcel of cultivated land') and pan ('on top of').

There are many uses of corn in Mexico, but the most important is for masa, or corn dough. It is estimated that the average Mexican eats 335 kg (740 lb) of corn per year!

I am strong-willed person and wanted to make my own masa and tortillas from scratch in my little restaurant. Our tortilla supplier told us to go for it but that we'd come crawling back to them. We never did, but it's been quite the journey. Sourcing corn and developing a method for making fresh masa every week in Australia has been challenging; we're constantly learning. But the smell and feel of fresh masa is so rewarding.

On our last trip to Mexico, we wanted some local feedback. We went to Tepoztlán to visit my friend Lucía, and she organised for us to have a session with local legend Doña Blanca. She is an expert on nixtamal, and taught us to make masa and tortillas from scratch.

Making masa the traditional way is not as simple as grinding corn into flour and adding water. The corn needs to be nixtamalised before it can be ground, wet, into masa. Nixtamalisation is a chemical process where the corn is heated to about 80–90°C (176–194°F) in an alkaline water solution (with calcium hydroxide added; see page 262), then left to soak overnight. Nixtamalisation is important. It makes the corn more nutritious, releasing proteins for human absorption. During nixtamalisation, the seed coats dissolve and the whole kernel swells up and becomes gelatinised, improving the taste and the texture of the masa. The smell of nixtamal takes me back to those small villages in Mexico where everything is still done traditionally.

Once you have rested the corn overnight, you have nixtamal. The word comes from nextli ('lime from ashes') and tamalli ('cooked dough from corn'). The liquid is called nejayote. Nixtamal is now ready to be ground into masa. Traditionally, this is done on a metate, a large grinding stone that is worked by hand, but these days an electric stone mill is the norm.

Most villages have molinos comunitarios, or community mills. The molinos are machines with a big motor and two volcanic stones. A sort of screw pulls the corn between the stones with centrifugal grooves, and the masa is then pushed through the sides of the stones. We have one at La Popular, too. Making masa is a noisy affair!

Once you've got masa, you're free to make everything you know and love about Mexican cooking. We're talking tamales, gorditas, tlacoyos, atole, huaraches, panuchos, sopes, tostadas, totopos, tetelas, memelas, empanadas, quesadillas, molotes, salbutes, chochoyotes, tlayudas, chalupas, dobladas, chileatole, tascalate, tejuino, pozol, tejate, champurrado, guarapo and, if you can believe it, much, much more!

Makes 650 g (1 lb 7 oz)

Preparation time 15 minutes

Cooking time Nil

Dietaries Gluten free, vegan

Difficulty Easy

Masa

–

Corn dough

Masa is the starting point of so many dishes in this book. You ideally get masa that is nixtamalised in-house at a local tortillería, but you're highly unlikely to find this outside of Mexico. So to make our lives less complicated, I use nixtamalised maize flour or masa harina (instant masa) to make our corn dough in this book. The nixtamal process of the flour is different and industrial, but it will beat any shop-bought packaged tortillas or tostadas for flavour and texture.

280 g (10 oz) masa harina (nixtamalised maize flour)
¼ teaspoon table salt (optional)
about 375 ml (1½ cups) warm water

In a mixing bowl, combine the masa harina and salt (if using). Gradually add the warm water while stirring with your hands. Continue to add water until the dough comes together and becomes soft and pliable.

The dough should hold together but not be overly sticky. If it feels too dry, add a little more water. If it's too wet, add a bit more masa harina.

Knead the dough for about 10 minutes to get the best result. It should be smooth and well combined. It must have a Play-Doh–like consistency, quite soft and a little bit sticky. A good test is to make a tortilla in a press between two sheets of thin sandwich-bag plastic (see page 253). If the edge of the tortilla has deep cracks, the masa is too dry. A rough edge is normal.

You can keep masa for a couple of days in the fridge in an airtight container. If you want to use it, take it out of the fridge about an hour before you plan to use it. Knead thoroughly with your hand and add some water if necessary.

01

02

03

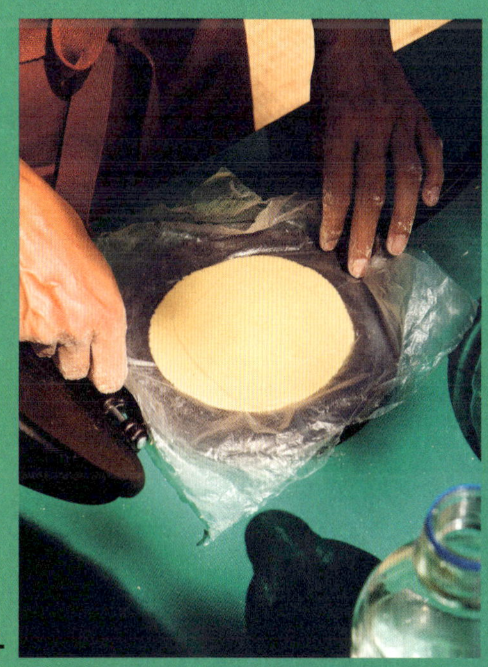

04

Makes 800 g (1 lb 12 oz)

Preparation time 5 minutes

Cooking time 20 minutes

Dietaries Gluten free, vegan

Difficulty Easy

Totopos – Corn chips

Fun fact: corn chips (pictured on page 219) are made from stale tortillas. An even better fun fact: they are the perfect way to use up left-over tortillas (I mean, who doesn't love corn chips!). You won't go back to buying corn chips after you make your own (you can even use tortillas from a packet).

Tortillas, obviously, are the main ingredient here, and because totopos are fried, it's important to use stale tortillas. Moisture will puff them up and they'll split if fresh. If you're hampered with fresh tortillas, just leave them on a bench for a couple of hours and you're good to go. Serve totopos with salsa, guacamole or Refried beans (page 220). You will also need them to make Chilaquiles (page 30).

1 kg (2 lb 4 oz) stale corn tortillas (shop-bought or see opposite for homemade)
500 ml (2 cups) vegetable oil
10 g (¼ oz) table salt

Cut each tortilla into six triangles.

Heat the vegetable oil in a medium frying pan over medium–high heat, or heat in a deep-fryer to 180°C (350°F). I use a thermometer to test the oil, but if a piece of bread dropped into the oil browns in 15 seconds, the oil is the correct temperature.

Fry the tortilla triangles in batches until crispy and lightly golden, about 4 minutes per batch. Drain on a paper towel–lined plate and salt lightly while still hot.

They will keep for approximately a week, but you'll need to store them in a sealed container or they will lose their crunch.

Makes 16

Preparation time 5 minutes

Cooking time 25 minutes

Dietaries Gluten free, vegan

Difficulty Easy

Tortillas de maíz — Corn tortillas

Corn tortillas are the staple of Mexican cooking. They've been around for thousands of years and are so ubiquitous that the price for 1 kg (2 lb 4 oz) of tortillas is a cost of living/inflation measure! For this recipe, it helps to have a tortilla press and thin plastic sandwich bags. The dough will stick to the press if you don't use plastic sheets, and you won't be able to peel it off – trust me! Don't stress if you don't have a press, as there are alternatives you can easily find in your kitchen: just flatten the dough ball with a hardcover book or chopping board and use your hands to gently press and shape into a circle. But don't forget to use plastic sheets!

650 g (1 lb 7 oz) Masa (page 250)

Divide the masa into small balls (about 30 g/1 oz), slightly smaller than a golf ball. You can make them larger or smaller depending on your preference.

Preheat a comal, hotplate or non-stick frying pan over medium–high heat.

Place a ball of masa between two sheets of sandwich-bag plastic in the tortilla press (see the photographs on the following pages). Press down firmly to flatten it into a round tortilla shape. Rotate the flattened tortilla with the plastic sheets 180 degrees, then press again gently. The tortilla should be approximately 1–2 mm (1⁄16 inch) thick.

Carefully peel off one of the plastic sheets, then place the raw tortilla (with the plastic) on the palm of your hand. The tortilla should be half on your hand, half hanging freely. Peel off the second sheet of plastic.

Lay the tortilla on the preheated hotplate or in the pan by placing the freely hanging tortilla on the hotplate first, then letting the rest of the tortilla roll off your hands. You should come in with your hand, palm facing up, at an angle of about 45 degrees.

Once the tortilla has hit the hotplate, rotate your hands about 90 degrees, rotating your palm towards the hotplate, pulling away from the tortilla. This movement, if done smoothly, should release the tortilla from your palm without the tortilla falling on itself. This is a tricky movement, and I suggest practising this on the bench first (no heat).

Cook for about 30–60 seconds until the edge curls up slightly. Flip with a spatula and cook the other side for about 60 seconds, then flip again – if all goes well, it will puff up on the last flip. (Tip: Don't try to fix a wrongly placed fresh tortilla; it will get worse.)

Remove the cooked tortilla from the hotplate and stack it with the others in a clean tea (dish) towel in a chiquihuite. The stacking is important, as it will keep cooking the tortilla.

Serve the freshly made corn tortillas warm to make your tacos.

REHEATING CORN TORTILLAS

If you don't have the energy to make your own tortillas (no judgement!) or have left-over tortillas, here are some essential tortilla tips.

If you grab tortillas from a supermarket, make sure they are the best quality possible and made with nixtamalised corn. Try different brands to see which is the best.

Heating tortillas is just as important as making them. Here's what to do. Heat a comal, hotplate or non-stick frying pan and lightly moisten your tortillas (I use a spray bottle, or quickly dip them in a bowl with water) – this way the tortillas stay flexible and don't dry out. They should not be wet, just moist. Heat the tortillas for 10 seconds on each side on your preheated hotplate, then place in a clean tea (dish) towel in a chiquihuite to retain the heat. Listo: you're all set!

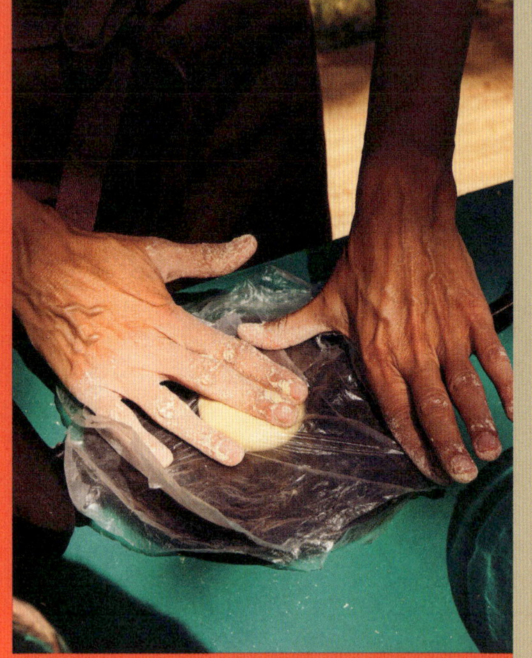

01

02

05

06

03

04

07

08

Makes 8

Preparation time Nil

Cooking time 10–20 minutes

Dietaries Gluten free, vegan

Difficulty Easy

Tostadas

—

While not as famous as tacos, tostadas play a vital role in Mexican cuisine. They are tortillas that are fried or oven-baked – both methods are delicious! If you bake them, they will have a slightly nuttier flavour and be less oily. I go oven-baked as a side for soups, and fried for tostadas with a topping, as they won't become soggy. Their versatility is their super power as you can enjoy them with toppings, such as Tostadas de cueritos (page 134) – my favourite – and seafood. Like taquerías, tostaderías are found all over Mexico, and you can enjoy tostadas on the street during the day as a snack or for lunch.

Be mindful that tostadas will shrink when you fry or bake them, losing 10–20 per cent of their original size. Check out the tostada recipes on pages 130–35 to make loaded tostadas. Or use a as a side with soups. Tostadas are really nice to crumble into a chicken soup; they give extra texture, like croutons.

8 stale corn tortillas (shop-bought or see page 253 for homemade)
300 ml (10½ fl oz) vegetable oil (if frying)

Use stale tortillas that are 2–3 days old (if they are fresh they will create vapour and puff up).

Heat the vegetable oil in a medium frying pan over medium–high heat, or heat in a deep-fryer to 180°C (350°F). I use a thermometer to test the oil, but if a piece of bread dropped into the oil browns in 15 seconds, the oil is the correct temperature.

Fry one side of the tostada and flip quickly (the tostadas will bend and be harder to garnish if kept too long on one side). Keep frying until they are golden brown and crispy; this will take about 4 minutes. Flip the tostadas a couple of times.

Another option is to bake the tostadas. Place the tortillas on one or two baking trays with baking paper. Preheat the oven to 160°C (325°F). Cover the tortillas with a sheet of baking paper and a second tray on top so they do not bend up.

Bake in the oven for 10 minutes. Remove the tray that is sitting on top of the tortillas and flip the tostadas. Bake for another 5 minutes until they are golden brown. If the tostadas are not crunchy yet, bake for a few minutes more.

Let them cool down before storing in a sealed container. You can make tostadas in advance, and they will keep crunchy for a day or two.

Makes 8

Preparation time 15 minutes

Cooking time 20 minutes

Dietaries Gluten free

Difficulty Medium

Sopes

—

Sopes are thick masa bases with a brim, which are traditionally topped with many ingredients. Pellizcadas is another term for them, as you need to pinch the edge of the sope to give it its characteristic shape. Pellizcar means 'to pinch' in Spanish, and the purpose of the raised edge is to keep the juices inside or to hold fillings such as refried beans.

Sopes are generally eaten for breakfast, but they can also be eaten as a snack or a starter. This recipe makes eight sopes about 10 cm (4 inches) in diameter, but you can make them larger or smaller. They are so versatile: they are a tasty canapé; you can serve them with shredded chicken or with chorizo with potatoes (see page 89); and they are delicious topped with basic ingredients, too – all you need are beans, lettuce, salsa and crumbled cheese for a tasty snack or light breakfast/lunch. Some places in Mexico go wild and pile loads of things on them, like Picadillo (page 164) or Rajas con crema (page 161).

300 g (10½ oz) Masa (page 250)
100 g (3½ oz) lard or vegetable oil
150 g (5½ oz) Refried beans (page 220)
200 g (7 oz) shredded chicken (see page 222)
¼ iceberg lettuce, thinly sliced
150 g (5½ oz) Salsa tatemada (page 241) or Salsa verde cocida (page 245)
½ white onion, finely diced
100 g (3½ oz) queso cotija or fresco

Start by making a small but thickish tortilla, about 12 cm (4½ inches) in diameter and 3 mm (⅛ inch) thick (see page 253). Cook for a bit longer than a normal tortilla, about 2 minutes (depending on the thickness).

Allow the tortillas to cool down a little until cool enough to touch. To make the sope, pinch the edges of the tortilla to create a little boundary around the edge. The tortillas will have a soft side and a harder side; place the soft side up.

Place the sopes in a container in the fridge – you can make these a day or two in advance. Make sure all your toppings are ready to go. The beans and (optional) fillings need to be warm.

Add the lard or oil to a small frying pan over medium heat and fry the sopes until golden brown, about 1 minute each side. Keep in a warm place on paper towel.

To build the sope, start with a layer of refried beans, then the shredded chicken. Next add some lettuce, salsa, diced onion and finish with a crumble of cheese.

Serve the sopes warm. You might want three for breakfast, but if you're serving them as a canapé or starter, serve one per person.

Makes 8

Preparation time 20 minutes

Cooking time 20 minutes

Dietaries Gluten free, vegan

Difficulty Easy

Gorditas

Gorditas, or little fatties, are little thick, puffy masa patties that are cooked on a comal or hotplate or in a non-stick frying pan. Gorditas are cut through the side to make a pocket and are filled with a guisado (a precooked filling), such as Rajas con crema (page 161) or chorizo with potatoes (see page 89), some salsa and crumbled queso fresco or other fresh cheese.

400 g (14 oz) Masa (page 250)

Divide the masa into small balls (about 30 g/1 oz), slightly smaller than a golf ball. Flatten them between two sheets of sandwich-bag plastic in a tortilla press (see page 253), or with a chopping board on a kitchen bench, to make thick tortillas, about 5 mm (¼ inch).

Cook the gorditas on a comal, hotplate or in a dry non-stick frying pan for about 6–7 minutes until cooked all the way through.

Keep the gorditas in a chiquihuite with a clean tea (dish) towel. Leftovers will keep in an airtight container for up to 1 week.

Makes 1

Preparation time 5 minutes

Cooking time 10 minutes

Dietaries Gluten free, can be vegan

Difficulty Medium

Huaraches

—

Huaraches can be one of two things in Mexico: traditional leather sandals/loafers, or a thick masa patty filled with beans that is fried on a hotplate. This book isn't a guide to casual Mexican footwear, so I'm going to talk about the latter. I love huaraches. And whenever I return home to visit my parents, I always look forward to my dad asking me: 'Hey Dani, would you like some huaraches for breakfast tomorrow?' I always answer, 'Yes, a green one for me, and a quesadilla de huitlacoche, please!' (Huitlacoche is also known as corn smut or Mexican truffle.) My dad has been getting huaraches from the same little stall around the corner from their house for the past 35 years.

There are many ways you can serve your huarache. The simplest is with some fried eggs and Salsa verde cocida (page 245) – see Huaraches con huevos y salsa verde (page 35). But you can also use Salsa roja (page 238), or serve them divorciados (divorced): half with salsa verde and half with salsa roja. For a more substantial meal, grill a thin steak or nopal or fry some chorizo, then finish with diced onion, coriander (cilantro) and a sprinkle of queso fresco or other fresh cheese. Below is a recipe for one huarache – just multiply by the number you need if making them for a group of people.

40 g (1½ oz) Refried beans (page 220)
100 g (3½ oz) Masa (page 250)
drop of lard or vegetable oil

For this recipe, you need refried beans that are dry and feel like paste, similar to or drier than masa. If the beans are too runny, reheat them in a dry frying pan. Left-over beans should be the right consistency.

With your hands, ply the masa into a ball, then roll into an oval/cylindrical shape. With your fingers, push into one side of the masa to create a cavity large enough to fit the refried beans in. Fill with beans and close the cavity so that no beans are visible.

Now we are going to make the huarache, which should be a flat, oval piece of dough filled with beans. You can try to do this with your hands, like the ladies at the market in Mexico. You can also place the to-be huarache between two chopping boards or books with two thin sheets of sandwich-bag plastic, as for with tortilla making (see page 253), and flatten with your hands until you have the right shape and it is about 1 cm (½ inch) thick. I make them oval, about 20 cm (8 inches) long and about 15 cm (6 inches) wide, but at the markets you can get much bigger huaraches.

Place the huarache on a hot comal, hotplate or in a non-stick frying pan over medium heat with a little bit of lard or oil and cook for about 5 minutes on each side. Make sure they are cooked in the middle. Serve immediately.

If you made it in advance then, once it's time to plate, rub the huarache with some lard or vegetable oil. Reheat the huarache in a hot frying pan and finish to your liking.

You can make your huarache the day before to store in the fridge in a container or a snaplock bag. You can even freeze them. Just don't store it too long, as it will dry out.

Los menús

Drinking food (snacks you can eat standing)

Charales enchilados (page 74)
Shot of Cantina-style prawn stock (page 62)
Chicharrón de queso (page 81) with Guacamole estilo mercado (page 72)
Codzitos (page 92)
Pescadillas (page 94)
Tostadas de paté de pescado ahumado (page 130)
Panuchos (page 99)
Sopes (page 257)
Churros con chocolate (page 182)

Dinner with friends

Chile ancho relleno de queso de cabra (page 88)
Mole con pollo (page 165)
Red rice (page 225)
Corn tortillas (page 253)
Helado de chocolate (page 190)

Dinner with family (traditional main meal)

Sopa de migas (page 50)
Tostadas de salpicón (page 131)
Flan de queso (page 180)
Agua de limón (page 205)

Carne asada (BBQ) with friends

STARTER

Guacamole (page 70)
Cacahuates enchilados (page 73)

APPETISER

Ceviche de pescado con mango y aguacate (page 104)

MAIN

Camarones zarandeados (page 156)
Carne asada (see page 114)
Chiles toreados (page 230)
White rice (page 224)
Refried beans (page 220)
Corn tortillas (page 253)
Salsa tatemada (page 241) or/and Salsa verde cocida (page 245)

DESSERT

Paletas de chocolate mexicano (page 197)

Taquiza (for large groups)

Guacamole (page 70) with Corn chips (page 252)
Salsa tatemada (page 241) with fresh cheese
Red rice (page 225)
Refried beans (page 220)
Corn tortillas (page 253)
Rajas con crema (page 161)
Bistec en salsa de chile pasilla (page 162)
Picadillo (page 164)
Chicharrón en salsa verde (page 160)
Carne de puerco con calabacitas (page 168)
Cochinita pibil (page 146)
Salsa verde cruda or cocida (pages 242 or 245)
Salsa roja (page 238)
Habanero hot sauce (page 247)
Cebolla curtida (page 228)
Agua de jamaica (page 202) or Agua de horchata (page 204)
Pastel tres leches (page 186)

Some useful words

Aguardiente A distilled alcoholic spirit, literally meaning 'fire water'.

Calcium hydroxide powder Slaked lime or pickling lime used for nixtamalisation. If you dissolve calcium oxide (also known as cal in Spanish) in water, you get a milky liquid or limewater, which is dissolved calcium hydroxide.

Carne asada Meaning 'grilled steak' but also used as a term for a barbecue.

Chalupa In real life a sort of canoe, but in Mexican food terms this is a small round or oval tortilla. It's thicker than a standard tortilla, boat-shaped and topped with shredded meat, salsa, onion and queso fresco. Similar to a Sope (page 257), chalupas differ in shape depending on geographical zone.

Champurrado A type of atole (see page 184), made with nixtamalised masa (corn dough) and Mexican chocolate, sweetened with piloncillo or sugar.

Chileatole A savoury atole (see page 184). From the Nahuatl chīlli ('chilli') and atolli ('corn drink'). Made with fresh corn, masa (corn dough), chillies, epazote and water. The recipe varies by region.

Comida Food or meal. Also a term used to refer to the main meal.

Comida corrida Literally a quick meal, generally served at a fonda as menu of the day.

Dīa de Muertos Day of the Dead, a Mexican holiday where families honour and welcome the souls of our departed loved ones with food, drinks and joyful celebration. Celebrated on 1 and 2 November.

Doblada Literally meaning 'folded', this is a folded tortilla (corn or wheat) that is filled, then shallow-fried.

Memela In some parts of Mexico, this is a thick, toasted corn tortilla topped with ingredients such as refried beans, cheese and chorizo, eaten as a snack or meal. Very similar to Sopes (page 257). In Mexico City, this is a type of Huarache (page 259).

Milpa A traditional permaculture plot where corn, beans, pumpkins and chillies are grown.

Molote A stuffed, plantain and/or corn-based pastry usually served as an appetiser or snack.

Nixtamalisation The process of heating corn kernels in water with calcium hydroxide. The result will be nixtamal, which is then ground into masa harina (corn flour). This chemical process improves the nutritional quality and texture of the masa.

Pancita Tripe soup. Also called menudo.

Panela (sugar) Raw cane sugar; same as piloncillo.

Piloncillo Raw cane sugar; same as panela.

Romerito A traditional dish served at Christmas dinner, which has a type of seaweed or quelite (edible greens) cooked in mole poblano with potatoes, nopal and dried prawns (shrimp).

Salbute Originally from the Yucatán Peninsula, a thick tortilla that has been fried.

Tamal A traditional dish made of soft masa (corn dough), filled with savoury or sweet ingredients, wrapped in corn husks or banana leaves, then steamed.

Taquiza A buffet-style party where people make their own tacos with guisados (stews) and meats that are served with beans, rice and tortillas.

Tascalate A drink from Chiapas made with toasted maize, cacao, achiote paste and cinnamon, and sweetened with piloncillo. Often served cold.

Tejate A drink from Oaxaca made with toasted corn, fermented cacao beans, toasted mamey pits (sweet orange creamy fruit with a large pit) and cacao flowers. It is known for its frothy texture.

Tejuino A fermented drink made primarily from masa (corn dough). It has a unique sweet, sour and slightly salty taste, and is popular in western and northwestern Mexico.

Tlacoyo A thick pastry made from masa (corn dough), often stuffed with cheese, broad beans or refried beans, then fried or toasted.

Tlayuda A large (30–40 cm/12–16 inch) tortilla that has been cooked until leathery/toasty, then covered with different toppings. Originally from Oaxaca.

Tetela A thick, round masa patty folded inwards to make a triangle. These are generally filled with refried beans or stringy queso oaxaca or quesillo.

Stockists

Australia

Chile Mojo chilemojo.com.au
El Cielo elcielo.shop
Fireworks Foods fireworksfoods.com.au
La Tortilleria latortilleria.com.au
Latin Market SA latinmarketsa.com
Mexico City Foods mexicocityfoods.com.au
Poblano poblanomexican.com.au

UK

CoolChile coolchile.co.uk
LaTiendita latienditamex.co.uk
MexGrocer mexgrocer.com
Mextrade mextrade.co.uk
Sous Chef souschef.co.uk
The Asian Cookshop theasiancookshop.co.uk

US

Amigo Foods amigofoods.com
Best Mexican Foods bestmexicanfoods.com
MexGrocer mexgrocer.com
MexMax mexmax.com
Vallarta Supermarkets vallartasupermarkets.com

Acknowledgements

Never in my wildest dreams did I think I'd end up writing a book – let alone a cookbook – and in another language, in another country! When I was younger, I had a few big dreams: one of them was living in Australia, working in conservation and protecting nature. And, funnily enough, when I finally made it to Australia, that dream came true. However, while I was achieving this goal, it was also the moment I felt I had to change paths, completely switching gears, to follow my heart straight into the kitchen.

And now here I am 14 years later, writing the acknowledgements for this book. I still can't quite believe it's real. There are so many amazing people I need to thank for helping make this happen. With your support, I get to share one of my biggest passions: showing the world just how wonderful Mexico is through its food and culture. So, my hope is that this book not only fills your kitchen with delicious aromas but also sparks your curiosity, makes you smile, and maybe inspires you to fall a little in love with Mexican culture, too.

The birth of this book started a couple of years ago, when we had our first meeting with Super Studio (our marketing team for La Popular Taqueria) to discuss our goals. They had a long list of things we could do and one of the items was: would you like to work on a cookbook? This was when the seed was planted. Over time, I started thinking about it more and more, and a few months later we started working on a proposal. So, thanks to Tamrah Petruzzelli, David Knight and Selena Battersby for all your ideas and support. And a very special thank you to David, my co-writer, who had to sit through (very patiently – or at least you made it look that way!) all my long stories and overly detailed explanations about what we eat, when we eat it, and why we definitely don't eat certain things in Mexico. You have now become an expert on Mexican food. Thank you for helping me take all that chaos and turn it into something clear and beautiful. This book wouldn't be what it is without you!

And then there's one person who worked just as hard (maybe even harder some days!) on this book – my husband, Kor. Thank you for always believing in me, for jumping into this adventure with me, for helping me brainstorm, create, test (and test again!) recipes, and for happily eating all of them. Thank you Rok (yes, I call him Rok), for encouraging me, for your endless patience, and for loving me so much through all the chaos, late nights and kitchen disasters.

Thanks to everyone on the Murdoch Books team for helping me create this beautiful book. But a special thank you goes to Jane Willson for believing in my cooking, seeing what I wanted to achieve and convincing her team that this was a risk worth taking. And to Loran and Kristy, thank you for keeping me on track, on time (mostly!), and for helping turn all these ideas and recipes into something real. You made the whole process so much smoother; I couldn't have done it without you! And to Ariana Klepac, my copyeditor – who I haven't even met in person! – thank you for all your thoughtful questions and spot-on comments that helped shape this book into what it is now. You really made me stop and think, because I kept assuming everyone would just get what I was trying to say. But you gently (and wisely!) showed me that I needed to slow down and explain things more clearly – without losing my cheeky tone, of course! I'm so grateful for the way you helped make this book more fun, more accessible, and just ... better. Finally, thank you to Lucy Sykes-Thompson for the beautiful design; you really captured my personality and essence, so it feels perfect to me!

I'm a firm believer that when you are having fun, and everybody is enjoying themselves, things will turn out great. And this is what happened at the book's photoshoot; everyone involved loved what they were doing, and you can see it reflected in the pictures. It was hard work. We did the shoot in only six days at our home in Semaphore – no fancy studios or kitchen equipment. We had some crazy ideas – some worked, some didn't – but the process was so enjoyable, and we had lots of laughs creating some seriously amazing photos.

David, my co-writer, and me; Me and my husband, Kor.

Big thanks to Simon Bajada. You're an amazing photographer to work with! Your beautiful work, styling and photos are just marvellous. Come back for a swim in the ocean soon! Andy Nowell, thanks for your trenchant way of being and helping Simon with his work and making everything run more smoothly; this would have been a different book without you. Thanks to Michelle Gration and Karah Wertz for all your help maintaining all the equipment and keeping the kitchen shiny and ready to go! Thank you to the Dutch Coffee Lab for providing the caffeine to keep us going.

Also, I've got to thank my amazing team at La Popular Taqueria. You guys really held down the fort while I was caught up in book land! I know it wasn't always easy, but you made it all work, and I'm so grateful for that. Thank you for stepping up, for your hard work, and for keeping everything running smoothly while I was juggling recipes, writing, and probably making a mess somewhere else. You're the best!

To all my friends and my beloved sister, Maru, who helped me, with their support, comments, testing and cheers in this process – Karla Peregrina, Guille Echeverría, Lucía López de Medrano, Melina Soto, Diana Gonzalez, Kate Turner, Amanda McKinnon and Coco Cox. To my Mexican chat group, thanks for all the food discussions (especially on the topic of pico de gallo!).

I would also like to thank all our regulars at the restaurant. It still amazes me how caring you are, always checking in, asking how the book is going, and getting just as excited about it as I am. Your excitement makes me feel so happy and gives me the energy to keep going, to not give up on this journey and the battle (yeah, sometimes it feels like that) to showcase traditional Mexican food in Australia. I really appreciate you!

And finally, thanks to you, the reader. I hope to see photos of your creations soon. Make sure you tag me: @daniella_guevara_

¡Muchas gracias y provecho!

Index

A

Acapulco fish fritters 94
achiote paste 18
  Achiote marinade 223
  Adobo chicken tacos 119
  Cochinita pibil torta 126
  Panuchos 99
  Yucatán-style achiote grilled fish in banana leaves 154–5
  Yucatán-style chicken soup 58
  Yucatán-style pulled pork 146–7
Adobo chicken tacos 119
Agua de horchata 204
Agua de jamaica 202
Agua de limón 205
Aguacatadas 172
Aguachile 84
aguardiente 262
Albóndigas 140
allspice 18
ancho chillies 21
  Kangaroo tail barbacoa 148–9
  Mexican tomato sauce 164
  Minced meat stew 164
  Stuffed ancho chilli with goat's cheese 88
  Stuffed banana chilli with picadillo 142
añejo cheese *see* queso añejo
árbol chillies 20
  Adobo chicken tacos 119
  Cantina-style prawn stock 62
  Corn in a cup 75
  Crispy chilli oil 244
  Mexican bread soup 50
  Mixed tacos 115
  Simple quesadillas 45
  Taquería-style salsa 239
  Tomato tostadas with salsa macha 133
Arroz blanco 224
Arroz rojo 225
atole 184
Atole de vainilla con regañadas 184–5
avocados 18
  Avocado enchiladas 172
  Avocado ice blocks 197
  Basic torta with no filling 124
  Fish ceviche with mango and avocado 104
  Green pork hominy soup 56–7
  Guacamole 70
  Market-style guacamole 72
  Mexican prawn cocktail 106
  Panuchos 99
  Pickled beef tostadas 131
  Pickled pork skin tostadas 134–5
  Pork loin in adobo torta 125
  Pork schnitzel torta 125
  Raw tomatillo salsa 242
  Simple quesadillas 45
  Tortilla soup 55
  Valentina sauce 134–5
  Yucatán-style chicken soup 58

B

bacon
  Beef in a tomatillo broth 145
  Black bean soup 64
  Steak on a skewer, without a skewer 118
  stew 145
Baja-style fish tacos 116–17
banana chillies 20
  Stuffed banana chilli with picadillo 142
Barbacoa de cola de canguro 148–9
Basic torta with no filling 124
batter, fish 117
beans 19
  Basic torta with no filling 124
  Beef in a tomatillo broth 145
  Black bean soup 64
  Chipotle dry pasta 86
  Cooked pot beans 218
  Eggs with machaca 44
  Huarache with eggs and salsa verde 35
  Huaraches 259
  Motul-style eggs 38
  Panuchos 99
  Pickled pork skin tostadas 134–5
  Pork loin in adobo torta 125
  Pork schnitzel torta 125
  Pot mole soup 61
  Ranch-style eggs 32
  Refried beans 220
  Sopes 257
  Stuffed ancho chilli with goat's cheese 88
  Toasted bread roll with beans and cheese 41
  Tomato tostadas with salsa macha 133
beef
  Beef in a tomatillo broth 145
  Dried shredded beef 232
  Eggs with machaca 44
  Minced meat stew 164
  Mixed tacos 115
  Pickled beef tostadas 131
  Pot mole soup 61
  Slow-cooked short rib in tomatillo 167
  Steak and cheese torta 126
  Steak in pasilla sauce 162
  Steak on a skewer, without a skewer 118
  Steak tacos 114
  stew 145
  Stuffed banana chilli with picadillo 142
  Traditional Mexican meatballs 140
beer
  Baja-style fish tacos 116–17
  fish batter 117
  Michelada 208
berries: Three milk cake 186–7
biscuits
  Pig-shaped raw sugar biscuits 193
  regañadas 184
Bistec en salsa de chile pasilla 162
Black bean soup 64
Blistered chillies 230
Boiled chicken 222
bread
  Basic torta with no filling 124
  Cochinita pibil torta 126
  Mexican bread soup 50
  Mole eggs 42
  Pork loin in adobo torta 125
  Pork schnitzel torta 125
  Steak and cheese torta 126
  Toasted bread roll with beans and cheese 41
  Traditional Mexican meatballs 140

C

cabbage
  Acapulco fish fritters 94
  Baja-style fish tacos 116–17
  Panuchos 99
Cacahuates enchilados 73
cake, Three milk 186–7
Calaveritas 189
calcium hydroxide powder 262
Caldito de camarón – estilo cantina 62
Caldo de pollo 221
Caldo de pollo estilo Yucatán 58
Camarones al ajillo 152
Camarones zarandeados 156
Cantina-style prawn stock 62
capsicums
  Smoked fish tostadas 130
  Steak on a skewer, without a skewer 118
carne asada 262
Carne de puerco con calabacitas 168
Carne en su jugo 145
carrots
  Basic torta with no filling 124
  Cantina-style prawn stock 62
  Chicken stock 221
  Kangaroo tail barbacoa 148–9
  Minced meat stew 164
  Pickled beef tostadas 131
  Pickled jalapeños 229
  Poblano chilli soup 52
  Pork loin in adobo torta 125
  Pork schnitzel torta 125
  Red rice 225
  Simple quesadillas 45
  Stuffed banana chilli with picadillo 142
  Stuffed jalapeño tacos 120–1
  White rice 224
  Yucatán-style chicken soup 58
cauliflower
  Basic torta with no filling 124
  Pickled beef tostadas 131
  Pickled jalapeños 229
  Pork loin in adobo torta 125
  Pork schnitzel torta 125
  Simple quesadillas 45
Cebolla curtida 228
Cebollitas cambray 78
celery
  Chicken stock 221
  Poblano chilli soup 52
Ceviche de pescado con mango y aguacate 104
ceviche, Fish, with mango and avocado 104

chalupa 262
Chamoy 19
champurrado 184, 262
Charales enchiladas 74
Charred tomato salsa 241
chayote *see* choko
cheese 19
Cheese crackling 81
Cheese flan 180
Corn in a cup 75
Motul-style eggs 38
Steak and cheese torta 126
Stuffed ancho chilli with goat's cheese 88
see also queso cotija, queso fresco, queso oaxaca, queso panela, queso sopero
cherries: Three milk cake 186–7
chicharrón 20
Green pork hominy soup 56–7
Mixed tacos 115
Pork crackling in salsa verde 160
Tortilla soup 55
Chicharrón de queso 81
Chicharrón en salsa serde 160
chicken
Adobo chicken tacos 119
Avocado enchiladas 172
Boiled chicken 222
Chicken mole 165
Chicken stock 221
Mole enchiladas 173
Panuchos 99
Sopes 257
Swiss enchiladas 174
Yucatán-style chicken soup 58
chickpeas: Kangaroo tail barbacoa 148–9
chilaca chillies 20
Chilaquiles 30
Chile ancho relleno de queso de cabra 88
Chile güero relleno de picadillo 142
Chile relleno 151
chileatole 262
Chiles en escabeche 229
Chiles toreados 230
chilhuacle chillies 20
chillies 20–1
Acapulco fish fritters 94
buying 20
Crispy whitebait with chilli 74
Grilled corn on the cob 76
Grilled marinated prawns 156
Michelada 208
Spicy peanuts 73
see also chilli varieties ancho, árbol, banana, chipotle in adobo, guajillo, habanero, jalapeño, mirasol, mole poblano negro paste, morita, pasilla, poblano, serrano
chipotle in adobo 21
Baja-style fish tacos 116–17
Chipotle dry pasta 86
chipotle mayonnaise 117
meatball sauce 140
Smoked fish tostadas 130
Traditional Mexican meatballs 140
chochoyotes 64
chocolate 22
champurrado 184
Chicken mole 165
chocolate dip 182
Churros with chocolate dip 182–3
Mexican chocolate ice cream 190
Mexican hot chocolate 206
Mexican chocolate ice blocks 197
mole 165
Mole eggs 42
Mole enchiladas 173
Chocolate caliente mexicano 206
choko: Pot mole soup 61
chorizo 22
Basic torta with no filling 124
Chorizo and potato gordita 89
Mexican bread soup 50
Mixed tacos 115
Churros con chocolate 182–3
Churros with chocolate dip 182–3
cilantro *see* coriander
Cochinita pibil 146–7
Cochinita pibil torta 126
Cochitorta 126
Cóctel de camarones 106
Codzitos 92
cola: Mixed Cuba libre 213
comida 262
comida corrida 262
Cooked green salsa 245
Cooked pot beans 218
coriander 22
Adobo chicken tacos 119
Avocado enchiladas 172
Beef in a tomatillo broth 145
Cantina-style prawn stock 62
Charred tomato salsa 241
Cooked green salsa 245
Corn chips with salsa 30
Fish ceviche with mango and avocado 104
Garlic chilli prawns 152
Guacamole 70
Huarache with eggs and salsa verde 35
Market-style guacamole 72
Mexican prawn cocktail 106
Mixed tacos 115
Pepita dip 82
Pickled beef tostadas 131
Pickled pork skin tostadas 134–5
Pico de gallo 246
Prawns in chilli water 84
Raw tomatillo salsa 242
Red salsa 238
tomatillo salsa 145
Steak tacos 114
Tortilla soup 55
Yucatán-style chicken soup 58
corn 248–9
Corn in a cup 75
Grilled corn on the cob 76
Poblano chilli soup 52
Pot mole soup 61
Stuffed poblano chilli 151
see also corn chips; hominy; masa harina; tortillas, corn; tortillas, wheat
corn chips
Corn chips 252
Corn chips with salsa 30
Fish ceviche with mango and avocado 104
Guacamole 70
Market-style guacamole 72
Pepita dip 82
Prawns in chilli water 84
cotija cheese *see* queso cotija
courgettes *see* zucchini
cream 22
cream cheese
Cheese flan 180
Smoked fish tostadas 130
Crema de chile poblano 52
Crema de frijol 64
Crispy chilli oil 244
Crispy potato tacos 100
Crispy whitebait with chilli 74
Cuba libre campechana 213
cucumbers
Baja-style fish tacos 116–17
Prawns in chilli water 84
cueritos 134–5

D

Día de Muertos 262
dips
chocolate dip 182
Pepita dip 82
doblada 262
Dried shredded beef 232
drinks
atole 184
champurrado 184
Fresh lemonade 205
Grapefruit tequila long drink 212
Hibiscus water 202
Horchata 204
Margarita 209
Mexican hot chocolate 206
Michelada 208
Mixed Cuba libre 213

E

eggs
Cheese flan 180
Corn chips with salsa 30
Eggs with machaca 44
Huarache with eggs and salsa verde 35
Mexican bread soup 50
Mole eggs 42
Motul-style eggs 38
Ranch-style eggs 32
Stuffed jalapeño tacos 120–1
Traditional Mexican meatballs 140
Elote callejero 76
enchiladas 170
Avocado enchiladas 172
Mole enchiladas 173
Swiss enchiladas 174
Enchiladas suizas 174
Enmoladas 173
Entomatado de res 167
Esquites 75

F

fish
Acapulco fish fritters 94
Baja-style fish tacos 116–17
Crispy whitebait with chilli 74
Fish ceviche with mango and avocado 104

Smoked fish tostadas 130
Yucatán-style achiote grilled fish in banana leaves 154–5
Flan de queso 180
flan, Cheese 180
Flautas de papa 100
Fresh lemonade 205
Fried quesadillas 96
Fried tortilla rolls with Yucatán-style tomato salsa 92
Frijoles de la olla 218
Frijoles refritos 220
fritters, Acapulco fish 94

G

Garlic chilli prawns 152
gorditas 258
Chorizo and potato gordita 89
Mushroom 'chorizo' gordita 91
Wheat tortillas and gorditas 234–5
Gorditas de chorizo con papa 89
Gorditas de chorizo de hongos 91
Grapefruit tequila long drink 212
Green pork hominy soup 56–7
Grilled corn on the cob 76
Grilled marinated prawns 156
Grilled spring onions 78
Guacamole 70
Guacamole estilo mercado 72
guacamole, Market-style 72
guajillo chillies 21
Adobo chicken tacos 119
Cantina-style prawn stock 62
Crispy chilli oil 244
Garlic chilli prawns 152
Kangaroo tail barbacoa 148–9
Mixed tacos 115
Mushroom 'chorizo' gordita 91
Pork loin in adobo 150
Pork loin in adobo torta 125
Simple quesadillas 45
Taquería-style salsa 239
Tomato tostadas with salsa macha 133
Tortilla soup 55
güero chillies 20
see also banana chillies
guisados 158

H

habanero chillies 21
Beef in a tomatillo broth 145
Cochinita pibil torta 126
Fish ceviche with mango and avocado 104
Fried tortilla rolls with Yucatán-style tomato salsa 92
Habanero hot sauce 247
Margarita 209
Motul-style eggs 38
Panuchos 99
Pepita dip 82
Pickled red onions 228
Yucatán-style chicken soup 58
Yucatán-style pulled pork 146–7
Yucatán-style tomato salsa 240
ham
Motul-style eggs 38
Simple quesadillas 45
Helado de chocolate 190
Helado de mango 192
Hibiscus water 202
hominy
Green pork hominy soup 56–7
pork stock 56
hot sauce, Habanero 247
Huarache with eggs and salsa verde 35
Huaraches 259
Huaraches con huevos y salsa verde 35
Huevos con mole 42
Huevos motuleños 38
Huevos rancheros 32

I

ice blocks
Avocado ice blocks 197
Mango ice blocks 197
Mexican chocolate ice blocks 197
ice cream
Mexican chocolate ice cream 190
see also ice blocks, sorbet

J

jalapeños 21
Avocado enchiladas 172
Basic torta with no filling 124
Beef in a tomatillo broth 145
Blistered chillies 230
Charred tomato salsa 241
Chorizo and potato gordita 89
Cooked green salsa 245
Corn chips with salsa 30
Crispy potato tacos 100
Eggs with machaca 44
Fried quesadillas 96
Green pork hominy soup 56–7
Huarache with eggs and salsa verde 35
Market-style guacamole 72
Mixed tacos 115
mole verde 56
Mushroom 'chorizo' gordita 91
Pickled beef tostadas 131
Pickled jalapeños 229
Pork crackling in salsa verde 160
Pork loin in adobo torta 125
Pork schnitzel torta 125
Prawns in chilli water 84
Ranch-style eggs 32
Raw tomatillo salsa 242
Red salsa 238
tomatillo salsa 145
Simple quesadillas 45
Sopes 257
Steak on a skewer, without a skewer 118
Steak tacos 114
Stuffed jalapeño tacos 120–1
Swiss enchiladas 174
Jamaica flowers 23
Hibiscus water 202
jars, sterilising 229

K

Kangaroo tail barbacoa 148–9

L

lamb: Kangaroo tail barbacoa 148–9
lemonade, Fresh 205
lettuce
Chorizo and potato gordita 89
Crispy potato tacos 100
Fried quesadillas 96
Green pork hominy soup 56–7
Mushroom 'chorizo' gordita 91
Panuchos 99
Pickled pork skin tostadas 134–5
Sopes 257
Tomato tostadas with salsa macha 133
Yucatán-style chicken soup 58
limes 23
Acapulco fish fritters 94
Avocado ice blocks 197
Baja-style fish tacos 116–17
Beef in a tomatillo broth 145
Blistered chillies 230
Cantina-style prawn stock 62
Cochinita pibil torta 126
Corn in a cup 75
Crispy whitebait with chilli 74
Fish ceviche with mango and avocado 104
Fresh lemonade 205
Garlic chilli prawns 152
Green pork hominy soup 56–7
Grilled corn on the cob 76
Grilled marinated prawns 156
Grilled spring onions 78
Guacamole 70
Mango paletas 197
Mango sorbet 192
Margarita 209
Market-style guacamole 72
Mexican bread soup 50
Mexican prawn cocktail 106
Michelada 208
Mixed Cuba libre 213
Panuchos 99
Pickled pork skin tostadas 134–5
Pickled red onions 228
Pot mole soup 61
prawn cocktail sauce 106
Prawns in chilli water 84
Steak tacos 114
Valentina sauce 134–5
Yucatán-style chicken soup 58
Lomo adobado 150

M

Machaca 232
Machaca con huevo 44
maize *see* corn
mango
Fish ceviche with mango and avocado 104
Mango paletas 197
Mango sorbet 192
Three milk cake 186–7
Margarita 209
marinade, Achiote 223
Market-style guacamole 72
Masa 250
atole 184
Black bean soup 64
chochoyotes 64
Chorizo and potato gordita 89
Corn tortillas 253
Fried quesadillas 96
Gorditas 258
Huarache with eggs and salsa verde 35

Huaraches 259
Mushroom 'chorizo' gordita 91
Panuchos 99
Prawns in chilli water 84
Sopes 257
Vanilla corn drink with sugar biscuits 184–5
masa harina 23, 248–9
Corn dough 250
mayonnaise, chipotle 117
meatballs 140
memela 262
menus 260
Mexican bread soup 50
Mexican chocolate ice cream 190
Mexican cookware 14–17
Mexican hot chocolate 206
Mexican chocolate ice blocks 197
Mexican oregano 23
Mexican pantry 18–24
Mexican prawn cocktail 106
Michelada 208
milk
Rice milk 204
Three milk cake 186–7
milpa 262
Minced meat stew 164
mirasol chillies 21
Mixed Cuba libre 213
Mixed tacos 115
mole 23
Mole con pollo 165
Mole de olla 61
Mole eggs 42
Mole enchiladas 173
mole verde 56
mole poblano negro paste
Chicken mole 165
mole 165
Mole eggs 42
Mole enchiladas 173
Molletes 41
molote 262
morita chillies 21
Crispy chilli oil 244
Kangaroo tail barbacoa 148–9
Mexican bread soup 50
Pork loin in adobo 150
Pork loin in adobo torta 125
Simple quesadillas 45
Tomato tostadas with salsa macha 133
Motul-style eggs 38
mozzarella
Adobo chicken tacos 119
Fried quesadillas 96
Poblano chilli in cream 161
Simple quesadillas 45
Steak tacos 114
Stuffed jalapeño tacos 120–1
Stuffed poblano chilli 151
Swiss enchiladas 174
Toasted bread roll with beans and cheese 41
Tortilla soup 55
mushrooms
Fried quesadillas 96
Mushroom 'chorizo' gordita 91
Simple quesadillas 45

N

nixtamalisation 262
nopal 23–4
Steak in pasilla sauce 162

O

oaxaca cheese *see* queso oaxaca
oil, Crispy chilli 244
onions, Pickled red 228
oranges
Achiote marinade 223
Adobo chicken tacos 119
Cochinita pibil torta 126
Habanero hot sauce 247
Mexican prawn cocktail 106
Panuchos 99
Pickled red onions 228
Pork loin in adobo 150
Pork loin in adobo torta 125
prawn cocktail sauce 106
Steak tacos 114
Yucatán-style achiote grilled fish in banana leaves 154–5
Yucatán-style chicken soup 58
Yucatán-style pulled pork 146–7

P

paletas 194
Paletas de aguacate 196
Paletas de chocolate Mexicano 197
Paletas de mango 197
Paloma 212
pancita 262
panela (sugar) 262
panela cheese *see* queso panela
pantry, Mexican 18–24
Panuchos 99
parsley: Poblano chilli soup 52
pasilla chillies 20
Mushroom 'chorizo' gordita 91
Pot mole soup 61
Steak in pasilla sauce 162
Pasta seca enchipotlada 86
pasta: Chipotle dry pasta 86
Pastel tres leches 186–7
peanuts
Crispy chilli oil 244
Simple quesadillas 45
Spicy peanuts 73
Tomato tostadas with salsa macha 133
peas
Minced meat stew 164
Motul-style eggs 38
Red rice 225
Stuffed banana chilli with picadillo 142
Stuffed jalapeño tacos 120–1
White rice 224
Yucatán-style chicken soup 58
pepitas 24
Crispy chilli oil 244
mole verde 56
Pepita dip 82

Pepito 126
pepper *see* capsicums, chillies
Pescadillas 94
Pescado tikin xik 154–5
Picadillo 164
Pickled beef tostadas 131
Pickled jalapeños 229
Pickled pork skin tostadas 134–5
Pickled red onions 228
Pico de gallo 246
Pig-shaped raw sugar biscuits 193
piloncillo 262
plantain: Motul-style eggs 38
plums: Three milk cake 186–7
poblano chillies 21
  Green pork hominy soup 56–7
  mole verde 56
  Poblano chilli in cream 161
  Poblano chilli soup 52
  Roasting poblano chillies 231
  Stuffed poblano chilli 151
  see also mole poblano negro paste
Pollo cocido 222
pork
  Cochinita pibil torta 126
  cueritos 134–5
  Green pork hominy soup 56–7
  Pickled pork skin tostadas 134–5
  Pork crackling in salsa verde 160
  Pork loin in adobo 150
  Pork loin in adobo torta 125
  Pork schnitzel torta 125
  pork stock 56
  Pork with zucchini 168
  Yucatán-style pulled pork 146–7
  see also bacon, chicharrón, chorizo, ham
Pot mole soup 61
potatoes
  Chorizo and potato gordita 89
  Crispy potato tacos 100
  Minced meat stew 164
  Mushroom 'chorizo' gordita 91
  Pot mole soup 61
  Steak in pasilla sauce 162
  Stuffed banana chilli with picadillo 142
Pozole verde 56–7
prawns
  Cantina-style prawn stock 62
  Crispy whitebait with chilli 74
  Garlic chilli prawns 152
  Grilled marinated prawns 156
  Mexican prawn cocktail 106
  prawn cocktail sauce 106
  Prawns in chilli water 84
Puerquitos de piloncillo 193
pumpkin seeds *see* pepitas

Q
quesadillas
  Fried quesadillas 96
  Simple quesadillas 45
Quesadillas de harina 45
Quesadillas fritas 96
quesillo cheese *see* queso oaxaca
queso cotija 19
  Corn in a cup 75
  Grilled corn on the cob 76
queso de hebra *see* queso oaxaca
queso fresco
  Avocado enchiladas 172
  Chipotle dry pasta 86
  Chorizo and potato gordita 89
  Corn chips with salsa 30
  Fried quesadillas 96
  Mole enchiladas 173
  Mushroom 'chorizo' gordita 91
  Pickled beef tostadas 131
  Refried beans 220
  Tortilla soup 55
queso oaxaca 19
  Fried quesadillas 96
  Stuffed poblano chilli 151
  Toasted bread roll with beans and cheese 41
queso panela 19
  Black bean soup 64
  Tortilla soup 55
queso sopero: Fried tortilla rolls with Yucatán-style tomato salsa 92

R
radishes
  Beef in a tomatillo broth 145
  Green pork hominy soup 56–7
  mole verde 56
  Pickled beef tostadas 131
Rajas con crema 161
Ranch-style eggs 32
Raw tomatillo salsa 242
Recado rojo 223
Red rice 225
Red salsa 238
Refried beans 220
regañadas 184
rice
  Horchata 204
  Red rice 225
  Stuffed jalapeño tacos 120–1
  White rice 224
  Yucatán-style chicken soup 58
ricotta salata
  Crispy potato tacos 100
  Eggs with machaca 44
  Fried tortilla rolls with Yucatán-style tomato salsa 92
  Grilled corn on the cob 76
  Huarache with eggs and salsa verde 35
  Pickled pork skin tostadas 134–5
Roasting poblano chillies 231
romerito 262
rum: Mixed Cuba libre 213

S
salbute 262
Salsa de habanero tatemada 247
Salsa macha 244
Salsa roja 238
Salsa roja yucateca 240
Salsa taquera 239
Salsa tatemada 241
Salsa verde cocida 245
Salsa verde cruda 242
salsas 236–7
  Charred tomato salsa 241
  Cooked green salsa 245
  Pico de gallo 246
  Raw tomatillo salsa 242
  Red salsa 238
  sterilising for storing 238
  Taquería-style salsa 239
  tomatillo salsa 145
  tomato salsa 120, 151
  Yucatán-style tomato salsa 240
sauces
  Habanero hot sauce 247
  meatball sauce 140
  Mexican tomato sauce 164
  prawn cocktail sauce 106
  Valentina sauce 134–5
  see also mole
serrano chillies 21
  Beef in a tomatillo broth 145
  Blistered chillies 230
  Chorizo and potato gordita 89
  Cooked green salsa 245
  Corn chips with salsa 30
  Crispy potato tacos 100
  Fried quesadillas 96
  Huarache with eggs and salsa verde 35
  Market-style guacamole 72
  Mixed tacos 115
  Mushroom 'chorizo' gordita 91
  Pork crackling in salsa verde 160
  Prawns in chilli water 84
  Raw tomatillo salsa 242
  tomatillo salsa 145
  Sopes 257
  Steak on a skewer, without a skewer 118
  Steak tacos 114
  Swiss enchiladas 174
shrimp *see* prawns
Sikil p'aak 82
Simple quesadillas 45
Slow-cooked short rib in tomatillo 167
Smoked fish tostadas 130
Sopa de migas 50
Sopa de tortilla 55
Sopes 257
sorbet, Mango 192
Spicy peanuts 73
spinach
  Green pork hominy soup 56–7
  mole verde 56
  Poblano chilli soup 52
sponge cake 186–7
spring onions, Grilled 78
Steak and cheese torta 126
Steak in pasilla sauce 162
Steak on a skewer, without a skewer 118
Steak tacos 114
sterilising jars 229
sterilising salsas for storage 238
stew 145
stockists 263
stocks
  Cantina-style prawn stock 62
  Chicken stock 221
  pork stock 56
Stuffed ancho chilli with goat's cheese 88
Stuffed banana chilli with picadillo 142
Stuffed jalapeño tacos 120–1
Stuffed poblano chilli 151
Sugar skulls 189
Swiss enchiladas 174

T

tacos 112
- Adobo chicken tacos 119
- Baja-style fish tacos 116–17
- Crispy potato tacos 100
- Mixed tacos 115
- Steak on a skewer, without a skewer 118
- Steak tacos 114
- Stuffed jalapeño tacos 120–1

Tacos campechanos 115
Tacos de alambre de res 118
Tacos de asada 114
Tacos de chile jalapeño relleno 120–1
Tacos de pescado estilo Ensenada 116–17
Tacos de pollo adobado 119
Tajín 24
tamal 262
Taquería-style salsa 239
taquiza 89, 263
tascalate 263
tejate 263
tejuino 263

tequila
- Grapefruit tequila long drink 212
- Margarita 209

tetela 263
Three milk cake 186–7
tlacoyo 263
tlayuda 263
Toasted bread roll with beans and cheese 41

tomatillos 24
- Adobo chicken tacos 119
- Avocado enchiladas 172
- Beef in a tomatillo broth 145
- Chorizo and potato gordita 89
- Cooked green salsa 245
- Corn chips with salsa 30
- Crispy potato tacos 100
- Fried quesadillas 96
- Green pork hominy soup 56–7
- Huarache with eggs and salsa verde 35
- Mixed tacos 115
- mole verde 56
- Mushroom 'chorizo' gordita 91
- Pork crackling in salsa verde 160
- Raw tomatillo salsa 242
- tomatillo salsa 145
- Slow-cooked short rib in tomatillo 167
- Sopes 257
- Steak in pasilla sauce 162
- Steak on a skewer, without a skewer 118
- Steak tacos 114
- Swiss enchiladas 174
- Taquería-style salsa 239

tomatoes
- Acapulco fish fritters 94
- Adobo chicken tacos 119
- Baja-style fish tacos 116–17
- Basic torta with no filling 124
- Black bean soup 64
- Charred tomato salsa 241
- Chicken mole 165
- Chipotle dry pasta 86
- Chorizo and potato gordita 89
- Corn chips with salsa 30
- Crispy potato tacos 100
- Eggs with machaca 44
- Fried quesadillas 96
- Fried tortilla rolls with Yucatán-style tomato salsa 92
- Guacamole 70
- Mexican prawn cocktail 106
- Mexican tomato sauce 164
- Michelada 208
- Minced meat stew 164
- Mixed tacos 115
- mole 165
- Mole eggs 42
- Mole enchiladas 173
- Motul-style eggs 38
- Mushroom 'chorizo' gordita 91
- Panuchos 99
- Pepita dip 82
- Pickled beef tostadas 131
- Pickled pork skin tostadas 134–5
- Pico de gallo 246
- Pork loin in adobo torta 125
- Pork schnitzel torta 125
- Pork with zucchini 168
- prawn cocktail sauce 106
- Ranch-style eggs 32
- Red rice 225
- Red salsa 238
- tomato salsa 120, 151
- Sopes 257
- Steak in pasilla sauce 162
- Steak on a skewer, without a skewer 118
- Steak tacos 114
- Stuffed banana chilli with picadillo 142
- Stuffed jalapeño tacos 120–1
- Stuffed poblano chilli 151
- Taquería-style salsa 239
- Toasted bread roll with beans and cheese 41
- meatball sauce 140
- Tomato tostadas with salsa macha 133
- Tortilla soup 55
- Traditional Mexican meatballs 140
- Yucatán-style achiote grilled fish in banana leaves 154–5
- Yucatán-style tomato salsa 240

Torta de lomo adobado 125
Torta de milanesa 125

tortas 122
- Basic torta with no filling 124
- Cochinita pibil torta 126
- Pork loin in adobo torta 125
- Pork schnitzel torta 125
- Steak and cheese torta 126

Tortilla soup 55

tortillas, corn
- Acapulco fish fritters 94
- Adobo chicken tacos 119
- Avocado enchiladas 172
- Baja-style fish tacos 116–17
- Beef in a tomatillo broth 145
- Corn chips 252
- Corn tortillas 253
- Crispy potato tacos 100
- Fried tortilla rolls with Yucatán-style tomato salsa 92
- Green pork hominy soup 56–7
- Mixed tacos 115
- Mole eggs 42
- Mole enchiladas 173
- Motul-style eggs 38
- Pickled beef tostadas 131
- Pickled pork skin tostadas 134–5
- Poblano chilli soup 52
- Pot mole soup 61
- Ranch-style eggs 32
- reheating 253
- Smoked fish tostadas 130
- Steak on a skewer, without a skewer 118
- Steak tacos 114
- Stuffed jalapeño tacos 120–1
- Swiss enchiladas 174
- Tomato tostadas with salsa macha 133
- Tortilla soup 55
- Tostadas 256
- Yucatán-style chicken soup 58
- Yucatán-style pulled pork 146–7

Tortillas de maíz 253

tortillas, wheat
- Eggs with machaca 44
- Simple quesadillas 45
- Steak on a skewer, without a skewer 118
- Steak tacos 114
- Wheat tortillas and gorditas 234–5

Tortillas y gorditas de harina de trigo 234–5

tostadas 128
- Pickled beef tostadas 131
- Pickled pork skin tostadas 134–5
- Smoked fish tostadas 130
- Tomato tostadas with salsa macha 133
- tostadas 134–5
- Tostadas 256

Tostadas de cueritos 134–5
Tostadas de jitomate y salsa macha 133
Tostadas de paté de pescado ahumado 130
Tostadas de salpicón 131
Totopos 252
Traditional Mexican meatballs 140

V

Valentina sauce 24

vanilla 24
- Cheese flan 180
- Mexican chocolate ice cream 190
- sponge cake 186–7
- Three milk cake 186–7
- Vanilla corn drink with sugar biscuits 184–5

W

wheat tortillas *see* tortillas, wheat
White rice 224
Worcestershire sauce 24

Y

Yucatán-style achiote grilled fish in banana leaves 154–5
Yucatán-style chicken soup 58
Yucatán-style pulled pork 146–7
Yucatán-style tomato salsa 240

Z

zucchini
- Basic torta with no filling 124
- Pickled beef tostadas 131
- Pickled jalapeños 229
- Pork loin in adobo torta 125
- Pork schnitzel torta 125
- Pork with zucchini 168
- Pot mole soup 61
- Simple quesadillas 45

Published in 2025 by Murdoch Books, an imprint of Allen & Unwin

Murdoch Books Australia
Cammeraygal Country
83 Alexander Street
Crows Nest NSW 2065
Phone: +61 (0)2 8425 0100
murdochbooks.com.au
info@murdochbooks.com.au

Murdoch Books UK
Ormond House
26–27 Boswell Street
London WC1N 3JZ
Phone: +44 (0) 20 8785 5995
murdochbooks.co.uk
info@murdochbooks.co.uk

For corporate orders and custom publishing, contact our business development team at salesenquiries@murdochbooks.com.au

Publisher: Jane Willson
Co-writer: David Knight
Editorial manager: Loran McDougall
Design manager: Kristy Allen
Commissioning Editor: Justin Wolfers
Designer and illustrator: Lucy Sykes-Thompson
Layout designer: Madeleine Kane
Editor: Ariana Klepac
Photographer and stylist: Simon Bajada
Photography assistant and model: Andy Nowell
Props: James Brown
Production manager: Natalie Crouch

Murdoch Books acknowledges the Traditional Owners of the Country on which we live and work. We pay our respects to all Aboriginal and Torres Strait Islander Elders, past and present.

EU Authorised Representative: Easy Access System Europe, Mustamäe tee 50, 10621 Tallinn, Estonia, gpsr.requests@easproject.com

The front cover features traditional Mexican cookware. Clockwise from top left: molcajete y tecolote (volcanic stone mortar and pestle); molinillo (wooden milk frother); two cazuelas (handmade clay cooking pots); exprimidor de limõn (lime press); prensa para tortillas (manual tortilla press)

ISBN 978 1 76150 063 3

A catalogue record for this book is available from the National Library of Australia

A catalogue record for this book is available from the British Library

Colour reproduction by Splitting Image Colour Studio Pty Ltd, Wantirna, Victoria
Printed in China by C&C Offset Printing Co., Ltd

OVEN GUIDE You may find cooking times vary depending on the oven and oven setting you are using. For fan-forced (convection) ovens, as a general rule, set the oven temperature to 20°C (25–50°F) lower than indicated in the recipe.

SPOONS We have used 20 ml (4 teaspoon) tablespoon measures. If you are using a 15 ml (3 teaspoon) tablespoon add an extra teaspoon of the ingredient for each tablespoon specified.

10 9 8 7 6 5 4 3 2 1

Where to eat in Mexico City

In Mexico, certain dishes are typically served in certain types of restaurants. This guide is based on my experience growing up in a working-class neighbourhood of Mexico City – though someone from another part of the country, or even the city, might have a different experience. These places exist because there is a need for them. Street food, for example, thrives due to the pace of city life; the bigger the city, the more puestos you will find. Mexico City, with its 25 million inhabitants, is one of the biggest and best street-food cities in the world. Commutes can be enormous, a couple of hours each way, so people don't have time to cook and eat at home. It is common to stop at a puesto to grab an atole and a tamal – brekkie on the go; to have your main meal at lunchtime in a fonda; and then in the evening to buy some sweet bread in a panadería (bakery) or stop at a tortería or taquería for dinner.

Restaurante

These are generally open from morning to night, serving breakfast, lunch and dinner. Restaurants tend to have large menus and can specialise in a certain cuisine, e.g. Yucatán. Every city (and every mall) is packed with franchise restaurants that serve a mix of traditional Mexican dishes alongside popular 'worldly' foods, such as burgers and pasta.

Puesto

These are the places Mexico is famous for – the carts and stalls that sell street food. A puesto (stand) specialises in one or two dishes. You'll find carnitas, tamales and guajolotas (tamal sandwiches), as well as garnachas, such as tlacoyos and gorditas.

Specialty restaurante

This one's easy to explain, as their names signify what you're going to get. A taquería specialises in tacos, a tostadería in tostadas, and a pozolería in pozole, while a tortería will sling tortas. These can be well-established places, holes in the walls or someone's garage or house.

Cantina

A cantina is a bar, watering hole and restaurant rolled into one. They are also known as centros botaneros and salones familiares. A traditional cantina serves small dishes for free while you keep ordering drinks, such as the Cantina-style prawn stock (page 62). There are fewer and fewer cantinas in Mexico City, but hopefully a revival is on its way. One of the most famous is La Ópera, where you can still see a bullet hole made by Pancho Villa in the ceiling.

Fonda

Fondas, also known as a comida corrida, loncheria and antojería, are more affordable than restaurants. They have simple lunch counters and are where most regular working folks eat. Despite this, fondas serve some of the freshest and best prepared foods in Mexico. A fonda is generally a casual family-run restaurant that is only open for lunch, which is eaten around 2–3 pm. This is where you will find guisados that are sometimes served in cazuelas (clay cooking pots) in a buffet-style setup. Other fondas serve the comida del dia (meal of the day), a simple set-lunch menu with a starter (such as soup), main and dessert. When I was working as a biologist in Mexico City, I used to go to these places a lot. I have fond memories of a lady in a ute (truck) who would park outside our offices. She had a booth full of guisado buckets and a huge basket of tortillas, to serve tacos for lunch. What do you call this? Fonda on wheels? Street food? I don't know. But it is a classic example of how we eat in Mexico.